'A useful manual for navigating friendships, a touching account of the various ways women connect – and a welcome non-fiction counterpart to novels such as Elena Ferrante's Neapolitan Quartet or the TV series *Girls* and *Big Little Lies*' *Evening Standard*

'A wealth of cultural insight ... Men will enjoy and profit from this book as much as women will ... The moral of these stories [is that] the need for friendship is forever, no matter what forms it takes. Friends come and go, but those who allow us to be unselfconsciously ourselves? Hamlet understood. We grapple them to our souls with hoops of steel' *Wall Street Journal*

'A book about friendship that is also interested in the miscommunication that can so complicate it ... The language, in this book about language, is saturated with concepts that apply equally well to romance in its more traditional forms. The language, too, celebrates friendship in its frustrations and its rewards and, above all, its wonderful complexity. It is promoting friendship from a supporting character into a starring role ... The loves that the linguist explores in her romantically named book are not merely ones that comfort and sustain women until, one day, the real thing comes along. They are the real thing' *The Atlantic*

'At a time when the messages we give and get have so many more ways to be misconstrued and potentially damaging, a book that takes apart our language becomes almost vital to our survival as friends' *Washington Post*

D0316276

By Deborah Tannen

You're the Only One I Can Tell: Inside the Language
of Women's Friendships

You Were Always Mom's Favorite!: Sisters in Conversation
Throughout Their Lives

You're Wearing THAT?: Understanding Mothers
and Daughters in Conversation

I Only Say This Because I Love You: Talking to Your Parents,
Partner, Sibs, and Kids When You're All Adults

The Argument Culture: Stopping America's War of Words

Talking from 9 to 5: Women and Men at Work

You Just Don't Understand: Women and Men in Conversation

That's Not What I Meant!: How Conversational Style
Makes or Breaks Relationships

You're the Only One I Can Tell

Inside the Language of
Women's Friendships

DEBORAH TANNEN

virago

VIRAGO

First published in the United States in 2017 by Ballantine Books
First published in Great Britain in 2017 by Virago Press
This paperback edition published in 2019 by Virago Press

1 3 5 7 9 10 8 6 4 2

Copyright © 2017 by Deborah Tannen

A CIP catalogue record for this book
is available from the British Library.

ISBN 978-0-349-01219-3

Printed and bound in Great Britain by
Clays Ltd, Elcograf S.p.A.

Papers used by Virago are from well-managed forests
and other responsible sources.

Virago Press
An imprint of
Little, Brown Book Group
Carmelite House
50 Victoria Embankment
London EC4Y 0DZ

An Hachette UK Company
www.hachette.co.uk

www.virago.co.uk

To Addie and Al Macovski
my parents-in-law
and -in-love

Contents

Introduction

Best friend, old friend, good friend, close friend, good strong friend, bestie bestie, go-to core friend, close close friend, very very very very close friend, bff, my sweet angel from heaven: as I interviewed over eighty women about their friendships, and spoke casually about the topic with dozens more, I heard a seemingly limitless range of words and phrases that women used when referring to—and thinking about—the women friends they cherish. And explanations of why they cherish them were equally vast—and inspiring: "Women friends are the people you turn to emotionally. They are the most sustaining thing in my life"; "I've been protected and defended and shielded by my women friends"; "My friendships with women are as essential as air"; "My women friends are my life."

But I also heard comments like, "With women, throughout my life, the hardest part is getting to be friends at all. Once we cross the line and become friends, it's great, but it hasn't happened often"; "I find female friendships a difficult terrain to negotiate, to navigate"; "I don't have women friends. I don't trust women." Though those who described more negative than positive experiences were in the minority, nearly everyone I spoke to mentioned ways that friends could frustrate or annoy, and told tales of heartache suffered when close friends disappointed or disappeared. Like all significant relationships, friendships among women can be the source of great solace but also of puzzlement and pain.

Conversations among women friends have much in common with the topics of my two previous books: *You Were Always Mom's Favorite!: Sisters in Conversation Throughout Their Lives,* and *You're Wearing THAT?: Understanding Mothers and Daughters in Conversation.* A journalist interviewing me about mothers and daughters once blurted, "Why are these relationships so fraught? After all, we're both women!" She was thinking of my book *You Just Don't Understand,* where I traced many conversational frustrations to differences in women's and men's ways of speaking. I had to think about that question for a moment. Then the answer seemed obvious: it's *because* we're both women. As I explained in that early book, girls and women, as compared to boys and men, tend to talk more—more often and at greater length—and to talk about more personal topics. All this talk can lead to more intimacy and closeness but also affords more opportunities to stir up emotions—both comforting and troubling—and to say the wrong thing.

Another way that women's friendships resemble relationships between daughters and mothers and among sisters is the source of hurt feelings. Just as with those family relationships—and in contrast to relationships among sons, fathers, and brothers—when women told me about being upset by friends, it was often because they hadn't been included in something or hadn't been told something. This reflects the sensitivity, common among women, to feeling left out or pushed away. (Men's sensitivities tend to lie elsewhere: to feeling put down or pushed around.)

In other ways, though, friendship is different from the family relationships I've written about. One big difference is the challenge of simply identifying who is a friend. When I asked women about their mothers, daughters, and sisters, they immediately knew who those were, and the number was limited. (Surprises in that regard—learning that you have siblings you didn't know about, or that the person you thought was your mother or sister really isn't—are the stuff of novels and life-changing personal drama, even trauma.) But when I asked about friends, I heard of a dizzying array of relationships. Women spoke of friends they see or speak to every day, and of friends they haven't seen or spoken to in years but still feel close to; they told me about friends they've known their whole lives, friends they met recently, and friends they've never met but have become close to through social media. And many women I interviewed, at one point or another, suddenly thought of someone they had forgotten but realized they should tell me about. A woman's concept of what constitutes friendship could vary within a single interview. One described a "couples friend" she values, but later in our conversation, she said that she didn't really have or need friends because she had her husband and the couples they see socially. In her first comment, the woman she sees as part of a couple is a type of friend, but in the second, "friend" seems reserved for someone she sees separately, one on one.

Despite how different the relationships with those called "friends" could be, hearing about them always gave me a window into a woman's world at the time of the friendship. For many, having friends was synonymous with having a good life. That was certainly true for my mother. Explaining why the period between getting married and having her first child was the happiest of her life, she said, "We went out; we had friends." When I asked about her childhood in Russia, she said she didn't remember much, but she was happy because she had friends. And it was clear, from her words and also from her life, that not having friends meant not being happy. Each time she had to move—from the house where she and my father had raised their children to a rented apartment, and later from the rental to a suburban condo—she was deeply unhappy until she succeeded in making new friends. In their eighties, my parents moved to a senior residence. Whenever I spoke to my mother in the months after that move, she'd end the conversation by saying, "I still don't have a friend." And if I asked about a social worker my sisters and I had hired to help her adjust, she'd say, "I wish she could find me a friend" or, more bleakly, "She can't find me a friend."

As I interviewed women for this book, I realized that my mother was not unusual. An octogenarian commented, when she heard that someone died, "I wish it had been me because my friends are gone." And a woman who told me that her mother, who was born in England, never adjusted to life in the United States, backed up that observation by saying that her mother never made friends here; she kept her friends in England and lived for the times when she could go back and see them.

Some women said they liked having lots of friends, and some said they needed only a few, but almost no one said she didn't want any. Those who told me they didn't have women friends always said it with regret. One woman articulated what many others implied: after her husband died, she went ahead and built the house they had planned to build together, and she lived in it for two years, but then she sold it and moved. "It did not make me happy," she said. "It was a perfect house, but it was just a house. I learned a very valuable lesson, that it's all stuff except people and relationships." That means relationships with family and also with friends.

In writing *You're Wearing THAT?* I came to understand that love between mothers and daughters can be like romantic love. In writing this book, I realized that the same is true of friends. Two of the most moving books I have ever read are memoirs of friendship and the acute pain of a close friend's death: Gail Caldwell's *Let's Take the Long Way Home* and Ann Patchett's *Truth & Beauty*. These memoirs capture how friendship can entail the same deep satisfaction and sense of connection that we tend to associate with romantic love, and how a friend's death can be as devastating as the loss of a life partner. In the same way, a first best friend can resemble first love, and breaking up with a best friend can be like breaking up with a romantic partner. A woman told me she had bad dreams for years about a close friend who summarily ended their friendship without saying a word; she learned she'd been cut off when an invitation to the friend's wedding never arrived.

Jeanne Safer, a psychoanalyst, begins a book of essays about "love lost and found" with a personal experience: she received a voice message from someone whose disappearance, two years earlier, had caused her great pain. Hearing the voice brought a flood of conflicting emotions that reminded her of the terrible suffering she had experienced as a college student desperately in love with a man who broke her heart. But the phone message was not from a former lover. It was from a woman who had been her best friend, "the one woman in the world who spoke my language," who told her, "I've never talked to anybody the way I talk to you." Hearing this voice from the past plunged Safer into a state of emotional turmoil. She even found herself singing songs of grief about failed love affairs. Wondering why, she realized that what she was experiencing— "the paralysis, the desperate attempt at self-control, the justifications that couldn't justify, the anxiety that a wrong move on my part could be fatal, the strangulated fury, the feeling that parting would be unendurable—was exactly the same."

A close friend can resemble not only a romantic partner but also a sister, a daughter, a mother, a mentor, a therapist, a confessor—or all at once. UCLA psychologist Shelley Taylor has shown one reason why friends are particularly important to women. For many years it was conventional wisdom, based on research conducted with men, that human beings under stress have two options: fight or flight. Taylor found that this is less true for women. In conditions of stress, her research shows, it is at least as common, maybe more common, for women to neither fight nor flee but to bond. Taylor calls this impulse "tend and befriend"— tending to offspring and affiliating with others. And there you have the enormous role that friends can play in women's lives.

Taylor's research also helps explain why troubles with friends can be more distressing for women than for men. Many hours of women's conversations with friends are devoted to problems with other women friends—as are hours of their conversations with therapists. One woman remarked that 25 percent of her time—costly time!—in therapy is spent on her relationship with a friend. And the resulting damage can be not just emotional but physical. Carnegie Mellon researchers Rodlescia Sneed and Sheldon Cohen found that negative social encounters with friends were associated with an increased risk of high blood pressure— for women but not for men.

When talking to women about their friendships—both in the extended interviews I conducted and in countless casual conversations I had while researching and writing this book—I tended to focus on women friends, because most of the friendships women told me about were with other women. But sometimes women told me about friendships with men, and I include examples of those in this book. In many cases, those friendships were with gay men. My own best friend, as I describe in Chapter 8, is a gay man, as was the dear friend whose loss I write about in the epilogue. Close friendships between women and gay men are common and in many ways resemble the friendships among women that I describe, especially the role played by talk about personal lives. The woman who said she finds female friendships a difficult terrain to navigate went on to say that a lot of her closest friends are gay men. "I suspect," she said, "that gay men are my girlfriends," because "I find gay men very easy to be around." And perhaps there is the added frisson of cross-sex companionship without the complication of sexual possibility—much as a lesbian told me that her closest friendships tend to be with gay men and straight women, since friendships with gay women can get complicated if one gets a crush on the other that is not reciprocated. I haven't tackled here the intriguing nuances of women's friendships with gay men; perhaps that will be a topic for another book. In this one, I just try to observe and describe patterns in friendships that I heard about from women who told me of their experiences, as well as my own.

All the examples I give of conversations and friendships—except for occasional examples from novels and short stories—are based on real ones. Most are from the interviews I conducted, while some are from casual conversations I had on the topic. Some are examples reported by students in my classes at Georgetown University, either in papers written for the class or in what I call field notes, where students describe interactions they took part in or observed, and analyze them using the concepts, theories, and methods they encountered in our course. To ensure that students feel no pressure to allow me to use their work in this way, I never keep copies of field notes when I grade them. If I come across a field note that I think I might want to cite in the future, I attach a photocopy to the original and return both to the student along with all the others. I keep no record of whose or which field notes I return with copies. Students who feel comfortable with the possibility that I might one day refer to their field notes in my lectures or writing can return the photocopies to me. Those who don't, don't. I can honestly assure them that I will have no knowledge or recollection of having been interested in a field note that I didn't receive back.

Regardless of the source, for every example that I include, I always show the person I got it from exactly what I wrote, and the context in which it appears. I ask, first, if it's okay to use it. If the answer is no, it's out, no explanation needed. If the answer is yes, then I ask whether I got it right and if there is anything I should change for any reason: accuracy, privacy, comfort. After making any requested changes, I show the source my rewrite, and if that's not quite right, I'll revise it again, until exactly what will appear in print has been approved. In most cases, I use pseudonyms or no names at all. Pseudonyms are always first names only. In the few cases where a source is identified with a specific example, I give her full name.

The examples I include come from girls and women of a broad range of ages (nine to ninety-seven) and backgrounds: African-Americans, Asian-Americans, European-Americans, and Hispanic-Americans from many different ethnic, geographic, economic, and religious backgrounds as well as sexual orientations and gender identities. I sought this diversity to ensure that I heard a broad range of experience, not to characterize or compare groups of people. Comparison of groups requires survey methods, which narrow the focus of questions in order to get responses from a large number of subjects. Such studies might find, for example, that 60 percent of one group compared to 40 percent of the other respond in a certain way; such findings never describe every individual in the groups compared. My academic discipline and training are in a field called interactional sociolinguistics, which uses a case-study method that allows for in-depth analysis of real-life examples. The goal is to discover and explain the subtle and complex workings of language in interaction. I therefore refrain from specifying the ethnic or cultural backgrounds—or ages, professions, or sexual orientations—of most of the individuals whose examples I use, unless those identities seem crucial to understanding the example.

Though I focus on women's friendships, I do not doubt that some of what I write might also be true of friendships between women and men, and among men. But friendships play a particularly large role, and a particularly complex one, in women's lives. Men are often surprised by the depth of women's friendships, the depth of their distress when those friendships go awry, and the sheer amount of time that women spend talking to—and about—their friends. In writing this book, I tried simply to listen to the many women who told me of their friendships, and to uncover what is wonderful and what is challenging in a relationship that plays such an important part in women's lives. The multiplicity of meanings encapsulated by the word "friend," and the many different forms that friendship can take, made getting to the bottom of these relationships more daunting but also more fascinating. Figuring out what it means to be a friend is, in the end, no less than figuring out how we connect to other people. Understanding women's friendships—how they work or fail, how they help and hurt, and how we can make them better—is the goal of this book.

You're the Only One
I Can Tell

1

Women Friends Talking

Kathryn and Lily, friends for over sixty years, hadn't seen each other in several weeks. They both felt this was too long, so they arranged to get together. When Kathryn arrived at Lily's home, they sat down and talked. And talked. And talked. They didn't stop, and they didn't get up, until two and a half hours had passed. They talked about books they were reading, their significant others, politics, movies, their children, their children's children, and how their bodies and their living situations were changing with age. Later, they exchanged emails. Lily wrote, "That was a wonderful and soul-lifting visit, my dearest old friend. Will let you know about the movie." Kathryn replied, "I felt the same way about our time together." Her email ended, "Let me know about the movie, and if we go to the other one I will let you know about that. Take care, dear friend."

Andrea recalls that she and her best friend in middle school, Joelle, walked home together every day. They could take a bus, but they usually chose to walk instead so they would have more time to talk. At one point, there was a chance that Joelle's family would move to another state. The prospect of losing her friend filled Andrea with dread. "I won't be able to live without her," she felt. "If she moves, how will I survive?" That feeling is usually associated with a life partner or parent. But a connection to a friend can be that strong, too. A deep sense of loss can result when a friendship ends. As with a romantic partner, losing a friend means losing a language. No one else can understand the particular meanings of words that you shared, the references that made you laugh or nod in understanding. That loss is a testament to the power of conversation—of talk—to create a connection, a shared world.

If a friend who is part of your daily life moves away, a hole is left that is palpable every day. Paula and her neighbor Nancy became fast friends by running together every morning before work. When Paula stepped out to pick up the paper in the morning, she faced Nancy's house. During the winter months when days were shorter and mornings still dark, seeing the light in Nancy's kitchen made her smile. It filled her with warmth to know that her friend was up, too, also preparing coffee and breakfast. Then Nancy and her family moved. Paula felt forlorn. She wasn't motivated to run before work if Nancy wasn't going with her. To her surprise, she found herself regarding the woman who bought Nancy's house as an interloper. Now if Paula steps out to get the paper and spies a light in the kitchen across the way, though she knows it makes no sense, she feels resentment toward the woman who is moving around in Nancy's kitchen.

A friend—just one single friend—changed the life of a girl named Maya. At eleven, Maya had never had a friend. Though she badly wanted one, she simply did not know how to relate to other children. As her much older sister, Chana Joffe-Walt, explained on the radio show *This American Life,* Maya had many of the traits associated with the autism spectrum: "sensitivity to touch, lack of eye contact, obsessive and intense interest in one topic, and difficulty with social emotional reciprocity, what many of us call conversation." Having struggled her entire young life, Maya "had amassed a team of therapists" and "a series of diagnoses that all seemed to take her most obvious character trait and add the word 'disorder' to it." Despite the efforts of these experts, Maya "stopped asking for play-dates altogether. She stopped reading. She stopped smiling, and sleeping. And she was on edge all the time, especially at school. A kid would take her pencil or brush up against her at the bus stop, and Maya would blow up. She had to be physically restrained. She broke a window. She was diagnosed with oppositional defiant disorder. She got hospitalized for a brief period."

Then the miracle happened. Maya went to a horse camp, race horses being her obsession. And there she met Charlotte, who became her friend. Charlotte and Maya had playdates. They laughed together. They had sleepovers. Until then, children had kept their distance from Maya. But Charlotte told her mother, "Maya is perfect." Maya's life changed so dramatically that her family referred to BC and AC, life Before Charlotte and After Charlotte. Maya herself explained that through Charlotte she learned how to relate to other people: "Be more flexible. Not just talk about what you want to talk about all the time. Do other stuff that your friend wants." After two years of their friendship, Maya at thirteen "feels the feelings that come when you're a girl and you have a friend who makes you laugh, and thinks about you when you're apart, and gets you." Maya was transformed. She "no longer regularly gets in trouble at school. She now does her homework and washes her hair without a struggle. She has not had one violent incident AC. She makes eye contact sometimes. She asks, 'How are you?' sometimes. She does chores. That felt impossible BC. All of it seemed impossible BC." A friend accomplished what a decade of experts and therapists couldn't.

She Was There for Me

Having a friend means feeling less alone in the world. You have someone to talk to, someone to do things with, someone you can call on when you need something—or, even better, who will come through without being called on. I heard accounts of friends volunteering help in vastly different contexts. When Aisulu Kulbayeva, a linguistics graduate student, talked to women in a village in Kazakhstan about their friendships, they told her of women coming through with help when needed, and of sharing what little they had. One woman, Valentina, explained that she has a niece who is also a friend. When either visits the other, she always brings something, like candy for the children. And if her niece's husband has gone fishing, she will bring Valentina a fish. When Valentina's father died, her niece came over as soon as she heard, helped at the funeral, and helped Valentina cook for the many guests who came not only for the funeral but also for traditional gatherings on the ninth and fortieth days following her father's death. Switching to present tense, Valentina explained that during that time, in order to be there for Valentina, her niece "leaves all her household chores. The only thing she goes home for is to milk the cow."

"She was there for me" is something many women said when telling me about friendships they treasured. Some of the most moving stories I heard were of friends who came through in difficult times, and they spanned the ages and stages of women's lives. One woman recalled how her friends rallied around her when she faced a challenging life circumstance—in the third grade. Her family was going through a difficult time that her classmates got wind of. Her close friends did not ask for details—that in itself was a gesture of friendship—and they worked as a team to protect her. If a too-curious classmate seemed poised to ask questions that might be hard for her to deal with, her friends would move in and encircle her, so the inquisitive intruder could not get to her—literally or figuratively. I heard many accounts of friends bringing over meals and providing rides to medical facilities when a friend fell ill. Several women told me of friends who lived in distant cities coming to help when they were recovering from surgery—and staying for a week or more. A woman described how, following a painful divorce, her friends helped her turn the run-down condo she moved to into a home: "They came over with their rubber gloves and their buckets. It was like the maid brigade. They showed up to get down and dirty and gritty, because I was sort of dysfunctional at that point. I could do stuff, but I couldn't organize it."

On the other hand, a woman, Shirley, talked of an opposite experience. When her husband began showing the debilitating signs of Parkinson's disease, Shirley said, "There were women friends—women I thought were my friends—who just disappeared." Particularly disappointing was the reaction of a couple who had been among their closest friends for years. As Shirley's husband's illness worsened, the wife's visits became more sporadic, and her husband's stopped altogether. The wife told Shirley: "My husband can't handle seeing your husband that way." The hurt in Shirley's voice was evident as she said, "We had to live with his Parkinson's every day, and she's telling me her husband can't stand it for an hour." The experience led Shirley to contemplate the meaning of friendship. "If a friend isn't there when you need her," she mused, "what is a friend?"

One woman answered this question by saying that a true friend is someone she could "call at three in the morning and say I need $100 for an airplane ticket." The same wee hour came to the mind of a woman who told me that if a friend called her at three in the morning and said, "I need bail," she'd reply, "Okay, can I come in my nightie? I'll be right there." These scenarios were hypothetical, but I heard many real-life accounts of friends who jumped in a car or on a plane when a friend faced dire circumstances, such as that most unimaginable loss, the death of a spouse. One woman, when her friend's husband died, flew across the country immediately and stayed to show her friend how to do the many things that he had done: write checks, balance a checkbook, shop for food and cook dinner. After returning to her own home, she called on the phone—and continued to call every day for a year. Even when she was physically distant, she was there for her bereaved friend—through talk.

The circumstances needn't be cataclysmic for friends to come through by being there to talk. Another woman recalled a next-door neighbor "who called me one day when her son had dropped a jar of mayonnaise and smeared it around all over the kitchen floor then put eggs in it because he was going to make a cake. And she just left the mess and came over. We drank coffee and commiserated with each other."

It's All Talk

"For girls and women, talk is the glue that holds a relationship together."

When my book *You Just Don't Understand: Women and Men in Conversation* was published, I said this so often in interviews that my mother would tease me by chanting the sentence back to me. I'd always go on to add, "For boys and men, it's activities that are central. For girls, your best friend is the one you tell everything to. For boys, your best friend is the one you do everything with—and the one who will stick up for you if there's a fight."

Studies of children at play, such as Marjorie Harness Goodwin's *He-Said-She-Said*, found that girls and boys tend to play with others of the same sex, and to use language differently when they do. Typically, girls' social lives are centered on a best friend, and they spend a lot of time sitting and talking, especially exchanging secrets. Boys talk, too, of course, but they tend to do it differently and for different purposes. Typically (though, obviously, not every child is typical; patterns should not be misconstrued as norms), boys use language to take center stage by boasting, telling stories, making jokes, or telling others what to do—all ways of establishing their status in the group, and also ways of talking that girls find unacceptable in other girls. A boy who issues commands to others and gets them to stick is the leader. A girl who tries to tell others what to do is bossy, and the other girls don't want to play with her.

Observing the ways children use language in same-sex play sheds light on differences in how women and men tend to use language among friends as adults. Students in my classes observing their own conversations frequently describe contexts where the young women talk and the young men use action. Here's an example provided by Erika Duelks.

> Saturday night, after a party, a group of us went to Matt's house to hang out before we went home to bed. I (and the other girls) proceeded to sit down on the couch and we began talking about the night: what we thought was fun, what we wished had happened,

etc. I was in the middle of giving my friend Sarah advice about a
boy when all of a sudden the coffee table was pushed out of the way
and the guys began to wrestle, throwing each other onto the couch
and pushing each other off chairs. It was funny for me to see my big
guy friends wrestling as if they were five-year-olds, but it also struck
me that this is how we chose to relax: the girls began talking . . .
and the guys got up and started play-fighting.

If the boys were acting like five-year-olds by roughhousing, Erika and her
friends were also acting like five-year-olds—five-year-old girls—by sitting
and talking.

I've often asked audiences, "When did you last communicate with
your closest friend?" Most women raise their hands to indicate "this
morning," "yesterday," or "within a week." A few women's hands go up to
show "within a month." But many men, and very few women, raise their
hands to indicate it has been a year or more. When I ask this question in
conversation, men often say, "I haven't spoken to him in a year—but if I
needed him, he'd be there." If talk is the glue that holds a relationship
together, you have to talk to your friend to maintain the friendship. If
friendships are focused on activities, then there's not much to gain by
talking to friends who aren't there.

Journalist Jeffrey Zaslow was intrigued by the close friendships he saw
his mother, sister, wife, and daughters enjoying—and sometimes suffering from. Like an anthropologist who goes to live among members of a
different culture, Zaslow followed a group of women who had been
friends for forty years, to figure out what drives their friendships. As he
recounted in his book *The Girls from Ames,* he quickly realized that talking about their personal lives was key to their friendships—and completely different from the kind of talk he and his friends engaged in. "I've
been playing poker with a group of friends every Thursday night for
many years," he wrote in his introduction to the book. "About 80 percent
of our conversations are focused specifically on the cards, the betting, the
bluffing. Most of the rest of the chatter is about sports, or sometimes

our jobs. For weeks on end, our personal lives—or our feelings about anything—never come up."

Zaslow wasn't unusual. Two couples, for example, had parallel friend-ships: the husbands played tennis regularly, and the wives met regularly for lunch. One day one of the wives remarked to her husband how bad she felt that the other couple were getting divorced. This was news to him—shocking news: though they'd met to play tennis week after week, the state of his friend's marriage had never come up.

Women are often surprised by what men don't know about their friends—and by what they don't talk about when they talk. A mother, chatting with her son who had recently graduated from college, asked if he'd spoken to one of his friends lately.

"Yup," he said. "We spoke yesterday."

She followed up, "How is he doing?"

He replied, "I don't know."

"But you just spoke to him," she said. "Didn't he say?"

"Nope."

"Well, how's his job?"

"I don't know."

"How's his girlfriend?"

"Don't know."

"Well, what did you talk about?"

"Football."

"Did you only talk about football?"

"Nope. Soccer, too."

The contrast in how women and men tend to talk to friends emerged in a couple's experiences. The wife and several other women got together weekly to talk. Seeing how much their wives enjoyed these meetings, their husbands decided to do the same. But it didn't work as well for them. When the men got together, they were uncomfortable; the conver-sation just didn't flow. Finally, they found a fix: they decided they needed a prearranged topic to talk about. This contrast also underlies the experi-ence of a transgender man who told me that his best friend is a man who, like him, was born female and transitioned to male in his early thirties. He generally hasn't had close friendships with men born male, and he suspects this may be because their ways of being friends tend to differ from his. Although he did not want to generalize about trans men, he feels that his own socialization as a girl shaped the way he maintains friendships: meet for coffee, take a walk, call on the phone—and talk. He has found that men born male generally (obviously there are exceptions) don't meet for coffee or schedule other meetings primarily to talk; they tend to get together to do something, and talk while they're doing it.

Telling Secrets, Making Friends

There is a type of talk that has a special place in girls' friendships: telling secrets. I have seen pictures from all over the world of two little girls sitting together, one whispering in the other's ear. (I have never encountered a similar picture of two little boys.) The role of secrets in their friendships helps explain why girls are often cliquey: you can't tell secrets in front of a girl who isn't a friend. (By contrast, boys have no reason to exclude a boy they don't like. They can let him play, but stick him in an undesirable position in a game or otherwise give him a hard time.) For girls, and later for women, closeness can be gauged—and negotiated—by who knows what secrets, and how and when they know them. If a girl reveals her best friend's secret to another girl, she might find herself with a new best friend.

"I define close," a woman said, "as someone who knows things about me that other people don't." Often that closeness begins in a breakthrough conversation where something deeply personal is revealed. As one young woman put it, sharing personal information is like a first step toward friendship: "Here's this little piece of me. This means I like you." A friendship grows if the listener reciprocates. Another woman recalled an acquaintance becoming a friend that way: "We'd never really just *talked,* like about personal things. Then she opened up about some mental health issues she's had. And so I opened up, too. And it was just a strong bonding experience. And ever since then I've felt so much closer to her." Yet another explained that a friendship formed when she could talk about heartbreak and use pronouns—that is, she let her friend know that the lover who broke her heart was a woman, and thereby learned that her friend had been questioning her own sexuality: "My revealing that was the deepest conversation we have had, and her revealing that to me brought us closer, opened up the doors to deeper conversations."

Exchanging secrets can be a litmus test of friendship. "If they're true friends," a woman said, "I tell them everything I feel and everything I think." And they are expected to do the same. For many women, failing to tell what's going on in your life is a violation of friendship. Trudy was stunned when her friend Pam revealed that she had been having an affair and was separating from her husband—and wanted Trudy to reassure her that she was doing the right thing. During the months leading up to this revelation, Trudy and Pam had traveled together; Trudy had helped Pam deal with problems at work; and she'd been open about what was going on in her own life. In all ways, she'd been treating Pam like a friend. But by keeping this crucial aspect of her life secret, Pam had not acted like one. Trudy felt betrayed: "I felt like she had lied to me. She hadn't confided in me when she was going through this. I felt like, if I'm one of her closest friends, she could have bounced some of this off of me. I felt very slighted." In Trudy's view, and that of many women, not telling a friend what's really going on is tantamount to lying; it's not being a true friend. And if Pam hadn't been one, she shouldn't expect Trudy to be: "I felt like, now she wants me to be on board without having led me through any of this."

Not every woman seeks closeness through sharing secrets, and no woman seeks it with everyone or with anyone all the time. The sharing of secrets may not be welcome with a particular friend, or not welcome at that point in the friendship. Like wanting to slow down a suitor who is going too fast, a college student, Jill, recalled a roommate who one night "just shared a lot and I was like, 'Ahhh!' It was too much for me." Jill went on to explain that she is like a nut, so it takes time to crack through her shell. In time, though, she and her roommate became friends—and she did, as she put it, crack open her shell, that is, become comfortable with sharing personal information.

Whispers in the Night

The importance of exchanging secrets is inextricable from a ritual that has a unique place in the lives of many young girls: sleepovers. An eleven-year-old told me, by way of explaining the difference between a best friend and a good friend, "With a best friend you invite her over for a sleepover every other weekend. A good friend, you might invite her over for a play-date sometimes." Sleepovers entail a special intimacy, because of the hours of uninterrupted time the girls have to spend together, the self-revelation of pajamas and of shedding day clothes to get into them, and the physical proximity that usually prevails. One woman described a scene from her childhood sleepovers: the hair circle. She and her friends would sit in a circle, each one combing and braiding the hair of the one in front of her, while her own hair was being combed and braided by the one behind. The intimacy of touch—a girl's fingers grooming another's hair while someone else's fingers groom hers—is intensified as all the girls experience it at the same time. By bringing them together in a single shape, a circle, the shared experience connects them all the more tightly as a group—as do the matching braids that result. And because the physical intimacy of a sleepover takes place during the night, it sets the stage for exchanging secrets, like extending the scene of a little girl whispering in another's ear.

For roommates at college or boarding school, every night is a sleepover. One woman explained the deep connection of a boarding-school friendship by describing this scene: "I was really upset and we were lying in bed at night—our two cots were very close to each other—and she was so supportive. I don't remember what I was upset about. All I remember is the warmth that came from the opposite bed."

The kind of talk that can be uncovered by the cover of darkness is the subject of Sarah Orne Jewett's story "Miss Tempy's Watchers," which was published in 1888. Night-talk constitutes the story, which consists entirely of a conversation between two elderly women, friends since high school, in a small New England farming town. The Miss Tempy of the title is a third high school friend who has died; as her "watchers," the two friends are spending the night in Miss Tempy's house so her body will not be left alone until it is buried the next day. The setting allows Jewett to articulate the women's inner lives as they fill the otherwise silent house with their conversation. And, thanks to the embrace of night, "the two women had risen to an unusual level of expressiveness and confidence. Each had already told the other more than one fact that she had determined to keep secret; they were again and again tempted into statements that either would have found impossible by daylight."

The women's conversation in Jewett's story, like the talk that often takes place at girls' sleepovers, is an archetypal version of the exchange of secrets that is typical of girls' and women's friendships. When a little girl is whispering in another's ear, the contents of the words whispered may not always be literal secrets: personal thoughts, feelings, and confessions that would be compromising if others knew them. As often as not, what the girl is whispering about is something trivial that would not especially interest or compromise anyone were it said aloud. Rather than keeping a tidbit of information private, the main point may be what the action of whispering makes public: their closeness. Since girls tell secrets only to friends, sharing a secret can be a way of initiating or nurturing—and displaying—a friendship. All who see them are reminded that the pair are friends, bound together in a way that excludes others. And this display of connection is enhanced by the girls' physical proximity: the whisperer has to get close enough to touch her friend, who has to allow that closeness and that touch.

Knowing each other's secrets—intimate thoughts, feelings, confessions—is both currency and evidence of closeness. Who knows what, and who knows first, can come to represent who is the closer and more valued friend. The desire to know is inseparable from a desire to have others know that you know. Conversely, it can be humiliating when your not knowing is known. In *The Social Sex*, their history of women's friendship, Marilyn Yalom and Theresa Donovan Brown quote an upper-class French woman living in the seventeenth century who complained, in a letter to a friend, of just such a betrayal: "Being your friend to the extent that I am, it is ridiculous that I am always the last to know the things that concern you, and that I am ashamed to let others know I am ignorant of them." Inseparable from this woman's wish to know is her wish for others to know she knows—a public representation of her closeness to this friend, rather like the display of little girls' whispering.

Why Didn't You Tell Me?

Cassie and Meg had been dear friends for decades—ever since they'd met when they both lived in the Midwest, and continuing long after Cassie had moved to Los Angeles, and Meg to Philadelphia. They were the kind of friends who felt like family: each referred to the other as the sister she never had. They had no secrets from each other, and every Thanksgiving Meg came to stay with Cassie—first with her daughter, and then, when her daughter was grown, by herself. But one year something seemed very wrong—so wrong that Cassie closed herself in her bedroom and wept. She had the dreadful feeling that her dearest friend had lost interest in their friendship; Meg was treating Cassie's home not like her own home, but like a hotel.

During her visit, Meg had a single afternoon completely free, but rather than spending it with Cassie, she was going to have lunch with a high school classmate she barely knew. Meg asked Cassie to help: Could she drive her to meet this friend? Could she pick her up? These requests felt to Cassie like exploitation; even worse, it felt like Meg was asking her to facilitate her own exclusion. She demurred. Meg persisted: if Cassie couldn't drive her, could she tell Meg how to get there on public transportation? Cassie was baffled: why would her dearest friend squander their one chance for time together by spending the afternoon with a casual acquaintance? It didn't make sense. Cassie's meltdown, like the depth of her hurt, was less about feeling passed over in favor of another than about feeling that Meg either was hiding something or was no longer the friend Cassie had known her to be. She couldn't say which of these deeply upsetting prospects was the more disturbing.

Cassie said nothing during that visit, but because she treasured the friendship, she expressed her dismay over the phone—in an after-the-fact, let's-work-this-out conversation that is common among women (and baffling to many men). Meg's explanation made everything fall into place, like a fuzzy picture that suddenly comes into focus. Meg's grandson had been having problems with drug abuse, and Meg had recalled that this high school classmate had married a psychiatrist specializing in teenagers and substance abuse. Meg had contacted the friend, who had connected Meg's daughter with her physician husband, who had been very helpful to her son. Meg felt so grateful to this friend that she wanted to thank her personally by taking her to lunch. But she didn't feel it was her place to tell Cassie, since it was more her daughter's and grandson's secret than her own.

Secrets are at the heart of this story, and of the shifting alignments that they can create and threaten: who knows, who tells? Had Meg told Cassie what was going on, Cassie would not have been hurt by her friend's decision to spend her free afternoon with the high school classmate, and she would have been more than happy to drive Meg to the meeting and pick her up. Instead of feeling that she was being asked to help her best friend neglect her, she would have felt like she was playing a part in something important in Meg's life. And being told something so private, especially something potentially compromising, would have reinforced their closeness, while sensing that something was being kept from her had undermined it.

Troubles Talk: Don't Tell Me What to Do

Differences in how women and men tend to use talk in close relationships lie behind a mutually frustrating scenario that often plays out in conversations between women and men. (Of the many scenarios I described in *You Just Don't Understand*, this one is among those that sparked the most enthusiastic recognition.) A woman tells a man about a problem she is having, and is frustrated when he tells her how to fix it. She wasn't looking for a solution. She had hoped for what a woman friend might say, something like "The same thing happened to me" or "I know how you feel; I'd feel the same way." He is frustrated, too: why does she want to talk about it if she doesn't want to do anything about it? He may even feel wrongly accused: he thought he was supplying what she asked for; why would she tell him about a problem if she didn't want his help fixing it?

The answer is the type of conversation, so common and so valued among women friends but so unfamiliar to most men: troubles talk. From her point of view, "The same thing happened to me" is an expression of understanding and a reassurance of sameness, both of which are treasured benefits of friendship. But that's only the start of the conversation. A friend would go on to ask for more details: And then what did you say? And what did she say? And why do you think she said that? And how did that make you feel? And what did you say next? The failure to ask those follow-up questions may be the most frustrating thing about his telling her how to fix the problem. By describing the problem, she meant to start a conversation. Offering a solution shuts the conversation down. This result, disappointing to her, might be a secondary gain for him, because he finds it frustrating to take part in a conversation that seems to have no point. It seems that way because he's looking for the point in the message, while it lies elsewhere: in the metamessage.

Every utterance has meaning on two levels: message and metamessage. The message is the meaning of the words; the metamessage is what it says about the relationship that these words are spoken in this way in this context. The message of follow-up questions and extended answers is clear to everyone. It's their metamessage that means so much to many women (and can be opaque to many men). Taking the time to explore a problem, to ask questions and listen to the answers, and then use the answers in formulating further questions—all this sends a metamessage of caring. The one who tells of a problem feels less alone if someone cares enough to engage in troubles talk. Given this expectation, short-circuiting troubles talk sends the opposite metamessage: I don't want to hear any more about your problem because I don't care enough about it—or about you.

The frustration a woman might feel if she wants to talk about a problem and a man she is close to doesn't is commensurate with the magnitude of the troubles. Ironically, the greater the problem, the less eager he may be to talk about it, not because he doesn't care but because he cares so much. If someone he loves has a problem, he feels obligated to do something—he *wants* to do something. Since he doesn't feel, as women typically do, that listening and expressing understanding *is* doing something, talking about a problem he can't fix aggravates his feelings of helplessness. A woman who was recovering from a double mastectomy and undergoing breast reconstruction was disappointed that she could not talk about what she was going through with her husband, but she understood that he needed to focus on something he could do. He suggested that they take advantage of the time she'd be home to renovate their kitchen. So instead of talking about cancer they talked about cabinet colors.

A new kind of taxi service, SheTaxi and SheRides, allows passengers to request a woman driver. An article about the service reports that customers rave about it—and so do the drivers. One driver, Martha Pitterson, explained that she prefers women riders because she prefers their conversation. When men ride in her cab, she said, they tell her to drive faster or talk about sports, a topic that doesn't interest her. Women talk about their lives—and often their troubles. One passenger, for example, confessed she was having an affair, while another complained about her grandchildren. I'd be curious to know (the article doesn't say) how Ms. Pitterson responds to her passengers' troubles: by just listening or by offering matching troubles of her own.

It is almost an obligation for women to come up with matching troubles, to fulfill their part in this conversational ritual, even if, as one woman recounted, a friend's troubles are difficult to sympathize with. Following a disastrous divorce, Hannah was living in subsidized public housing, so it was hard to feel sympathy for a friend who was complaining about the inconvenience caused by workers adding a screened-in porch to her house. Yet Hannah knew that she had to find a trouble to offer up in the conversation. Luckily, she could always find something about her son or her grandchildren to complain about. In a parallel way, a graduate student was relieved that she could always complain about school when her friend complained about a boyfriend's thoughtlessness and other offenses that her own boyfriend was not guilty of. ("My boyfriend wouldn't do that" is not an acceptable response.)

Finding matching troubles to offer can be a delicate business—and can easily backfire. A woman devastated by her husband's accidental death was not comforted when a friend said that she, too, had experienced the pain of learning to live alone, following her divorce. Though the friend began by saying, "I know it's not the same," her comment gave the impression that she did think the losses were comparable, and this reinforced the widow's conviction that her friend didn't understand what she was going through at all, and had no idea how much more painful it is to lose—suddenly and irrevocably—a partner with whom she had lived in near-perfect harmony.

The need to find matching troubles can also be challenging when a friend's circumstances change for other reasons. For example, if friends are in the habit of commiserating over their dating woes, it can be awkward when one of them commits to a monogamous relationship and no longer has dating problems to talk about. She may hesitate to talk about the relationship problems she does have, because she feels a sense of loyalty to her partner that she did not feel toward those she dated: she might not want her friend to get a negative impression of her partner, who might object to being talked about for the same reason. This is especially true for men who wouldn't talk to their own friends about problems in their relationships, and don't see why anyone else would either.

Troubles Talk: Please Tell Me What to Do

The apparent explanation of why women's troubles talk often backfires with men—she doesn't want a solution; she just wants to talk about it— isn't quite right. In many cases, a woman who initiates troubles talk does want advice. She just doesn't want it right off the bat; she wants it to emerge after, or in the course of, talking about it. Before you know what advice to give, you need to know more about the situation. That's why women typically ask follow-up questions. While on the metamessage level asking questions and listening to the answers shows caring, on the message level, troubles talk provides crucial information that is necessary to figure out what advice would be best.

Advice is not anathema to troubles talk; it's inextricable from it. But it's not always clear when someone wants advice, when she just wants someone to listen, and what advice she'd appreciate if she is open to any. Sometimes confiding in a friend is a plea for encouragement to do what she fears or hesitates but really wants to do. But sometimes it's not. Louise, for example, was having a hard time now that her son had graduated from college and taken a job in a distant city. He had found an apartment, but it was still empty, because he hadn't managed to shop for furniture. When they spoke on the phone, he told her that he was sitting in the dark because his apartment had no overhead lighting; he hadn't taken her suggestion to buy a lamp. Louise felt an almost irresistible urge to do what she did when he was in college: go and help him buy furniture. She was describing this impulse to a friend, who advised, "Well, get on a plane and go!" In a different situation, Louise might have appreciated being encouraged to act on her impulse. In this case, though, she didn't. "That's not helpful!" Louise protested. "He's twenty-two. I'm trying to fight this obsession, not give in to it!"

There are other times, though, when women appreciate friends' advice—even if they haven't been doing troubles talk. Grace, for example, mentioned that from the time she moved into her home, her mother made it clear that she doesn't like a narrow carpet that runs up the stairs. Grace has left it there nonetheless—maybe even, she admitted, to be contrary. Then she added, "But let me say this. If one of my friends was like, 'Have you thought about not having a runner there? It would look so much more crisp,' I'd probably get a box cutter and take it up." Advice from mothers is often suspect because it feels like criticism, so a daughter may resent and therefore resist it. But (to her mother's dismay), the same advice from a friend may be valued: if she thinks I should do this, maybe I should.

Sometimes advice from friends is resented, too, either because it feels impractical or, worse, because it reveals insulting assumptions. That happened with a young professor, Terry, who suffered the setback that all junior faculty members fear: being denied tenure. If Terry didn't find another university position, all the years and money and effort she had invested in earning a PhD and developing a research program would go down the tubes. Among the pieces of advice that friends offered Terry, one stuck in her craw: "Maybe you should try teaching high school instead." This advice implied that Terry was not capable of the career she had chosen, trained for, and worked so hard to build. (In fact, she found a position at another college, where she earned tenure and went on to establish a successful academic career.) The problem wasn't that her friend gave advice instead of offering support, or even that she gave advice that Terry wouldn't take, but that the advice she gave seemed to reflect a lack of confidence in Terry's abilities.

Whose Back Do You Have?

The closer a friend is, the more you might trust her advice—or the more suspicious you might be, because you know that your decision will affect her, too. In a novel aptly titled *Friendship,* Emily Gould portrays these complications. The eponymous friendship begins when Bev gets a job at a New York publishing company where Amy has been working for a year. Among the many conversations that create a friendship between them is Amy giving Bev "practical advice about how to appease her boss." The benefit of such advice is clear-cut. But personal advice can be more complicated than the practical kind, especially as the two women become best friends. When Bev tells Amy that her boyfriend is moving to Wisconsin to go to law school, and she is going to quit her job to go with him, Amy tells her that she is making a mistake. It eventually becomes clear that Amy was right: after two years of working in a restaurant while her relationship with her boyfriend deteriorates, Bev learns that he has been having an affair with a fellow law student. She packs up and returns to New York—with no job and no self-esteem.

Following her boyfriend to Wisconsin made a mess of Bev's life. But it had a significant impact on Amy's life, too. When Bev left New York, Amy lost her constant companion, her confidante. And it affected Amy in another, more material way, too. When Bev returns to New York, depressed and destitute, she goes to her friend Amy's tiny New York apartment, intending to stay temporarily but in the end staying for months. Had Bev listened to Amy, her life would have been better—and so would Amy's! The way that decision played out, the reader—and the friends—can't know to what extent Amy's advice was based solely on what was best for Bev, or also on what was best for herself. They don't have to ask, because staying in New York rather than quitting her job to follow her boyfriend would have been best for both of them. But the next big decision that Bev has to make—the one that becomes the core of the novel's plot, and the challenge to the friendship—is not so clear.

Back in New York, Bev discovers that a single night of sex with a man she barely knows has left her pregnant. Once again, her friend offers advice: she points out that Bev has no partner or family who could share the responsibility of raising a child; no money, only debts; and no job or career prospects: she is barely managing to pay rent in a shabby living situation by occasional work through a temp agency. Obviously Bev's only viable option is to have an abortion. In this case, too, Bev does not listen to Amy. She decides to have the baby—a decision that turns out to be the right one, though it becomes so thanks to developments that Amy could not have foreseen: a chance meeting with a former professor leads Bev to the perfect, well-paying, health-insurance-providing job, and another near stranger turns out to be a wealthy woman who is happy to take on the role of co-parent and source of limitless, no-strings-attached-no-particular-due-date loans.

Though these deus ex machina plot twists are idealized, the challenge to the friendship when Bev chooses a path that differs from Amy's, and that Amy advised against, is realistic. And it forces Amy to examine her own motives in formulating that advice. After a period of separation, she sends a soul-searching and conciliatory email to Bev. In it, she writes: "I never imagined that you would have a child. I must have thought we would always stay essentially the same as we were when we met." She goes on to say that though she had many fantasies about her future, she knew she was doing nothing to make them real, and "I was counting on you to be the same way, which was what made it so hard when it turned out you were going to be a mother. You were right: I was jealous! And I feel horrible about feeling jealous . . ." As for the advice she had proffered, "I thought I was just trying to help you realize what was best for you." But in fact, she now realizes, "the whole time, I was only thinking about what was best for me."

Amy confesses that she fears Bev won't forgive her for letting her down, for "not being there" when Bev gave birth. But she also fears that "I won't be able to fit into your new life." She closes the email by explaining why she let so much time pass without contacting Bev, and in the process also explains the inextricable combination of caring and selfishness that is part of any close relationship. If she reached out, Bev might reject her: "I was scared of how it would feel if you picked up the phone and sounded disappointed to hear my voice. Which in and of itself is selfish." The novel has a happy ending: Bev replies immediately to Amy's email by texting "YT" for "You There?"—the way they had routinely checked whether the other was available to chat. Amy's heart leaps. By responding in their private language, Bev signals that she is not disappointed to see Amy's name on her screen—and the reader knows, as Amy does, that the friendship has survived.

Amy made that happy ending possible by acknowledging the complex motivations that underlay the advice she gave her friend. Though ideally a friend is someone who selflessly wants only the best for you, it can't always be as simple as that, because of the nature of closeness. In close friendship, as in romantic relationships, one person's actions significantly affect the other. Knowing that someone cares deeply about you is comforting, but it is also confining, because taking into account how your actions will affect someone else limits your freedom. It can—and often does—affect the advice that person gives you.

The Trouble with Troubles Talk

A gynecologist and obstetrician, Frederica Lofquist, cautions her pregnant and trying-to-get-pregnant patients never to join a group of women in the kitchen at a party. In those kitchen conversations—or similar backstage gatherings in any context—women will offer what seem like the usual well-meaning matching troubles. But the troubles they dredge up are often exaggerated if not unfounded and in any case upsetting. Here are some examples that Dr. Lofquist gave me, a few among innumerable such comments that her patients have recounted to her.

- You look really small. Does your doctor think everything is going okay?
- You look really big. Are you having twins? Do you think you are further along than what they say? Does your doctor think everything is going okay?
- I was in labor for five days before my baby was born, and then they had to do an emergency cesarean and I almost bled to death. It was so horrible!
- How long have you been trying to get pregnant? I had to have five IVF cycles before I got pregnant and then I ended up with an ectopic pregnancy and almost died from internal bleeding. None of my five best friends have been able to get pregnant, even my sister who started trying when she was twenty-five.
- I hope everything goes well. My sister's best friend lost her baby a week before she was due. She still hasn't recovered.
- My cousin's best friend recently died in childbirth. It was so terrible; it went on for a week. All these things went wrong and for some reason the doctors let it happen.

Disaster stories like these—whether they are accurate, exaggerated, or apocryphal—play into and magnify the fears that plague pregnant women anyway. They may be motivated by a desire to help by alerting someone to potential danger she might be able to avoid if made aware of it. But hearing such stories can be deeply disturbing.

When I heard Dr. Lofquist's list of scare stories, my first reaction was to think, How could anyone say things like that? My second was to realize I had just done something comparable! I'd been at an event that was winding down; a few of us late-leavers were strolling down the hall when a friend tripped and fell. My husband and I rushed to help her up, find her a seat, and ask if she was okay. She said she was but would like to put ice on her elbow. As someone went for ice, I told my fallen friend to be cautious, because her arm might be broken—a caution I backed up by relating an experience of my own: I'd tripped and fallen at an airport, and though the EMS team that showed up had assured me my arm didn't seem broken, the next day my doctor insisted that I go to the emergency room and get an X-ray, which showed that it was.

After talking to Dr. Lofquist, I was mortified to realize I had done exactly what she described—told a disaster story that probably upset my friend further when she was no doubt badly rattled by her fall. My motive, I was sure, had been to prevent her from overlooking a potentially dangerous situation. But how helpful could my warning have been? My doctor had recommended I go to the emergency room because the morning after I fell, I could not straighten my arm, whereas my friend assured me the next day that her arm was fine. In addition to making me ashamed of myself, the realization reminded me that good intentions do not always guarantee good effects. Though I sincerely thought I was being helpful, what I really was doing was free-associating, thinking out loud. My friend's fall reminded me of my own. In a way, offering my disaster story was a perversion of the troubles-talk rejoinder that would be welcome in other contexts: "The same thing happened to me." Dr. Lofquist's advice to her patients to avoid groups of women is a valuable warning to all of us, especially us women: conversational rituals that might be appreciated in one context may be far from constructive in others.

Gossip

There is another way that troubles talk, which can be deeply comforting, must be handled with caution. Troubles talk and secrets are inextricably intertwined; in many cases, they're the same. You want to discuss a problem with a friend, to feel that someone knows and understands what you're going through; to think through how to handle it; to seek support—either the emotional kind that comes of caring or the pragmatic kind that consists of offering to help. But telling troubles, like telling secrets, entails a risk. If you tell a friend something you don't want everyone to know, you must trust her not to repeat it. One woman, talking to me about a friend, put it this way: "She has told me some very personal things, and she knows it stays in the vault. There's nobody I would tell. And I feel the same with her."

"The vault" is an apt metaphor; secrets can be that valuable. But it can never be guaranteed that personal information will stay in the vault if someone else holds the key. A friend might not realize that something you told her was meant as a secret; she might let it slip inadvertently; she might repeat it intentionally, in the spirit of sharing news or to let someone else know how close she is to you; and she might use it against you if your friendship ends or was never as true as you thought it was. Women are aware of these risks, and must constantly monitor them. One young woman explained, in an overheard conversation, "I have two close friends. I can tell one of them anything. I know it will stay with her. But if I tell the other one something, everyone will know about it." Yet she considers them both close friends. I heard a similar comment from a nine-year-old, who described two friends this way: "Me and Tina, we feel like we can trust a secret with each other. But I don't really feel like I can trust a secret with Rachel, because she goes over to someone else and might tell someone."

Several women said they prefer men as friends because guys won't repeat their secrets. I don't think this is because men are inherently more trustworthy, but because secrets don't have the currency in boys' and men's friendships that they have in girls' and women's: men have nothing to gain by repeating secrets. Because girls and women tend to vie for closeness—to a popular girl or a particular friend—what better way to prove you are close to someone than to show that you know her secrets? So friendship, even true friendship, can lead inevitably to gossip.

Women's fear of gossip seems to be as universal as their desire to talk about troubles. It was the primary concern that Aisulu Kulbayeva heard about when she discussed friendship with women in a small Kazakh village. The same fear is common in the United States. An American woman recalls that her mother advised her to be careful about sharing personal information, especially with women who play bridge or get their hair done every week. "When they run out of things about themselves to say," her mother warned, "they'll move on to talking about you."

Underlying this caution are two assumptions: first, that friends will tell each other personal and potentially embarrassing or even compromising things, and, second, that when women get together, they talk, and their preferred topics are personal, about their own or others' lives. The result is that having friends entails the risk of gossip—both because of women's desire to have material for conversation and because of their desire to open their hearts to a friend. A Kazakh woman who, on one hand, told Kulbayeva, "I don't share the difficult stories of my life with anyone," also said, "When you have talked to someone, it is lighter on the soul. The day seems sunnier, and troubles step back and start seeming smaller." That is the inescapable conundrum of women's friendship: talk about personal problems is both its greatest gift and its biggest risk.

Good Gossip: Talking About

Gossip! That damning word inextricably associated with women talking. Gossip has a bad rep, which gives women a bad rep. Or maybe it's the other way around: the association with women is part of what makes gossip suspect. Women talking are often assumed to be gossiping, and to be doing something unsavory. Norman Rockwell's classic painting *The Gossips,* featured on a *Saturday Evening Post* cover in 1948, depicts the spreading of a rumor in a series of two-person conversations. Each pair includes a speaker who was a listener in the previous pair. The rumor (and the painting) begins with a woman speaking and ends with a man—apparently the one who is the subject of the rumor—wagging his finger at the same woman, who looks chagrined to be identified (fingered!) as its source.

There are two very different ways of discussing other people—that is, of gossiping: talking about and talking against. It's the "against" kind that gives gossip its bad rep. But often, and more commonly, people talk about others' lives without putting them down: just talking *about*. This kind of gossip simply reflects an interest in other people's lives, exactly what lies at the heart of academic disciplines like anthropology, sociology, psychology, and my own, sociolinguistics. It's also the stuff of which novels and short stories are made. Fiction writer Cynthia Ozick points out that gossip is simply an interest in people: talking about people—gossiping—is being a philosopher; it's being human.

Being interested in a friend's personal life is a show of caring, a way to create closeness. A college student described a friend she especially appreciates by describing their conversations: "When something's wrong she will sit there and make eye contact the whole time and really take things in." Talking about others can be an extension of just this kind of interest and caring. We ask a friend how another friend is doing, and are happy to hear if the news is good and saddened if it's bad. If it's neither good nor bad but just filling in—what college did her daughter decide on? Did she take a new job?—knowing what's going on in her life makes you both feel more connected. Just asking is a sign of connection. That kind of talking-about is at least benign, often constructive.

Given the role of talk about personal lives in women's friendships, it's not surprising that the original meaning of the word "gossip" was, simply, a close friend. It's easy to see how the word could have morphed to mean talking about others' personal lives. And it's also easy to see how talking about personal lives can morph from good gossip—talking about—to bad gossip: talking against.

Bad Gossip: Talking Against

The kind of talk that the word "gossip" most often calls to mind is talking *against*. Bad gossip was one of the main reasons some women told me they don't trust other women, and the reason they don't have women friends. But protecting yourself from gossip by not revealing personal information can mean losing the chance to make friends. A Greek woman's comments illuminated the connection between fearing gossip and missing out on friendship. She used to live in Athens, but now she lives in a small town. It's harder, she said, to make new friends in the small town, because people living there are less open than Athenians. That goes for herself, too: she is less likely to talk about her problems to friends in the small town because they gossip. Consequently, she has fewer friends there than she had when she lived in the city.

Carly formed the opinion early on that women can't be trusted because they gossip: during summers when she was a child, her mother would take her to work, and she'd hang out in the lounge where her mother's colleagues gathered during breaks. "I'd watch them be snide and catty and backstabbing," Carly said. "And I was like, 'Wow, this is what it means to be a grown-up?' I was watching and listening and feeling disgusted by it. I just didn't want that." Carly feels this explains why she became a private person: "I don't like my business in the street." Her wariness of gossip, and of girls, was reinforced in middle school when a friend, Deanna, deliberately made up and spread rumors about her:

> One time I got on the school bus, and I sat next to this older guy. I didn't even talk to him. I was really shy. But there was nowhere else to sit. And he had a girlfriend, and I was seeing somebody, so it wasn't like we were even flirting. It just pissed her off so much that I got to sit next to him. So another friend told me that Deanna was spreading rumors about me to this guy so he wouldn't like me.

Burned by experiences like this, Carly concluded that girls backstab and gossip, especially in competition for boys. She made up her mind to have none of it: "I'm not playing that game; I'm not doing the backstabbing, the gossiping, the going after the boys stuff. And I'm not sharing myself with you either because I don't trust you." She realized, however, that this decision got in the way of her making friends: "And so because I removed myself that way, I kind of had to remove my whole self. And so then I didn't have a certain closeness or intimacy with some of my peers that I now know that other people had." Happily, this has changed. "As I've gotten older," Carly said, "my friendships have gotten better, deeper, more comfortable. I've learned how to be a better friend."

Another woman, Lauren, could also pinpoint the reason that a middle school friend—in her case, a former friend—spread rumors about her. Lauren's mother had decided, for reasons of her own, that Lauren should stop spending time with her best friend, Olivia. Lauren had no choice but to obey her mother. She knew Olivia would be hurt, as she herself was deeply hurt to lose her best friend. But she did not expect Olivia to "retaliate"—by spreading rumors. Lauren recalls, "All of a sudden, 'Lauren isn't good enough for Olivia. Lauren is bad. Lauren is snobby.' There was a whole drama surrounding it." Spreading rumors is an easy way to cause others harm—because they hurt you, because you are jealous, or just because.

As adults, women must find ways through this minefield, balancing the desire, on one hand, to share secrets in order to form friendships and to think through problems with the need, on the other hand, to avoid providing fodder for gossip. One way is to be careful about whom to trust with troubles talk. One woman, for example, confides in a neighbor who is not in her social network. A high school student explained that when she's upset, the first friend she calls is one who is already in college: "My friends at school, if I call them it could get out, but she has literally no one to tell." In these cases, a confidante feels safe because she doesn't know others who know you. In other cases, it might be a matter of personality, or character—or past experience. About a friend who had repeated a confidence, a woman said: "I don't want to give her any material to chew on and spit out to someone else." A friend can also violate a confidence by bringing it up to you in a way that hurts. Another woman to whom that happened made up her mind that henceforth she would reveal nothing to that friend; she would always claim to be fine.

The destructive potential of bad gossip is amplified in the digital age, especially among kids in school. Through social media, rumors can be spread with lightning speed and to vast numbers of listeners, their viciousness amped up by anonymity. Look no further than the smart phone app Yik Yak, which seems specifically designed to spread gossip, with such devastating effect that many high schools and colleges have banned its use.

Deliver Me Not into Conversation

The potential for gossip is not the only reason that some women, in some circumstances, prefer to avoid the kind of talk that is common among women friends. Another reason is time. A woman in her sixties, to illustrate how important her friendships were to her when she was young, told me of a conversation she had with her women friends in which they'd all said they could sooner imagine living without their husbands than without each other. I asked if she felt the same way now. Implying she didn't, she said that many things had changed in the intervening years. When she was younger, she talked to her closest friends every day—voice to voice, at length, on the phone. "As much as I love certain people," she said, "and feel very close to them, I can't imagine putting that burden on myself today." Several other women I spoke to used the same word, "burden," to explain the downside of close friendships. One confessed that when a close friend moved away, though she felt sad, she also felt relieved: it was one less burden.

Many women share, or feel they can learn from, something that is more common among men: focusing less on talk and more on doing things together. Explaining that preference, one man commented that the reason many men like fishing is that they can be together, bond, and not have to talk. Since telling secrets is less likely to be an issue for men, what are the benefits of not talking? For one thing, if there's no talk—especially no troubles talk—the company of others is a chance to get your mind off whatever is bothering you. Equally important, not talking about troubles means you don't let others know that you have any: why display weakness if you don't have to? And, too, if others aren't talking about their problems, you don't have to worry about how to react, what to say, or what to do to help. These benefits of not talking don't always hold the same appeal for women as they do for men (and women may not feel that because they're doing something, there's no need to talk). In particular, fewer women may share the desire not to appear weak. And they are less likely to feel they're supposed to do something about what they hear—or, rather, they are more likely to feel that listening and expressing concern *is* doing something.

There are also times, though, when women can see the value in avoiding conversation. Several women mentioned their distaste for troubles talk as a reason they prefer the company of men. One explained that, to avoid such conversations, when someone asks how she is, "I've learned to say, 'I'm fine,' even if I'm falling over on my face." Another commented that the great thing about being friends with men is that you don't always have to talk. This might be particularly precious when the subject of talk is upsetting. Yet another woman said that when she was going through a divorce, she particularly valued time with her men friends—as a way to escape her women friends' talk. She recalled one man who had also recently divorced, so there was an understanding—a silent one—between them that they shared this pain but didn't have to talk about it. They would just ride their bikes together until they were exhausted.

If there are women who sometimes avoid talk, there are men who sometimes indulge in it. A man in his thirties told me that he didn't recognize himself in my description of men who don't talk to their friends at length. He has a friend, he said, that he can talk to about anything—but then he added, so long as they have a Nintendo between them. The conversations they have resemble those I have described as common among women: "We talk about the whole world," he said, "including our problems and feelings and our friends' problems and feelings, as well as politics, music, books, movies, and freewheeling nonsense." But their time together is still focused on an activity, and he explained why: "It does help diffuse the intensity to be playing video games" at the same time.

The reference to diffusing intensity is significant, for women as well as men. Because women friends tend to talk frequently, at length, and about very personal topics, their friendships are indeed often intense, which may be both nourishing and also potentially fraught: more talk and more personal talk mean more opportunity to say the wrong thing, to have complicated and confusing emotions stirred up, or to feel uncomfortable later about what, or how much, was revealed.

Doing or Talking or Both

There are certainly friendships between women that are made more of doing than of talking. One woman, for example, in telling me about her friends, gave me a catalog of activities: golf, cooking, kayaking, walking, riding bikes. Many women spoke of friendships formed and maintained through groups focused on an activity—a community chorus or a church committee—or activities planned, like going to movies or plays, dancing, or shopping. And doing and talking are not mutually exclusive: activities are often opportunities to talk. Shopping, for example, might entail offering honest opinions about what looks good and what doesn't, encouraging a friend to buy things she really likes—and talking while walking between stores or stopping for lunch.

For women as well as men, some of the most satisfying conversations take place while doing something. The activity makes it easy to switch topics effortlessly, and fills the space when you're not talking. One woman told of spending time with a friend on a small island in a lake. The two would go swimming together, making their way around the island: periodically, they'd find a rock that was smooth enough to stand on, where they'd rest and talk before returning to the water to swim. Their conversations ranged from professional topics to more personal ones. Swim, talk, swim, talk: the perfect combination of doing and talking.

There's a special closeness that comes from doing and talking in turn, or at once, like the two working mothers who had what they called cooking playdates. They'd get together every two weeks to plan and prepare their families' meals. Each would choose two or three recipes—more complicated ones than they'd make on their own—then cook together at one or the other's house, talking the whole time. And between cooking playdates, they'd stay connected by collaborating on when they'd serve the dishes they'd prepared together: "We're having the fish tacos with mango sauce tonight." "We will, too." Doing and talking, each feeding into the other as they fed their families, allowed these mothers to feel less alone—to be less alone—while doing the otherwise one-person work of cooking for their families.

The domestic chores that women in industrialized societies typically do alone were often done in traditional societies by women together, like going down to the river to do laundry. I had the privilege of seeing women engaged in a traditional joint activity in Greece, where several women were preparing fillo dough, the paper-thin leaves of pastry that are layered with nuts and honey to make baklava. It was the 1970s; even then Greek women in the cities bought packaged fillo at the store. But this was a small village on the island of Ikaria. Working together at the kitchen table in one of their homes, the women spread the dough across the top of the table, gradually—very gradually, very carefully, very skillfully—pulling it thinner and thinner, till it covered the table and draped over the sides. I didn't hear anyone tell anyone else what to do; they all seemed to know exactly how to coordinate their moves. And as they worked, they talked, and they laughed.

This scene brings to mind another one, though it is one that I didn't observe myself. A Turkish friend recalled with nostalgia the many times in her childhood when she watched the women in her family gather to remove their body hair. They heated sugar till it melted, spread the burning hot liquid on their bodies, and waited while it cooled and hardened.

Then they pulled it off, and the hair with it, leaving their skin perfectly smooth. My friend recalled watching in delight as the women worked together, talking and laughing. She longed for the day she'd be old enough to join their group. She wasn't nearly as scared by the prospect of pain as she was enticed by the women's palpable joy in each other's company. The pain was a price worth paying to be so closely connected to the other women.

What Is a Friend?

Though these specific activities—making fillo dough, removing body hair with melted sugar—are particular to given cultures, all societies have evolved ways of bringing people together, to do things and to talk. The perspective of cultural differences and cultural universals made me think again of the question posed by Shirley, whose husband suffered from Parkinson's: "If a friend isn't there when you need her, what is a friend?" I wondered if cultures—and individuals—might have different ways of being there for a friend. Haru Yamada, who grew up alternately in Japan and the United States and has written books comparing the two cultures, has friends in both countries, so I put the question to her. In answer, she compared how a Japanese and an American friend were there for her when she had to make a sad journey back to Japan, because her mother was nearing the end of her life. The American friend offered comfort by lending an ear, lightening Haru's mood when they talked, and going with her to buy presents to take on her trip to Japan. The Japanese friend did not say anything about what Haru was feeling, nor did she expect Haru to. She just went ahead and did things for Haru's mother in her place, like buying things she might want and taking them to the hospital.

Yamada sees her friends' different ways of being helpful—both of which she appreciated—as reflecting cultural patterns. Japanese go to greater lengths to help friends, she explains, which is precious but also has a downside: the beneficiary of such efforts incurs an obligation to reciprocate, and feels deeply a debt that she may or may not be able to repay. The American way of friendship leaves individuals freer; Japanese friendships, while more thoughtful, are also heavier to carry. If the concept of "being there" helps explain what it means to be a friend, Yamada's Japanese and American friends were both there for her when her mother died, though in different ways.

Friends needn't be from different cultures to embody different ways of being there in troubling times. For some, "being there" means being available to talk. For others, it means coming through with action. And both are invaluable. A young woman told me of a time when she was extremely upset: she was having trouble with her girlfriend; it looked like their relationship was going to break up (and it did). Her two closest friends helped her get through that difficult time. One came over and stayed with her for two days. The other was out of town, but kept in close touch by texting frequently. She was grateful that both friends were there for her.

Perhaps most dramatic are accounts of women in truly dire circumstances for whom friendships with other women literally saved their lives. Studying memoirs by survivors of Nazi concentration camps, Myrna Goldenberg observed that just about all of those by women describe how friendships with other women helped them survive. Many of these accounts included concrete ways that friends helped each other, like sharing their meager rations of food, and nursing or otherwise protecting a friend who was sick. Joan Ringelheim, for example, quotes an Auschwitz survivor, Susan, whose friends saved her life by standing close and holding her up during roll call when she came down with typhus. "These women," she said, "supported me physically . . . emotionally and spiritually." Perhaps most of all, their connections to their friends gave them a sense that their survival mattered. Isabella Leitner said of her time as a prisoner at Auschwitz that having connections to other women meant having "the absolute responsibility to end the day alive."

Among the many types of relationships that can be referred to as "friends," the quintessential one is a best friend—in modern terms, a bff. The initialism "bff" (best friends forever) has worked its way into the language—globally. I saw it scrawled on a wall in a village on a small island in Greece! And people use it in conversation: "she's my bff," "I have my bff." Yet many, maybe most, bffs turn out not to be forever, which can make the use of the initialism seem naïve, if not hypocritical. But that view misses the point. When friends call each other bffs, it is not a prediction but a description of what they mean to each other now. Jenna Wortham feels this so strongly that she has inscribed it on her body, starting in middle school when she and her best friend tattooed identical hearts on each other's ankles by heating a pin with a Bic lighter, dipping it in ink, and outlining a heart with a series of dots. The feeling of closeness that the matching tattoos engendered was so satisfying, Wortham explained in an essay, that she went on to get matching tattoos with five different friends at different times of her life. The friendships that inspired all those tattoos have since grown more distant, and Wortham is no longer in touch with her middle school friend at all. But she doesn't believe that means it was a mistake to get the tattoos. They have fulfilled their purpose: not to predict the second "f" in "bff," but to commemorate the "b." The tattoos make her smile, reminding her of friends she treasured when they got the matching tattoos.

Few of us have our friendships literally burned onto our bodies, but we all have them burned into our hearts. That many of the friendships (like tattoos) fade over time does not rescind the beauty and comfort they gave us. Maybe each one taught us how to be friends—as well as how to be cautious about friends—and laid the groundwork for the friendships that followed.

2

That's Not What I Meant!

The Invisible Influence of Conversational Style

"She never asks anything about me," a woman said, explaining why an acquaintance isn't a friend. Another made a similar complaint about a friend: at a time when she felt it was obvious that she was "struggling," the friend "never once asked me, 'Hey, how are you doing?'" And a woman who'd told her friend how worried she was because her mother was in the hospital was upset that the friend never asked how her mother was doing. These comments, like many others I heard from women, assume that a true friend shows caring by asking personal questions; not asking means not caring.

Yet I also spoke to women who believe it's intrusive to ask personal questions: if someone wants to tell you something, she'll volunteer it. That was the explanation given by the woman who didn't ask after her friend's mother: "My family taught me it's rude to ask personal questions." One woman recalled that, from the time she was a child, her mother cautioned her never to pry into others' personal lives: "People will let you know what they want you to know." Even volunteering isn't a guarantee that they want you to show interest by asking questions. As someone I interviewed said of a friend, "She'll drop a bomb"—that is, refer to a serious personal problem—"but then she doesn't want to talk about it. I don't push her because she's not the type that would want to open up more if you gave her a push."

Are personal questions a welcome, even requisite, show of caring or unwelcome pushing? Though troubles talk is typically the coin of the realm in women's friendships, there are vast differences in individual women's assumptions about when and how to engage in it. If someone turns up with a sore on her face, should you show concern by asking about it, or refrain from asking so as not to embarrass her? And if you do ask, how deep should you probe? How many follow-up questions should you ask? Asking questions—how many, in what form, and in what circumstances—is just one of many ways of speaking that make up what I call conversational style, an aspect of language that I have focused on in my research and writing for four decades. I've shown that many frustrations in human relationships, both private and public, can be traced to differences in conversational styles. Such frustrations are also frequent among women friends, for whom conversation typically plays such an important role. Understanding how conversational style works, and how differences in style can be the invisible causes of trouble, is the first step toward overcoming such trouble and strengthening women's friendships.

When we open our mouths to speak, we focus on what we want to say, yet we need to make decisions about how to say it—and we make them automatically: what tone of voice, what pitch, what intonation patterns to use; how loudly or softly to speak; how to get the floor or yield it to others or let them know we're not ready to yield it; how we get to our point—say it right out or build up to it?; how relatively direct or indirect we're going to be ("Shut the window!" or "It's cold in here"); whether and when to tell a story, what it can be about, and how we get to the point of the story; whether we'll use humor, and what type (sarcasm, irony, telling or making a joke); and innumerable other choices that must be made every time we say anything. All these linguistic mechanisms—every aspect of how we say what we mean—make up what I call conversational style.

"You're Not Listening!"

Conversational style is also at play when we're not speaking. As listeners, too, we tend to focus on meaning: What are others trying to tell us? What does that say about who they are and how they feel about us and about our relationship? To answer these questions, we tend to assume that they must mean what we would mean if we said the same thing in the same way in a similar context. When conversational styles are relatively similar, that assumption is likely to be accurate. But when they differ, it may not be accurate at all. And conversational styles often differ, because ways of speaking tend to vary not only by gender—which women friends share— but also by geographic region, ethnicity, class, age, and a myriad other influences that friends may or may not share, such as place in the sibling hierarchy (why are oldest sisters so often called bossy?), profession (imagine an accountant talking to a psychotherapist), sexual orientation, and individual personality. Any conversational style difference can lead to missed signals, miscommunication, and, most damagingly, misjudgments about others' intentions, and the kinds of people they are. When misjudgments arise between friends, it's especially hurtful, since feeling understood is one of the main reasons women have and treasure friends.

Ruth and Jesse were taking a walk by a lake, a lovely setting replete with the beauties of flora and fauna. Jesse was telling Ruth about something going on in her life, and Ruth was listening with attention and empathy. But Ruth was also enjoying the natural surroundings, and the pleasure of sharing them with her friend. So whenever they passed a particularly pretty or interesting sight—a duck gliding on the surface of the lake with a string of tiny ducklings behind her, or a patch of flowers with extraordinary color—Ruth pointed it out. Suddenly Jesse exclaimed: "You haven't listened to a word I've said!" Ruth was stunned—and stung. Of course she'd been listening. Calling attention to sights she thought Jesse would appreciate did not mean she wasn't. If she didn't point them out while Jesse was talking, her friend might miss them: by the time her story was over, the thing of interest would be long gone.

For Ruth, sharing the appreciation of their surroundings was a treasured part of their time together, just as surely as was listening to her friend's story. She did not regard quick comments about something in their environment as interruptions, any more than, at dinner, a muttered request to pass the salt would be perceived as interrupting another diner's story. In both cases, the remarks are obviously fleeting parenthetical asides. But here's where conversational style differences wreak havoc: to Jesse, listening means not talking, so anyone who is talking is not listening. If that means a listener must forgo sharing the beauty of a passing sight—or salt on her food—it's a price she has to pay. Jesse was hurt that her good friend would show so little interest in what she was saying, and Ruth was hurt that her good friend would accuse her of not listening when she was.

How could two friends have such different views of something so basic, so mundane, as how to show you're listening? The answer is conversational style. Each learned basic habits and assumptions about how to have a conversation—how to say what you mean and show how you feel—as they learned to talk, from family members and the people they spoke to, growing up. And each had a lifetime of evidence that her own conversational style makes sense, because many of those she spoke to had similar styles. Of those who didn't, she could draw conclusions, faulty or not, about the kinds of people they were or their intentions in a given conversation—including conclusions like "You're not listening."

Don't Just Sit There! Interrupt!

Trouble can start with the most basic building block of conversation: taking turns. When two people are having a conversation, first one person speaks, then the other speaks, then the first speaks again. But how do we know when the other's turn is over and it's our turn to begin? We judge by an array of signals like whether she seems to have stopped or be winding down by lowering her pitch or volume or otherwise trailing off and whether she has made her point. But where in another's talk are you looking for the point—early on, or only after a slow buildup? And will the point be explicit or implied? Does falling intonation and lower pitch really mean she's finished, or could it mean that she's made a subpoint on the way to her main point? And how long does a pause have to be before it means "I'm finished" rather than "I'm catching my breath" or "I'm pausing for dramatic effect—stand by, the clincher is coming"?

That tiny matter of how long a pause must be to signal "I'm finished" can throw the whole turn-taking system—and the relationship between the speakers—into disarray. Imagine a conversation between two friends, Jordan and Rhonda. Jordan expects a slightly longer pause between turns than Rhonda. The shorter pause comes first, so Rhonda gets the impression that Jordan has finished—and takes the floor. Jordan assumes it's obvious that she hasn't finished, so she feels interrupted and protests, "Let me finish!" But Rhonda is frustrated, too: "I thought you were done!" Jordan feels sure she was interrupted, but Rhonda feels sure she was being a good sport, filling an uncomfortable silence.

"Don't interrupt!" is a self-evidently justified protest. Few people would feel equally justified in demanding, "Don't just sit there! Interrupt!" But what constitutes an interruption is far from self-evident. If Carolyn is telling a story and Tammy encourages her with "yeah," "uh-huh" and "right," Carolyn probably will assume that's listener talk, and won't feel interrupted. But what if Tammy says whole sentences like "I know what you mean; the same thing happened to me." That could feel like listener talk, too—or like an attempt to grab the floor and start telling her own story. And how about if Tammy meant it as listener talk and Carolyn takes it as an attempt to steal the floor? Carolyn might stop talking, thinking she was interrupted, and Tammy might start her own turn, interpreting Carolyn's silence to mean she was finished. Who created that interruption? Tammy, because she began speaking? Or Carolyn, because she stopped? I'd say neither created the interruption single-handedly. It resulted from the differences in their conversational styles.

This sort of misfire can happen in any conversation, but it's especially hurtful between women friends, because listening—and showing that you care about what you hear—is a big part of what most women expect and value in friends. That's what's at issue with interruption: Are you listening? Do you care? So it may come as a surprise that women are actually more likely than men to talk over each other in casual conversation. I asked all the women I interviewed what sometimes annoys them about their friends. In response, some described ways of talking, such as "She's argumentative," "She always knows what's right," and "She talks all the time." No one mentioned a tendency to interrupt. At first this surprised me, but then I realized that it goes along with something I observed in my research, and other studies have found as well: while men tend to interrupt women more often than the reverse in formal settings like meetings, women actually tend to "interrupt" each other more than men do when having casual conversations with others of the same sex. I put "interrupt" in quotation marks because, in most cases, the overlapping voices in women's casual conversations are not experienced as interruptions. Instead, women tend to talk along—latching on to each other's sentences, adding their own experiences or perspectives, showing understanding or appreciation of the other's words—and show no sign of resenting the intrusion of others' voices when they hold the floor. The choral voices seem to add to everyone's enthusiasm and enjoyment.

A linguist, Alice Greenwood, found evidence for this gender pattern when she recorded and analyzed conversations among teens and preteens. One interchange that Greenwood observed took place among two girls and one boy. Dara was twelve, and Stephanie was eleven; Max, at fourteen, was a guest of their older brother. The girls tried to amuse Max by performing a funny routine that culminated in a tongue twister. Although this routine sparked laughter when the girls performed it for other friends, Max did not laugh and claimed not to get the joke. The girls tried to explain it to him, but Max objected, recalling instead a tongue twister that he knew. Dara rushed to assure Max that the two tongue twisters were essentially the same, but Max did not take this reassurance in a positive spirit. Throughout this conversation, the girls cut into, overlapped, and finished each other's sentences, and their doing so never stalled the conversation, nor did either of them show any sign of objecting to the verbal intrusions. It was apparent that they regarded the "interruptions" as welcome signs of enthusiasm. Max's objection, in contrast, was explicit: "You keep interrupting me."

High-Involvement and High-Considerateness Styles

Though no two people's conversational styles are exactly alike, there are patterns that tend to characterize styles. Expecting shorter pauses between turns, and perceiving long pauses as uncomfortable silences, tends to go along with other linguistic habits that together make up what I call high-involvement style. Expecting longer pauses and being more comfortable with silence are among the linguistic habits that make up what I call high-considerateness style. Think about it this way: we all want to be considerate, and we all want to show that we're involved in a conversation, but speakers of one style tend to place more emphasis on showing involvement, while speakers of the other style tend to emphasize showing considerateness. Let's go back to the hypothetical conversation I described between two friends, Tammy and Carolyn. By filling a pause that threatened to become an uncomfortable silence, Tammy was showing enthusiastic listenership, as high-involvement style requires: a good person makes sure to show she's involved. By expecting a listener to be relatively wordless, Carolyn was exercising a high-considerateness style: a good person makes sure to leave plenty of room for others to talk.

Linguistic habits that go along with high-considerateness style also include standing farther apart (in other words, giving more physical as well as verbal space); speaking more softly and with relatively level pitch and minimal gestures; talking more about impersonal topics and less about personal ones; being relatively indirect about conveying something negative or getting your way; and—to return to the example I started with—not asking personal questions. Linguistic habits that go along with high-involvement style include expecting shorter pauses between turns—or maybe no pause at all: to avoid an uncomfortable silence, a speaker signals she's ready to relinquish the floor by winding down, expecting a listener to chime in before she comes to a complete stop. It also includes standing closer when you talk; speaking in a more animated way and often more loudly; telling more personal stories and making the point of the story relatively dramatic; being more relatively direct; and asking personal questions to show interest and caring. Differences in habits and assumptions about any of these ways of talking can lead to frustration, even between good friends, because the same way of speaking can have different meanings. Being quiet while listening really can mean you're not interested—and so can starting to speak before your friend's finished.

We learn conversational styles at the same time that we learn language, as children growing up, so experience tells us that the way we show good intentions is the right way, and those who play by other rules are wrong. Actually, we rarely realize they are playing by other rules; we think they're breaking rules. (The title of Haru Yamada's book about communication between Japanese and Americans, *Different Games, Different Rules,* can also apply to communication between people who speak the same language but have different conversational styles.) Of course a listener should be quiet! That's the definition of listening. Of course a listener should talk along to show enthusiasm and involvement! Otherwise how do you know she's paying attention? Both styles make sense, each in its own way. A good listener can emphasize considerateness by being silent, even if it means forgoing observations that she thinks the speaker would appreciate; and a good listener can emphasize involvement at the same time that she's listening—by talking.

Talking across styles is all the more difficult because each style fosters its own capabilities. If you're used to hearing listeners talk while you're speaking, it doesn't distract you; it encourages you. But if you're used to listeners being quiet, it does: you can't keep your focus if someone who's supposed to be listening keeps talking. It's hard to believe that what wouldn't distract you might distract someone else, or that someone else—especially a friend—wouldn't be distracted by what distracts you. Conversational style differences cast doubt on the adage "Do unto others as you would have others do unto you." If your conversational styles differ, what you would have others do unto you may be the very thing that bugs them when you do it unto them.

Not Imposing Is So Offensive

In developing my concept of conversational style, I was inspired by the work of my professor at the University of California, Berkeley, Robin Lakoff, on what she called communicative style. Lakoff explained that people in different cultures show politeness—that is, concern for others' feelings—by observing different rules. What I call high-involvement style follows Lakoff's rule "Maintain camaraderie" or "Be friendly." High-considerateness style follows her rules "Give options" and "Don't impose." I was explaining these two styles to someone whose style was high-involvement. When I pointed out that she emphasizes "Be friendly," whereas those with a high-considerateness style emphasize "Don't impose," she said, "But the not imposing is so offensive."

How can that be? One way is by inserting distance where there should be closeness. For example, Sally repeatedly invited her friend Deena and her husband to visit Sally and her husband when they rented a cabin at a seaside resort. Deena finally accepted Sally's invitation, but started by asking: "Is it okay if we come?" "Yes!" Sally assured her. "I *want* you to come. That's why I keep inviting you." When Deena and her husband arrived, Deena asked, "Can we come to dinner tonight?" Sally was exasperated. "You're our guests, Deena! I expect you to come to dinner every night unless you get tired of us. Then you can take a night off. We love having you!" Being overly careful not to impose creates distance, because it's acting more like a stranger than like a friend. A friend who acts as if she were not one feels less like a friend.

At the same time, high-involvement-style speakers who give priority to the rule "Be friendly" can be off-putting to high-considerateness-style speakers, who tend to emphasize "Don't impose." Annette was surprised—and hurt—when her roommate Kristin said she found her intimidating. Annette shot back, "I'm five foot one and weigh a hundred pounds! How can I be intimidating?" Kristin replied, "Just like that." She wasn't referring to Annette's height and weight but to the swiftness, firmness, and what to her was the belligerent tone of Annette's challenge.

High-involvement and high-considerateness styles are not monolithic; they are two ends of a continuum along which each person's unique style falls. For example, conversational style is not simply a matter of being open or closed to talking about personal problems; it is a matter of when and how to be open or closed, and how open to be. A Greek woman, Marina, commented that with some friends, "We'll have to go out, talk for half an hour about other things, and then they'll get more personal. On the phone they don't do it at all. There are other friends who will pick up the phone and just say, 'Ah, Marina!' and they say everything."

Not in So Many Words

A linguistic mechanism that high-considerateness speakers tend to use more is indirectness, whereby meaning is not explicit in words but nonetheless comes across loud and clear. In the United States, at least, it is more common for women to use indirectness when trying to get their way. (In other contexts, such as apologizing, indirectness is more common among men.) Though indirectness can have many benefits and often works well, it can also complicate conversations between women friends. One woman put her finger on how this can happen in telling about messages she exchanged with a friend. Beth and Elaine had arranged to go running during their lunch hour one day. When Beth's boss told her she'd have to work extra hours that week, she thought she should get a jump on some of that work, so she sent Elaine a Facebook message suggesting they go running later than planned. Elaine's message came back, "I guess that's okay. Fine, see you then." For Beth that little opener, "I guess," and the unenthusiastic "okay" were signs that Elaine wasn't thrilled with the change of plans. She responded, "I'm sorry, I didn't mean to be difficult. I'm more flexible than I made it sound. I can actually just do one o'clock like we planned." That set off a back-and-forth that went four rounds—"No no no let's do the time you wanna do," "No no no let's do the time we said." In the end, they agreed to stick with their original time. Beth didn't much mind keeping the original time, but she felt there had to be a simpler way to get there! In commenting on this exchange, she said that she and her friends tend to "overthink" how they are going to say something because they're worried both about hurting the other person's feelings and about coming across as too demanding.

Aha! I thought, on hearing this. There's the rub. From the time they are children, girls learn from playmates, friends, and the world in general that if they tell others what to do or are "too demanding," they will be labeled "bossy." To be likable—and being liked is a major goal for most girls and women—they need to find ways to negotiate what they want or need without seeming to demand it. Equally important is the second motivation Beth mentioned: concern about hurting the other person's feelings. Since most girls and women share these values, the ways they learn to negotiate preferences are widely shared, too.

I regularly ask my students to observe their own conversations and analyze them in light of the theories and methods we have discussed in class. Over the years, many women in my classes have described and analyzed conversations in which they and their friends conveyed and accurately interpreted meaning by indirectness. Here's an example, one among many similar conversations in which roommates negotiate rights and responsibilities. Kate Bradley reported: "On a couple of different occasions last week I heard my roommates mention the fact that they wanted to have a party on Thursday. I didn't think much of it until Thursday afternoon, when I realized that I would be up all night writing a paper that was due Friday morning." How would Kate handle this conflict of interest? (How would you?) She could simply tell her roommates, "I just realized I have a paper due tomorrow, and I'll be up all night writing it. Would you mind nixing the party idea?" But Kate didn't feel comfortable making a demand like that; she explained, "I didn't want to be the annoying roommate that wouldn't allow a party, but at the same time, I didn't want distractions while I was trying to finish a paper under a deadline." Here's how she handled the dilemma: "As I was walking back from class with one of the roommates I asked, 'So, what are you guys doing tonight?' She responded, 'I'm not sure, we're thinking of having a party; what are you up to?' I told her that I had a big paper due on Friday. She responded with 'Oh, in that case we definitely won't have a party.'" Great, right? The matter was settled, exactly as Kate had hoped. But the conversation didn't end there. Kate described how it continued: "I told her that it would be fine with me, but she restated that they would not have a party. That time I didn't resist."

Why on earth did Kate say it would be fine for her roommates to have a party when it wasn't? Why did she start the conversation by asking, "So, what are you guys doing tonight?" when she knew perfectly well what they'd been planning? It goes back to what she wrote at the start: she didn't want to be the annoying roommate who wouldn't allow a party. And she didn't have to be. All she had to do was let her roommate know about her paper; the roommate would then make the decision not to have a party. Both women could walk away from the conversation feeling better about themselves and their friendship. Kate got what she wanted and needed without demanding it, and her roommate could feel she had been a good friend, accommodating to Kate of her own volition, not because it was demanded of her.

I encountered an example of a similar negotiation between two highly accomplished women friends that worked the same way. I had been invited to speak at a local conference for women in business. When I arrived, the conference organizer told me that one of the other speakers, a mutual friend, would not be appearing. She explained that the other speaker had called her that morning and said, "I'm feeling awful. I've got a terrible headache and I know I'm coming down with something. But if you really need me, I'll come and speak anyway." The organizer then told me she'd responded: "I need you to stay home and take care of yourself. We'll manage without you." I was thrilled to encounter this example of how indirectness had worked between women friends, so I asked if I could retell this conversation in my own lecture. "Absolutely!" she said. "It was perfect—clear, direct communication."

Then I asked if I could use that remark in my lecture, too. Though the conversation was indeed perfect, it was anything but direct. The speaker herself had not actually backed out; she had offered to deliver her lecture despite being sick. It was the organizer who told her to stay home. I believe that the organizer felt the communication had been "direct" because the meaning had been "clear": she had accurately interpreted her friend's phone call as backing out, and she knew that the offer to speak anyway was not meant literally: there was no way she was going to say, "I'm sorry you're sick, but I need you to give your talk anyway."

The beauty of this conversation—the beauty of indirectness—is that the speaker could feel she'd been a good person by offering to keep her commitment, and the organizer could feel she'd been a good person by putting concern for her friend's health first. The "meaning" of the speaker's phone call, and the knowledge of how the conversation would go, was obvious to both, so their communication didn't feel indirect; it just felt like communication. The satisfaction of conversations like this—knowing that your meaning came across without your having to hammer it home, and that you've accurately interpreted another's meaning, is one of the great pleasures of women's friendship, when they have similar conversational styles. It's like a verbal pas de deux.

I Said No, Didn't I?

If indirectness is satisfying when it works, it is also risky, because it depends on listeners to glean meaning not stated in words. If they don't glean it, or choose to ignore it, the indirect communicator is stuck. In theory, she could resort to directness, but most habitually indirect people don't feel comfortable speaking directly—and may not even be capable of it. This is a particular risk in conversations between women and men. I once saw this happen right before my eyes.

I was in an academic colleague's office when her telephone rang, and she answered it. I heard her say something like "Gee, I'd like to help you out, but I'm completely overwhelmed. I've made far more commitments than I can possibly fulfill. I've got two dissertation writers going full steam, I've taken on an overload course because the person who was supposed to teach it got sick, and I'm on the Rank and Tenure committee this year, which I knew would be a lot of work but is demanding more time than I could have imagined. There's just no way I could responsibly join another committee. Of course if you can't find anyone else, I'll do it, but honestly, I don't see how I could add it to what's already on my plate." When she hung up the phone, she turned to me with a look of astonishment and dismay. "I can't believe it," she said. "I told him I couldn't do it, but he put me on the committee anyway."

It's true that she told him she couldn't serve on the committee, but she did it indirectly, and therefore in a way that relied on him to grasp her meaning and do his part. By starting with a detailed explanation of the reasons she could not serve on the committee, she trusted him to understand that she was saying no, just as the speaker at the women's conference backed out by describing her illness and the student nixed a party by explaining that she had a paper due the next day. Given that premise, the professor also trusted her colleague to understand that her offer to help out if absolutely necessary was not meant literally—any more than the speaker really meant she could give her talk despite being sick or the student with a paper due really meant that it would be fine for her roommates to have a party. And just as the conference organizer told the sick speaker to stay home, and the roommate insisted there would be no party, the professor assumed that her colleague would assure her he would not add to her burden but would find someone else to join his committee. She found herself on the committee because he didn't do his part in that two-part ritual; her use of indirectness had backfired. You might say it was her own fault; she should have been more direct. But I'd say the fault lay with the difference between their conversational styles. And I don't think it was by chance that this frustrating conversation took place between a woman and a man.

But You Said It Was Fine!

The man who put his colleague on the committee might have been taking advantage of her indirectness to ignore what he knew was her intention to refuse. But I think it more likely that he knew she was saying it would be burdensome to serve on the committee but did not realize that she actually was saying no. In conversations between people with differing conversational styles, meaning that is obvious to one can be opaque to the other.

Three young women who shared a house were upset because their fourth roommate kept leaving dirty dishes in the sink, despite the house rule that each should wash her own dishes as soon as she used them. The three agreed that someone needed to tell the miscreant to clean up her act, and one of them volunteered to do it. The next day, there were still dirty dishes in the sink, so the two asked the volunteer why she hadn't followed through. "I did!" she protested. "Look at that!" She pointed to a note she had tacked up: "We love a clean sink." Clearly the fourth roommate had missed the meaning of the indirect message (or perhaps felt free to pretend to miss it).

Many women told me of problems finding the right way to tell a roommate that she is not clean enough. One said that she regretted not having been more direct. Her mother had cleaned houses for a living, and had instilled in her daughter high standards for cleanliness, so her roommate's very different habits irked her: "She would leave the dishes and she'd be totally okay with them being there for a week. I'm not a confrontational person, so I didn't tell her up front, 'I don't like your style.'" She put up with the discomfort: "I didn't think of it as something that was so grating that I had to tell her." But because she didn't, the situation continued—and continued to grate. She felt that over time her own cleaner habits did rub off on her messier roommate a bit, but she also felt, in retrospect, that directness might have saved her some grief—and her roommate from unknowingly annoying her. At the time, however, directness did not feel like an option.

I understand how indirectness can fail, because I've experienced its failure—with women friends. Years ago I went for a hike with a friend. We had not been on the trail very long before I realized that I was struggling to keep up. I let her know by saying something like "This pace is kind of fast for me." I was sure she would understand that I was asking her to walk more slowly, and that she'd graciously comply. Instead, she said, "This is a good pace"—and she didn't alter it. I continued to struggle for the rest of our hike, and had a serious case of charley horse the next day. Looking back, I have often wondered why, when my indirect request to adjust our pace failed, I didn't follow up with a more explicit demand: "I need to walk more slowly," or just "Slow down!" For some reason I didn't; somehow, I couldn't. I had communicated the one way I knew how to; when it didn't work, I was flummoxed. Our own conversational styles seem so self-evidently the right way to speak, and our linguistic habits so automatic, that speaking differently, which seems like it should be easy, can actually be unthinkable. By the same token, it's hard to understand why others don't speak in ways that we would.

Lynn was spending the day with Frank, a college classmate who was visiting from out of town. At one point Frank said that he'd love to see another of their classmates, Vicki, who also lived in that city. Lynn offered to find out if Vicki was available—and did so on the spot, by calling her on the phone. When Vicki answered, Lynn explained that Frank was in town and wanted to see her; Lynn would be glad to drive him over if Vicki was free and agreeable. Vicki said she was, and the visit took place. But the next day Vicki called Lynn to chew her out. She hadn't wanted to see Frank; she couldn't stand him. She had made that clear by the way she'd said it was fine, and she was furious at Lynn for bringing him over anyway.

Lynn was dumbfounded. "How could I have known you didn't want to see him when you said that you did? Why didn't you tell me you didn't want to?"

"I couldn't say that with him standing right there!" Vicki said.

"He was standing next to me, not you," Lynn protested. "He couldn't hear you. Why would you say yes if you didn't want to see him? All you had to do was say you were busy."

Vicki was adamant: "By calling me on the phone, you left me no choice. I had to say yes. But you should have heard in my voice that I didn't really mean it."

The disagreement was a true impasse because neither could conceive of speaking and acting the way the other had. For Vicki, indirectness was transparent: obviously she couldn't come right out and say, "Are you out of your mind? I can't stand Frank!" The only way to communicate her reluctance was to accept unenthusiastically. For Lynn, it would have been easy to say that—or to make up an excuse: "Gee, I have an appointment today. I was just about to go out." Since it was obvious to her that these options were readily available to Vicki, as they would have been to her, Lynn had no reason to question the sincerity of Vicki's words, or to look beyond the words to pick up nuances behind them.

Different assumptions about what is possible to say, and what should be said, might underlie the following complaint. A woman spoke with frustration of a friend who frequently asks her for favors but never reciprocates. When I asked how the friend responds to her requests for favors, she told me she never makes such requests; she couldn't. Someone who asks for favors might well assume that not asking means not needing help. And someone who never asks for help outright might well assume that not offering without being asked is implicitly refusing to provide the help that was needed but not requested.

That's What I Just Said

When friends have different habits regarding indirectness, misfires are particularly likely—and particularly resistant to repair, because each finds her own interpretation to be obvious and self-evident. And friends are likely to have different habits regarding indirectness if their cultural backgrounds differ, or if they grew up in different parts of the country.

I once asked a friend what she thought of someone we both knew slightly. She replied, "I don't really know him." I said, "I think he's a jerk." She responded, "That's what I just said."

Huh??!!

Here's how she explained: "I'm from South Carolina. In South Carolina you can't say you think someone is a jerk. You have to proceed on the assumption that if you know him you'll find something to like. So 'I don't really know him' means 'I haven't found anything to like about him.'"

As a scholar of conversational style, I was fascinated by this explanation. But as a native of Brooklyn, New York, I was a little incredulous. In Brooklyn—at least the Brooklyn where I was raised—it is perfectly acceptable to say you think someone's a jerk, so there's no reason to cloak such a judgment in roundabout words like "I don't really know him," or to look for hidden meaning in such words. Not long after, I was at a gathering where I was introduced to someone who said he was from South Carolina. I seized the opportunity to ask, "What would it mean if I asked you what you thought of someone and you said, 'I don't really know him'?" His answer was swift: "That means he's a no-good no-count."

If you looked up the words "I don't really know him" in a dictionary, you would not come up with that meaning. We don't learn our native languages from dictionaries; we learn what words mean by hearing them used in conversation. This generally works well: children begin using words and expressions the way they hear others using them, and others' responses let them know whether they're using them correctly. But when children grow into adults and have conversations with people whose styles differ, that all goes out the window. Their meaning can be missed; they can miss others' meaning; and both might conclude that there's something wrong with the other for having communicated in such an incomprehensible way.

Don't Start Up!

One reason that indirectness might fail, even among women friends—especially among women friends—is the desire to avoid conflict. A student in my class recounted an exchange among four roommates that shows how this can happen.

Four roommates shared an apartment in which the refrigerator and the stove were so oddly placed that if you didn't take extra care to make sure the oven door was fully shut, the freezer door wouldn't close properly either, and anything in the freezer door would defrost. One roommate was particularly negligent in this regard, and another was particularly eager to get her to be more careful. Approaching the problem in a way that is common among women, she began by consulting a third roommate about how to go about it without hurting their friend's feelings. Together they decided that direct communication—telling the offending roommate face to face or sending a text message only to her—would be too confrontational. They agreed it would be better to send a text message to the roommates' group chat, making it sound like it applied to everyone, including the sender herself. In composing the message, the determined roommate started with a disclaimer to head off the accusation she was being too critical, and ended with humor to sound less accusatory when complaining that her frozen pot stickers (gyoza) had been ruined. She wrote:

> Hey guys! I don't wanna be coming off as a bitch, but if everyone
> (including me) could really make sure that we're closing the freezer,
> I would really appreciate it. It was cracked open when I got home

and everything in the door is completely warm and defrosted
RIP Gyoza.

The sender was confident she'd found a considerate way to convey her concern to the negligent roommate. But her message was blurred, because the two other roommates rushed to change the subject. The first to respond acknowledged the admonition—humorously and cryptically—by beginning, "Aye Aye," but then sent an adorable picture of her one-year-old niece holding her four-month-old nephew. She wrote, "sorry 2 take away from the freezer, but how could I resist sending this?" The second roommate followed suit: she opened with a bitmoji—a cartoon character with a caption saying "Will Do!"—but immediately backgrounded the freezer topic with another bitmoji commenting on the picture: "totes ADORBS" (translation: the babies are totally adorable). The one who sent the picture then sealed the deal of deflecting attention from the freezer by raising the topic of what they should have for dinner. The fourth roommate then joined the conversation about dinner and ignored the original text about the freezer—the text that, though sent to everyone, had actually been meant for her. And the next day she again left the freezer door open.

The pot sticker buyer had failed to get her roommate to change her behavior. Her use of indirectness—not specifying which roommate her request was aimed at—had backfired for two reasons. First, by not naming her, it allowed the fourth roommate to ignore her request. And that outcome was further facilitated by the other two roommates, who apparently had a knee-jerk response to defuse the conflict by switching from a discordant subject—chastising a friend—to subjects that united them all in a positive spirit: an aww-inspiring photo of babies and the prospect of sharing a meal.

She Just Knows

I heard many complaints from women about friends who fail to pick up on meaning that wasn't expressed, and appreciation for friends who do. One woman pointed out that she might see two friends equally frequently, yet one feels like a close friend and the other doesn't: "There's something about a close friend," she said, that entails "understanding what's going on without being told." Another woman said that she and her best friend share that kind of understanding: "When something is wrong with me I don't tell people, I just get sort of quiet, and she picks up on that. And I do the same thing with her." I wondered whether her friend would ask her what's wrong; she said, "She'll ask me in the right situation, which—I don't know how to explain, but she'll just know. It's usually post the situation that was making me upset, but pre that it's been so long that I'm not upset about it anymore."

This benefit of indirectness, so prized by many women in their friends, can be puzzling to men. (What am I supposed to be, a mind reader?) But indirectness is commonly the norm not only among American women but also in communication around the world. The notion that true friendship means you "just know" without expecting to be told explicitly underlies Japanese assumptions about communication, according to linguist Haru Yamada. In her book *Different Games, Different Rules,* Yamada explains that Japanese tend to mistrust words, valuing silent communication instead. The word *haragei,* "belly talk" (literally, "belly art"), captures this idea: true communication is "visceral"—silent, wordless. That's the kind of communication, and show of caring, that was missed by the young woman who complained that her friend never asked, "Hey, how are you doing?" when she felt it was obvious she was struggling. Why didn't she just tell her friend, "I'm having a hard time. I need to talk about it." That wouldn't have provided what she wanted. A friend who asks, "Hey, how are you doing?" sends a metamessage of caring; noticing on her own that something is wrong shows that she knows her friend well enough to sense her unhappiness without being told, and cares enough to act on that sense. If you have to tell someone who's been around you that you're unhappy, you might as well be talking to a stranger, not a close friend.

Asking "How are you doing?"—what this young woman would have wanted from a friend—was not what another woman wanted; in fact a friend asking that question made her mad. The source of her anger, according to Raymonde Carroll, a French anthropologist who lives in the United States, was differences between French and American expectations of friendship. Carroll recounts and explains this experience in her book *Cultural Misunderstandings: The French-American Experience*. During a phone conversation, Carroll's French friend complained of being very tired and feeling worn out by her kids. Carroll offered to take care of them for a few hours, so her friend could rest. Her friend accepted readily and drove the kids over, but instead of leaving immediately to begin enjoying her rest, she stayed to express how much she appreciated Carroll's offer, and to contrast it with the failure of an American friend, and Americans in general, to do the same. Carroll writes that her French friend

> complained bitterly about the fact that her neighbor, an American woman whom she considered to be a good friend, had not made the same offer: "Do you think she said 'I'll take care of the children so you can rest?' Do you think she brought me a dish so that I wouldn't have to cook? No, nothing. She only asks me 'how I'm doing,' every day. . . . What a hypocrite!" A flood of similar reproaches followed. Then came some nostalgia for France, where people know what friendship is.

The accusation of hypocrisy always makes me prick up my ears, especially in a cross-cultural context. Hypocrites are people who act in ways that do not reflect their true feelings and intentions. Carroll and her French friend shared the assumption that a true friend, on learning of a friend's need, will offer to do something to help—without being asked.

Those who fail to make such an offer are not true friends; if they claim to be, they're hypocrites.

Carroll suspected that a cultural difference was at play, and she soon got corroboration in the form of another unsolicited complaint, this time from an American. (The assumption that friends tell each other when another friend frustrates them seems to be the same for both cultures.) When Carroll mentioned a mutual French colleague, her American friend said that she likes this colleague, and considers her a good friend, but "she has one fault that drives me crazy." The fault was offering to take care of the speaker's daughter so she could get a rest! This offer, exactly what her French friend expected and appreciated, struck the American as invasive and insulting, "as if I were incapable of taking care of my daughter and my work at the same time."

Both of Carroll's friends were drawing conclusions about another based on her way of speaking: she's a hypocrite for not offering to help me out; she's insulting me by offering to help me out. In both cases, they took a friend's way of speaking as evidence of her personal failings, unaware that they were dealing with cultural differences in expectations about how to be a friend.

Go On, Say It

Cultures can vary in other ways of showing friendship, too. Bharati Mukherjee, a writer born in India who now lives in the United States, was taking a medication that had the unfortunate side effect of causing her hair to thin. "When I run into old friends visiting the United States from Calcutta," she writes, "some will exclaim, with the shocking frankness that only Indian friends you have grown up with can, 'Bharati, you're getting bald! Good grief, what happened!'" It seems highly unlikely that American friends, whether or not they grew up together, would call attention to something unattractive, like thinning hair—especially not right off the bat and so explicitly. But the question "What happened!" is key: it shows that the reason for asking is not a lack of concern for a friend's feelings but rather concern for her health.

I experienced a similar cultural difference in a conversation with a former student who is now a friend: Susan Mather, who is a member of the Deaf community, a native speaker of American Sign Language, and a professor at Gallaudet University. I also had the opportunity to contrast her response with that of a hearing friend—and to benefit from her cultural style. At the time of these encounters, I had gained a significant amount of weight, which I felt rather bad about, though friends assured me it was not noticeable. The reaction of my hearing friend, whom I had not seen in a number of years, was typical. On greeting me, she said the requisite "You look great!" I responded, "No, I've gained weight," and she said, "It doesn't show. You look really great!" The very next day I was having lunch with Sue, who would be giving a guest lecture in my class that afternoon. (We were communicating with the help of an ASL interpreter.) Sue also began by saying, "You look great!" but when I said that I had gained weight, she agreed with me. Pointing to my waist, to the very bulge that I worried over when I looked in the mirror, she said, "You can't hide that."

The follow-up to this story is especially revealing. The class Sue Mather was about to address was Cross-Cultural Communication, and the topic of her lecture was differences between Deaf and hearing communication styles. I was delighted to have so recently encountered this example of a difference between Deaf and hearing cultures with regard to affirming or denying an undesirable characteristic. So when I introduced Dr. Mather, I told my class about her comment on my weight, and contrasted it with the comment of my other friend the day before. Since I invited her to give a guest lecture whenever I taught this class, I would repeat the story each time I introduced her to a new class. And each time, her reaction puzzled me. She showed no spark of recognition or agreement. She seemed not to know what I was talking about, as if the exchange had never taken place.

The mystery was solved a number of years later, when Sue recommended that I show my class a video, *See What I Mean: Differences Between*

Deaf and Hearing Cultures. One of the conversations dramatized in the video is similar to what Sue and I had experienced: a Deaf woman greets a hearing friend she has not seen for a while and says, right off, "You've gained a lot of weight! Are you pregnant?" This exchange is contrasted with a conversation between two hearing friends: when they meet, thought bubbles show that one is thinking, "I hope those few extra pounds aren't too obvious." The other is thinking, "Boy, she put on a little weight. She probably feels bad about it." But what she says is "I really like your earrings." The other says, "Thanks!" while thinking, "Whew! She didn't even notice!" In recommending this video, Sue explained that, until she herself saw it, she had been unaware of the cultural difference it explained: "In American hearing culture, it is considered rude to make a personal remark about someone's appearance, especially if it's negative." In contrast, "In Deaf culture, the rule is: if you can see it, you can comment on it." That's why Sue had never understood what I was saying about our own conversation. She also pointed out that her comment "You can't hide that" wouldn't have come across as blunt to a Deaf friend, who would see not only the words shaped by her hands but also her facial expression and body language, which would have shown empathy, much as tone of voice would if the words were spoken. And that metamessage of empathy might well have been lost as I heard the words in the voice of an interpreter.

Everyone must decide what to say (or not to say) about an undesirable characteristic in a friend—especially, for women, anything related to physical appearance. And, as with all assumptions about what's appropriate to say, our own habits and expectations seem self-evidently logical and reasonable. Obviously it's unkind to remind a friend of something she feels bad about; if you care about her, you'll reassure her that it's not so bad. When friends told me that my weight gain didn't show, I was (like the hearing woman in the video) genuinely reassured. But there is an equally convincing logic to the other approach: obviously, the reality is there for everyone to see, so it would be hypocritical to deny it; if you're a true friend, you'll express concern. Just so, by calling attention to my

waist, Sue was showing that she empathized with the concern I myself
had brought up. And her remark was a much appreciated reality check;
not long after, I made up my mind to take the extra weight off, and I did.
Sue had been a true friend.

I Was Just Trying to Be Nice

It is always disconcerting to say something and have the person you said
it to take it the wrong way. But the disappointment is especially deep
when the person who mistakes your intentions is a close friend. If you
thought you were being supportive, saying something nice, and she reacts as if you criticized or insulted her, it can undercut your sense of
being a right sort of person—or of your friend being one.

This happened to Sophie, who received a call from June, a former
neighbor who'd been a good friend until she moved away and they lost
touch. Sophie was pleased to hear from June, but saddened by the news
her old friend imparted: "I want you to know," June said, "that Greg and
I are getting a divorce." "Oh, I'm so sorry to hear that," Sophie said, safe
in the knowledge that she was expressing appropriate concern. But June
reacted as if Sophie had said something terrible. "Why are you sorry?"
she challenged, sounding angry. "I'm glad! I've got my own apartment,
which I love, and I'm happier than I've been in years." Sophie was caught
off guard and didn't know how to respond. Should she say "I'm sorry"
again—only this time as an apology rather than an expression of support? But apologizing would amount to admitting she'd done something wrong. Maybe June should apologize for making her feel like she
had, when she'd only said what any caring friend would have said in the
same conversation.

Another woman had a similar experience while having lunch with a
friend. Bridget was filling Gail in on what she'd been up to since they'd
last spoken. Her granddaughter had decided to transfer from a state college to a private one, and Bridget, along with her daughter, had helped

her move—and also was helping her daughter pay the increased tuition. "You do so much for them," Gail said. "They are lucky to have you." As soon as she spoke these words, Gail could see that Bridget wasn't pleased. "I don't do that much," she objected, her tone curt and her manner cold. "It's what any grandmother would do." Gail was puzzled, and hurt in turn. Why did her friend take offense at what was obviously a compliment? The conversation moved on, though the tense tone continued to chill it.

Gail emailed Bridget the next day, to ask why the comment had rubbed her the wrong way. Her friend explained that she'd heard "so much" to mean "too much" and therefore as criticism. Gail assured her that she truly meant her remark as praise, and Bridget seemed mollified. They put the disagreement down to a misunderstanding, and agreed to put it behind them. But misunderstandings like these can leave lingering discomfort, a tiny nagging suspicion. In Bridget's head, a voice may still whisper: "She's claiming to have meant it as a compliment, but Gail's comment let it slip that she really does think I do too much." And a similar small voice may be whispering in Gail's head: "She says she's put it behind her, but how can I know she isn't going to overreact and misinterpret something I say in the future?"

I Was Joking!

Did "You do *so* much" really mean "You do *too* much," as Bridget thought, or did it not, as Gail maintained? It's impossible to know what any remark "really" means—whether what a speaker intended or what a listener interpreted is the true, or truer, meaning. I have pondered this conundrum with regard to an interaction I witnessed in which a speaker and a listener interpreted a remark very differently. The fleeting exchange took place between two of my friends, one Black, one white, who were meeting each other for the first time. I'd invited them both to an event, and I offered to drive. As we were all about to get into my car, there was a moment of hesitation about the seating arrangement: which of them would take the seat in front beside me, and which would sit in the back? I no longer remember where they sat, but I will never forget what was said. In that moment of decision, my white friend made a joke about Blacks sitting in the back. There is no question in my mind that she meant this as an insider's joke, establishing solidarity with her new acquaintance by showing her awareness of the despicable racism that Blacks had faced in the past. But my Black friend didn't hear it that way. Though she remained cordial during our excursion, she told me later that she never again wanted to have anything to do with that woman, who was obviously racist.

I felt terrible, and still do, that I was responsible for subjecting a friend to a hurtful experience. But I felt bad for my other friend, too, because I know she does not think herself racist and her assumption that she isn't is precisely why she felt she could make the remark. I can't say, and can't know, what the "real" or "right" interpretation of her remark is. Clearly it was the wrong thing to say. And perhaps it's true that, though she intended her quip in the spirit of solidarity, it nonetheless revealed racist attitudes, if for no other reason than that she was referring to race with someone she didn't know, and making a joke about a devastating reality that has profoundly tragic consequences and is hardly a thing of the past.

It's possible to create solidarity by talking in a way that assumes you have it, but though that will work in some instances, in others it won't. An exchange like "Once I start eating potato chips I can't stop," "I know what you mean; I can't either," reminds both speakers of their shared humanity. But the assumption of solidarity based on references to an identity that characterizes one and not the other is likely to be distrusted by the one who inhabits that identity. The assumption "We're the same"—we both abhor racism—may not work if you really are not the same: I'm Black, you're white. In the context of racism, which remains painful, problematic, and pervasive, that's a world of difference. In that situation, speaking as if you're the same can have the opposite effect: it underscores the way that you're different.

There is an irony here—perhaps even a tragedy. Someone who sincerely wishes to avoid hurting others may fear inadvertently saying the wrong thing when speaking with those of different ethnic or racial backgrounds. Feeling uncertain about what is okay to say may discourage them from socializing with people who are different. The result is to make far less likely the very thing that could dispel or ameliorate such apprehensions: friendships across racial and ethnic divides.

I think it is not by chance that this well-intended but ill-received re- mark was made in a joking manner. When I recall my friend's comment about who will sit in the back of my car, I can still, in my mind, hear and see the way she said it—with a laugh. And I recall, too, that her laugh was met not with matching laughter but with grim silence. Shared laughter contributes to a sense of connection; one-sided laughter undercuts it.

That's Not Funny

Unshared laughter played a role in another conversation that went awry. A college student, Annie, returned from a weekend visit to her boyfriend at a college in a distant city—a trip that was meant to help celebrate his birthday but that unfortunately coincided with a major power outage, which disrupted and delayed train travel. When she arrived home on the Sunday following her trip, dragging her rolling suitcase behind her, Annie encountered three people sitting in the common room of her shared apartment. Two were her roommates; the third was a roommate's friend, who had come over so they could study together. The roommate who was hosting a friend greeted Annie: "Hey! How was your weekend?"

Annie replied, "Miserable."

"Oh!" the roommate said. "That's not what I expected to hear."

Annie then held forth: "It took me eight hours to even get there on

Friday. I missed his entire birthday party. And the only reason I left so early this morning was to get back in time for practice, which I missed anyway because of the delays. I think I spent more time in transit than actually with him. And the whole time I was so stressed about what I'd missed that I couldn't even enjoy my time there."

"Oh my gosh," her roommate responded—at which point Annie turned on her heel and retreated to her room. The second roommate who had been present rose from her seat and followed Annie to her room—to console her. She saw that Annie had been upset by the exchange. And she had sensed the reason—laughter.

When the first roommate responded to Annie's report that her weekend had been miserable by saying, "That's not what I expected to hear," she laughed. That's why Annie launched into a detailed account of why her weekend had been miserable—to let her roommate know that the experiences behind the word "miserable" were no laughing matter. And the reason Annie went silent and retreated to her room to lick her wounds was that her roommate had laughed again when she said "Oh my gosh" in response to Annie's account of her tribulations. In retrospect, Annie could see two reasons that her roommate had laughed. First, Annie's reply had caught her off guard. The question "How was your weekend?" was part of a greeting ritual, a formality to which the expected answer would be "Fine" or "Good." Second, the situation—doing homework with a visiting friend—was not conducive to a substantive answer. She probably laughed not because she was amused by Annie's suffering but because of those twin discomforts: the unexpectedness of Annie's reply and not wanting to disturb her visiting friend's studying by launching into an extended conversation with a suddenly appearing roommate.

Complementary Schismogenesis

Because Annie and her roommate had approached the interaction differently, each one's response drove the other to more exaggerated forms of the discordant approach. By answering "Miserable," Annie was responding as if her roommate's question had been substantive rather than ritual. Surprised to hear such a reply, her roommate laughed. Hearing a laugh rather than an expression of sympathy drove Annie to provide an even more substantive account, which drove her roommate to express even less sympathy and laugh again. And that was enough to push Annie over the edge.

There is a term for the way that Annie's and her roommate's divergent approaches led them to exaggerate rather than dial back those differences: "complementary schismogenesis." I adapted this term and concept from the anthropologist Gregory Bateson, who devised it to describe what can happen when cultures come into contact. A "schism" is a split, and "genesis" is creation, so complementary schismogenesis is the creation of a split in a complementary—that is, mutually enhancing—way. In the context of conversational style, speakers end up talking in ways they normally wouldn't, as each reacts to the other by increasing the very aspects of their styles that differed in the first place. For example, Noelle feels that her friend Tara talks too loudly in public places. So when they have lunch, Noelle will lower her voice to let Tara know that she should lower hers. But Tara feels Noelle is speaking too softly, so she'll do the opposite: raise her own voice to set a good example for Noelle. As each tries harder to get the other to speak at a volume that she feels is right, Noelle ends up practically whispering and Tara practically shouting—both exhibiting more extreme forms of their habitual behavior.

Let's go back to the exchange between Lynn and Vicki, whose friendship foundered when Vicki said it was fine to bring Frank over for a visit but expected Lynn to realize she didn't mean it. The seeds of discord in this exchange were probably planted by Lynn's decision to call Vicki on the phone. Given Lynn's high-involvement style, it made sense to get an immediate answer by that means. Given Vicki's high-considerateness style, a phone call put her on the spot; she couldn't think clearly about how to respond under that kind of pressure. Vicki communicated her reluctance to see Frank in an even more indirect way than she would have had Lynn instead sent a text or an email, as Vicki would have done had their roles been reversed. This is the sad irony of complementary schismogenesis: when conversational styles differ, speakers often end up doing more of the very thing that caused misunderstanding in the first place.

Here's another example. Becky remembers the last time she saw Liz. They had been standing and talking following an event they'd both attended, members of a group preparing to go to dinner together. Liz, who was married, told Becky, who was divorced, that she wanted to set Becky up on a date. Becky demurred, without giving any explicit reason. Liz persisted: why not? Becky was vague: she just wasn't really up for it. Liz continued to press: she was sure Becky would like this man. Finally, Becky said something she wouldn't ordinarily have said but that she felt would settle the matter: "Your friends are boring." Liz went silent, and maintained the silence through dinner.

Both Becky and Liz had heard words from the other that anyone might agree were unacceptable: Can you believe she told me my friends are boring? Can you believe she kept insisting I go on a date when I'd made it clear I wasn't interested? But neither of these offending remarks was uttered out of the blue; both were in response to the other's repeated conversational moves—and were traceable to Liz misreading Becky's indirectness. Liz continued to press because Becky had not made it clear—at least not to Liz—that her vague demurrals were in fact nonnegotiable refusals. Liz apparently heard them rather like ritual reluctance that really seeks encouragement, as when you offer someone something she wants but feels she shouldn't leap to accept: Please take this; No, I couldn't; Yes, please take it; No, really I shouldn't; Really, I want you to; Oh, all right, if you insist, thank you. And Becky's telling Liz that her friends are boring was sparked by her mounting frustration when more gracious attempts to turn down the offer didn't work. Becky had become increasingly vague in response to Liz's persistence, but Liz had become increasingly persistent precisely because Becky's refusals were so vague—you might say, indirect.

Avoiding Conflict—and Escalating It

If indirectness means communicating a message without making it explicit, the extreme form of indirectness is silence: communicating meaning by saying nothing. That's a tactic that many women use to avoid conflict, and it, too, can easily set off complementary schismogenesis.

Barbara and Annmarie had planned a weekend trip to Montreal. As the date neared, Barbara emailed Annmarie to nail down their plans, but she got no reply. She sent another email, with the same nonresult. Then she called and left a voice message. Nothing. Barbara kept calling, each time sounding more impatient and annoyed. She and Annmarie had been friends for a long time, so she was pretty sure she knew what was going on: Annmarie, no doubt, was too busy to go ahead with their plans, but was reluctant to disappoint Barbara, so she said nothing. Though Barbara knew that this was Annmarie's pattern, it was still infuriating.

Finally, the time came when Barbara called and Annmarie answered the phone, but she did it under special circumstances. A mutual friend of theirs was visiting, and Annmarie's wife was in the room, too. When she answered, Annmarie put the call on speakerphone! "I know what you're doing," Barbara said. "You put me on speaker so I won't yell at you, but it's not going to work!" Everyone was laughing, because they all knew Annmarie's tendency to hide at the first hint of conflict. But the irony is that it was only because of her turtle act that there was a conflict. Had Annmarie simply told Barbara as soon as she realized that she had to cancel their trip, Barbara would have been disappointed but not angry. What made her angry was Annmarie's not replying to emails or returning phone calls. Hearing her friend's mounting annoyance turn to anger made Annmarie less and less inclined to face her. It was a classic case of complementary schismogenesis. Whatever each one did in response to the other—Barbara leaving increasingly exasperated messages and Annmarie retreating further into silence—drove the other into more and more exaggerated forms of the opposing behavior.

Talk, Talk, Talk

Complementary schismogenesis can be a stealth culprit. When women told me what irritates them about certain friends and why certain others are not friends, a reason they often gave was too much talk. It might be talking when she should be listening: "I had just gotten back from Africa, so I'm saying, 'Oh, I just got back from Africa.' And she's like, 'Oh, I've been to Africa.' I haven't even gotten the words out and she's talking about her trip." Or it could be too many details: "She can't just say, 'April is coming over this afternoon.' She'll say, 'April is coming over this afternoon. She would have come this morning but she had to take her car in because the valve-thing was . . .' It'll go on for ten minutes." At times it's "constant harping on the same subject." And sometimes it's just a matter of filling the airspace with too many words: she talks nonstop!

Why would someone keep talking when listeners aren't interested? Part of the reason could be complementary schismogenesis. One woman articulated what is probably true for many: "I'm socially awkward, and don't know when it's appropriate to information-dump on people. Then the more I overtalk, the more awkward I feel. I sometimes can't discern whether this person would actually want this information before I start, and then I keep going because I'm already in the thick of it and not sure where to stop." In other words, someone who starts to "information-dump" (I love that term) might keep going even though she can see it's a bit much—maybe even more if she sees it's a bit much, because that makes her feel more awkward, the very reason she overtalked in the first place.

Sometimes, though, it's not obvious that a listener isn't interested, even one who thinks she's made that clear. For example, the woman who complained of a friend "harping on the same subject" described how she tries to convey "Enough already": "I usually keep quiet and sort of nod, which should be a signal but apparently isn't." Though a "sort of nod" should reveal lack of enthusiasm, the difference between nodding and sort of nodding can easily be missed, so the frustrated listener's way of getting the talker to stop—staying silent—may be perceived as encouragement to keep going. This is especially likely if someone assumes that those who want the floor will start speaking as soon as they sense a point has been made, without waiting for actual silence.

In a similar way, talking too much can result from differences in attitudes toward talk and silence that typically go along with high-involvement and high-considerateness styles. High-involvement style often entails the assumption that if you're together, someone should be talking. Three cheers for involvement. To someone who holds that view, silence in company is deeply uncomfortable, and the impulse to fill it is automatic—and irresistible. For others—especially those with high-considerateness styles—being able to sit comfortably in silence is eloquent evidence of a close relationship. When two people have these contrasting styles, it's a perfect storm for complementary schismogenesis. One talks to encourage the other to speak up, but her excessive talking has the opposite effect: the high-considerateness-style listener demonstrates her wish for the talker to stop by clamming up (and perhaps by sort of nodding). In the end, one is talking far more than she ordinarily would while the other is talking far less, and neither thinks that the other's annoying or mystifying behavior is in part a reaction to her own.

Fake Fights, Real Friends

There's another aspect of conversational style that tends to vary by gender but can also cause trouble between women friends: agonism. I first encountered this word in a book by Walter Ong, *Fighting for Life*. Deriving from the Greek word for war, agonism is ritual fighting—using adversarial or warlike words or stances when you are not literally fighting. Sports are agonistic: just as in a literal fight, teams or individuals vigorously oppose each other, each hoping to win. A debate is an agonistic way to explore ideas, pitting opponents against each other in a ceremonial battle

that one side wins. Ong demonstrates at length that agonism is fundamental to the social lives of boys and men in a way that it is not to girls'
and women's. An example of this is creating and maintaining friendships
through play-fighting. Ong's claim is not that girls and women don't
fight; they do, but they fight when they mean it. They are far less likely to
fight for fun. It's more common for boys and men to show affection—and
to accomplish a whole host of goals—by using adversarial formats. Think,
for example, of the iconic image of a man showing affection by playfully
punching another's upper arm or locking his head in a fake choke hold.
Men's ways of talking, too, are more likely to be agonistic.

Recall Kate Bradley's example of getting her roommates to cancel a
party by using indirectness. Here's an example, provided by Jeff Civillico,
showing how his roommates solved a similar problem. (Henle is the
name of a dorm.)

> I could not help but overhear a brief exchange between my
> apartment mates this week. I was doing something or other in my
> room with the door open. One of my apartment mates was in his
> room with the door closed, cramming for his organic chemistry test
> the next day. My other two apartment mates were watching the
> World Series in the common room, passionately yelling at every
> play. This went on for a while until the one studying opened the
> door and yelled out, "Guys, can you keep it down? I'm studying
> here." The response was "No!" The one studying followed with a
> quick "Go to hell!" The conversation concluded with a remark from
> the common room: "Fuck you!" And with that the problem was
> solved. They lowered the volume on the television and mellowed
> out considerably. No one was mad—just a typical way of problem
> solving in Henle 60.

The noisy television watchers said "No," they wouldn't keep it down, but
then they did. They pretended to be angry and belligerent when in fact
they readily accommodated their roommate's need to study, just as surely

as Kate's roommate accommodated her need to write a paper. By saying the opposite of what they meant, these young men used indirectness just as surely as Kate did. But the form of indirectness they used was mock hostility—as was the way the complaining roommate expressed his gratitude: "Go to hell!" Their indirectness worked because they all understood that the mock aggression was an expression of brotherly love.

Sisterly love can be expressed agonistically, too. A student in my class, Jo, described a scene where she was mistakenly the object of a mock insult that was meant for someone else. Jo was living in a shared house with five girls who had been good friends with each other since freshman year, whereas she herself had known them only since becoming the sixth roommate they needed to fill their house. One day Jo was on her way to do laundry, descending the stairs to the den, where one of her roommates was hanging out with two friends who did not live in the house. Seeing Jo's feet before the rest of her appeared, the roommate called out, "Go away! No one wants you here!" When the whole Jo came into view, the roommate laughed an embarrassed laugh and explained that she'd thought it was one of the other roommates—one who was a good friend. Jo wasn't hurt when her roommate called out, "Go away! No one wants you here!" because she knew the words were meant as a show of friendship—and not meant for her. If anything, she was sometimes hurt that her roommates *didn't* tease her the way they did each other.

In recalling this experience, Jo made a further observation about the way her roommate used the mock insult: Jo thought that calling out "No one wants you here!" may have been a bit of showing off, displaying for her visitors that she was such good friends with her roommate that she could insult her.

Getting Beyond Conversational Style

Conversational style helps explain the proverbial "birds of a feather flock together." In fact, it helps explain the behavior of actual birds, at least one species, parrots. Scientists who study parrots have observed that the highly intelligent birds cluster in permanent groups that keep up a steady stream of vocalizations. And each group has a unique way of calling, you might say their own dialect—or their own conversational style. In an enlightening (though a bit heartless) experiment, a team of researchers took a number of parrots from one group and moved them to another, eighteen miles away. They found that, much like children who quickly learn new languages, the youngest parrot picked up the call patterns of the new group and joined them. The older ones, though, continued to use their own ways of calling, and never socialized with the new group. They kept to themselves, forming what one of the researchers characterized as "a little immigrant enclave."

It's natural—for people as well as parrots—to prefer the company of those who will understand us when we talk, and whose talk we can easily understand. Beyond the agreement over what was meant—the message—there is also a reassuring metamessage about the relationship that comes across when styles are shared, in contrast to an uncomfortable metamessage when styles differ: if a friend keeps misjudging our intentions, and we have to keep figuring out why we miscommunicated, we are not on the same wavelength. As one woman commented, "I'm not really interested in having a girlfriend that I have to think twice about what I say." Yet we don't want to only have friends who are just like us—and, given the many influences on conversational style, that's pretty impossible. Realizing that negative impressions may be the results of conversational style differences can be a first step in bridging divides between friends of different backgrounds. Friendships do survive, and thrive, despite differences, including differences in conversational style. Understanding how conversational style works is a starting point to moving beyond it, so women friends can benefit not only from similarities but also from differences.

3

"We're a Lot Alike," "We're Very Different"

The Importance of Being—or Not Being—the Same

"We have the same sense of humor; we are both complete dorks."

"Something about the way that we were imbalanced made us mesh better. I was always loud and she was always quiet and willing to listen. She was funny in a way that I wasn't, and I'm funny in a way that she isn't."

"She has a personality and interests that don't necessarily overlap with mine, but we are both readers, and we trade books back and forth."

Almost everyone I talked to about friendship told me ways that particular friends were similar to or different from them. Sameness could be an explanation for why they're friends, but so could difference. And difference could be a reason why a friendship ended—or why it endured. A woman explained how differences can enhance connection: "One of the things that bonds us is that we come at things from different perspectives, so when we talk about things, we both come back with a greater understanding and appreciation for who we are, our personalities, our psyches, and our spirits." But sometimes talking to a friend who has a very different perspective can be irritating: "She'll say things that are just not anything I would ever do. It just doesn't resonate with me."

One woman made a comment that was startling at first: "The closer you are, the less you have to have in common to keep the bond." It's with casual friends, she observed, that you need things in common to motivate you to keep up the friendship. One of her own best friends is so different from her that they refer to themselves as yin and yang, but they are close because they grew up together. Friendship can flourish despite difference in many circumstances. The young woman who said that being "imbalanced" made her and a friend "mesh better" was referring to a roommate who had been randomly assigned. Had they not been, she said, they probably would not have become friends, because her roommate tends to be private, whereas most of her friends tend to be open about their personal lives. But by living together, she and her roommate got to know things about each other gradually. What this young woman referred to as "imbalance" sounds much like what another called the "balance" she finds in a close friend who, unlike herself, isn't a talker: "She helps me keep balance; it helps me kind of stand back and take a broader perspective, and not get caught up in all the feelings."

These contrasts—private or open, a talker or not—sound a lot like introverts and extraverts, or like someone shy and someone outgoing. A high school student attributed the success of her friendships to this difference: she said she gets along well with her three close friends because, in contrast to herself, they are "big extraverts," so she can "just kind of sit in a corner with them." But the introvert-extravert or shy-outgoing polarity can also have the opposite effect. Another high school student said of a friend, "She's much more extraverted than I am—more talkative and excited. She says what she's thinking and feeling, where I would just be thinking it. I wouldn't say it." For example, when she began hanging out with a different group of friends, her think-aloud friend told her that she was jealous. I asked whether she appreciated this friend's openness. No, she said; it made her uncomfortable.

The Same?!

Treasuring ways you're the same, measuring ways that you're not, typically play a special role in girls' and women's relationships, comparable to the way boys and men are often attuned to who's in the one-up or one-down position. This preoccupation, too, can be traced to the way children learn to use language as they play with other children of the same sex.

When I speak on this subject, I show video clips of children playing in a Minnesota preschool that illustrate this contrast. (The clips are taken from a workplace training video that I made.) In the first clip, four little boys are sitting together, talking about how high they can hit a ball. The exchange begins when one of the boys boasts, "Mine's up to there," and stretches his arm as high as he can. A second boy says, "Mine's up to the sky," and points upward. A third boy tops him: "Mine's up to heaven!" Then the fourth boy comes up with a way to top them all: "Mine's all the way up to God." Though it's incontestable that these boys' talk is competitive, there is nothing mean-spirited or belligerent about their conversation. It is apparent that they find it fun. After each comment, they all laugh with delight and exclaim in appreciation.

I then show a clip of preschool girls; their talk could not be more different. Two little girls are sitting together drawing at a small table when one looks up and says, "Did you know my babysitter, called Amber, has already contacts?" How will the other girl react to this announcement about contact lenses? She doesn't try to top it; the statement is not the sort that invites topping. It's not a boast, but an observation. The second girl responds, "My mom has already contacts, and my Dad does, too." With this comment, she not only matches the content of the first girl's remark—adults in her life wearing contact lenses—but also mirrors her odd syntax: "has already contacts." To this the first girl laughs with appreciation, and they both go back to drawing. But then she looks up again and exclaims in delight, "The same?!" Whereas the boys took pleasure in topping each other, she is taking pleasure in being the same.

When I show these clips as part of a lecture, and discuss the roles of competition among boys and seeking similarity among girls, audience members often tell me that these insights help them understand their children of the opposite sex. A mother said that the boys' clip reminded her of a conversation she'd overheard that had puzzled and troubled her. She was driving while her young son and two of his friends were in the backseat. She heard one of her son's friends say, "When we went to Disneyland, we stayed four days." The second friend responded, "When *we* went to Disneyland, we stayed *five* days." Then her little boy chimed in, "We're going to move to Disneyland!" His mother didn't want to embarrass him, yet she felt she should caution her son not to say things that aren't true. "Don't worry," I assured her. "The boys know you're not moving to Disneyland. But your son won that round."

In a parallel way, a man told me that the girls' clip helped him understand a conversation that he overheard and found puzzling. His young daughter was playing with a friend who remarked, "I have a brother named Benjamin and a brother named Jonathan." His own little girl responded, "I have a brother named Benjamin and a brother named Jonathan, too." But she didn't. He couldn't figure out why she would say that. I reassured him, too: his daughter's friend no doubt knew that she didn't; they probably both took the repetition, and the implication "I'm the same," as a way of saying, "I like you; we're friends." The videographer who recorded these conversations for my training video also told me that the clip helped him understand a conversation he'd had with his daughter. When he returned home from work one day, his little girl asked him (perhaps echoing what she'd heard her mother ask) what he had done that day. He replied, "I worked on my video." And she said, "I worked on my video, too." He'd found this charming, but odd, so he, too, was relieved to understand the logic—or rather the irrelevance of logic—to his daughter's remark.

A woman named Mali recalls her delight in being—or seeming to be—the same as her preschool best friend. Mali's name is pronounced like the name Molly, but its spelling derives from her full name, Amalia. Through kindergarten, though, she imagined it must be spelled differently. Because her best friend was named Lee, Mali decided that her own name must be spelled Malee, so she and Lee really had the same name.

Precious Sameness

Women of all ages, telling me about friends, ticked off ways they're the same. For example, one woman, referring to a friendship as "legendary," explained, "We were both in Egypt the same year and both had our first Coca-Cola in the same location; our fathers had worked in similar countries and both spoke nine languages." The unlikelihood of these overlapping details—having been in the same foreign country the same year, the precise number of languages their fathers spoke—lends an air of kismet to their friendship, a whiff of fate.

In other cases, the similarities that were mentioned to explain a friendship are the opposite of random. A college student said of a friend, "We're both from New York, we're both Dominican, we both have curly hair." These similarities indicate shared heritage, experience, and values. In addition to having grown up in the same city and having the same ethnic background, having curly hair is a reference to identifying with the natural hair movement that, as the student explained, represents "a reclamation of blackness," which "is true for Afro-Latinas generally, but is an especially important decision as a Dominican since wearing naturally curly hair has never been a positive thing for Dominican women." Establishing these points of similarity was like building a foundation of connection to support the ways they're different, which she went on to describe.

In his novel *Purity,* Jonathan Franzen parodies women's desire to be the same: a woman tells her husband that he shouldn't stand while using the toilet, because she can't; if she has to sit down, then he should, too. When radio host Terry Gross asked Franzen about this scene, he explained what he believes to be the motivation behind this absurd demand: "If we can totally merge our souls and be alike in everything, then I will never be abandoned." I think he's got a point: the value placed on being the same reflects the drive toward connection and is inseparable from the fear of being left alone.

There's a cultural conceit that if two women turn up at an event wearing the same outfit, they are horrified. But women often enjoy having matching clothes. I recall going shopping with a colleague who was also a close friend. We came across an outfit we both thought suitable for wearing to work, so we both bought it, but in different colors. Whenever one of us showed up in the department wearing the outfit, the other was pleased by the reminder of our shopping excursion (which turned out to be a one-off indulgence) and of our friendship.

It can also be satisfying—perhaps especially so—if choosing the same clothes happens by chance. A colleague recalled noticing, one day, that she and a grad student were wearing the same shoes. I asked how she'd felt on discovering this similarity. She said she felt pleased—and validated—that "this cool, stylish person made the same choice I did." Just the week before, she added, she and another faculty member had shown up in our department wearing almost identical outfits: skinny black jeans, black ballet flats, and a long chambray button-down shirt. This convergence delighted her, too. (They were so tickled, in fact, that they snapped a selfie, which she was able to send me.) Here, too, seeing that someone whose style she admires had made a choice similar to hers reinforced the rightness of her own taste and judgment. But it goes beyond that. My colleague said that she chooses what to wear in part based on her mood that day, so someone else who made a similar choice must be in a similar mood; that, too, is a comforting connection. Decisions about what to wear, like decisions about what to say, are reflections of who you are, so sameness with another can be deeply reassuring: if you're on the same page, then the page you're both on must be okay.

A woman I spoke to, Takako, said she was deeply touched when her best friend, Hiroko, told her that their friendship is one of three crucial relationships in her life; the other two are with her mother and her husband. Hearing this, Takako realized that the same three relationships were the most important in her own life, even though she is now divorced and her mother is no longer alive. As she told me about this friendship, Takako emphasized how they're the same: they are both writers, both Japanese (though one was born in Japan and one in the United States), and neither has children so they don't have to feign interest, as they do in other friends' children. And then, she said, they share what they refer to as the 3 Fs. One F is Fashion: they both have an interest in clothes. Another is Felines. When she first met Hiroko, Takako thought, I can't be her friend. She's too beautiful and too high-strung! But when the topic turned to their cats, she began to feel a connection. The third F is Fitness: they are both athletes, so they don't have to pretend that keeping in shape is a challenge. That they would feel the need, with other women, to pretend to be interested in children or to have problems staying in shape is itself evidence of the value women typically place on being the same.

I heard about multiple Fs from another woman, who was amused when a friend referred to a group they are part of as the "Fab Four." It reminded her of a four-member group she was part of when she was nine years old. She and her childhood friends called themselves, referring to their number as well as their Brooklyn neighborhood, the FFF: Four Flatbush Friends. Several women recalled that when they were in junior high (or middle school, depending on their age), they devised a name for their joint selves composed of parts of each of their names: in one case, Caren and Susan became Casan; in another, five friends became BECKK (said by doubling the final "k" sound), one letter each for Becka, Emma, Catherine, Kelly, and Kate.

Enshrining similarities in an acronym, and reifying friendships by merging initials or names, emphasizes the ways that sameness can be comforting. But we all have many sides and multiple selves; like Walt Whitman, we contain multitudes. Coming face to face with two different samenesses—friends with whom we have very different things in common—can shed light on who we are and who we can be. A college senior was having two simultaneous text conversations with two different friends. In one, she and a fellow senior were deciding what to wear, and whether or not to take an Uber, to meet with diversity recruiters for a company in Silicon Valley. In the other text exchange, she and a friend from home, a small town in Arkansas, were planning a baby shower for a mutual friend. Both pending events were potentially life changing: entering a professional career and entering motherhood. But the worlds into which the young professional and the young mother would enter could not be more different. Having these two conversations at the same time brought into focus how her life had changed, how different it now was from her friends' lives back home, and how her own life might have been had she not left her hometown to attend college in a distant state.

A Window on a Different World

Diana didn't recognize the number on her caller ID when she answered the phone. She felt a leap of excitement when she realized that the person calling was Kelsey, a childhood friend who had managed, after years of searching, to find her. Renewing their friendship as adults allowed them to learn what each had meant to the other when they were children, and how each had viewed the other's home and family as more wonderful than her own, an appealing world she could miraculously enter by walking across the street.

Diana and Kelsey were best friends for the four years that they were neighbors, when Diana was in fifth to eighth grades. When they learned to sew in school, they spread fabric on Kelsey's lawn, laid their patterns on top, then cut and sewed the pieces—and proudly posed for photos together in the dresses they'd made. They sang together—so often and so well that they appeared as a duet in the school talent show, singing, a cappella, all four verses of "Fairest Lord Jesus." The image of the two friends, side by side in their dresses and with their mingled voices, is a vision of how Diana described what her friendship with Kelsey meant to her. At the time, Diana felt that her household was in chaos: her family had just moved to San Antonio, having previously lived in Georgia and before that in Michigan. Her parents fought constantly, and her father often didn't come home until two in the morning. She also had three younger siblings, two of them brothers, who added to the commotion and uproar.

How different Kelsey's house was; it seemed to Diana an oasis of peace and stability. When she and Kelsey walked into the front room, Diana always knew what she'd find: Kelsey's mother would be sitting in a large upholstered chair, sipping iced tea and eating chocolates from a large box, watching soap operas on TV. When the girls appeared, she would look up, smile, and ask amiably what they were up to. To Diana, it was a comfort to know that Kelsey's mother would be there, and would smile, and would express interest in them. It wasn't until the friends reconnected fifty years later that Diana learned that Kelsey did not share Diana's appreciation of her mother's way of spending her time. For her, Diana's home was the oasis, though one of a very different sort: she admired Diana's mother for working outside the home, and relished the unpredictability of Diana's father and her wild younger siblings, since she herself had no siblings living at home. Kelsey recalled being smitten by Diana's tall, thin demeanor, while Diana recalled being smitten by Kelsey's "cute, smiling" presence: "She was rock solid, during a very sad and confusing time for me and my family." Their friendship had given both Diana and Kelsey entrée into worlds very different from their own.

When Different Means Better or Worse

It came as a surprise to Diana and Kelsey when they learned, decades later, that the other had admired—even envied—aspects of her family that she herself had regarded as anything but admirable. As friends negotiate and evaluate ways they're different and ways they're the same, they inevitably also are evaluating ways they feel equal and ways they fear they don't measure up. Any reminder of being different can feel like a put-down if you yourself feel that the quality assigned you is potentially compromising. I have often heard women who don't work outside the home express anger and hurt because they feel dismissed or dissed by women who do. As evidence, they often tell me of having met another woman at a social event and being asked the inevitable question, "What do you do?" Their reply "I'm at home raising my kids" is met with silence and, before long, the sight of the questioner's receding back. It is possible that the working woman's silence and swift departure mean what the staying-home woman thinks they mean: contempt for her choice, and for her. But I think there's another possible explanation, one I believe is more common. The person who summarily ended the conversation may simply have been at a loss as to what to say next. Had she been told, as expected, a job or profession, she could have asked another question: What company do you work for? What subject do you teach? What's your specialty? Or she could have come up with a point of connection: I taught English for a time, too, or My sister is also a nurse. Conversation is a ritual. We say the sorts of thing we have said many times before and have heard others say, so we have a pretty good idea of how to respond when someone says the sorts of thing we expect to hear. An unexpected comment can leave us flummoxed about how to respond. That discomfort, rather than contempt, might well explain the silence and the inclination to find a conversation which the questioner knows how to have. Though the vanishing conversationalist may indeed be responding to the fact of difference, whether that difference is better or worse may be more in the mind of the staying-home woman than in the mind of the one who walked away.

Years ago, I was part of a conversation in which something I felt was potentially compromising came into focus. I was a guest at a lunch gathering of about eight women, only one of whom I knew, and that one not too well. I was enjoying the conversation and the feeling of camaraderie when suddenly I felt different—and uncertain whether to speak up. The topic had turned to college experiences. In the course of recounting memories from their college days, the women who spoke named the colleges they had attended: Wellesley, Barnard, Bryn Mawr. "Gee," one of them said, "we all went to Seven Sisters schools." The "we" was clearly intended to encompass everyone present. But it didn't. And I had a split second to decide whether or not to say so.

It would have been simple to say, "No, not all. I didn't go to a Seven Sisters school." I would surely then have been asked where I did go, and would have answered, "Harpur College." In all likelihood that response would have met with puzzled expressions and the question "What's Harpur College?" The fact that they'd have to ask would in itself highlight that I had grown up in a world very different from theirs. I'd then have to explain, "It was a small liberal arts college that was part of the State University of New York." I could leave it at that, but I would probably have added, as I usually do when this comes up in conversation, that Harpur College has since grown into Binghamton University. That's a school they'd recognize. But then I'd hasten to add that when I went there, Harpur College had a total student body of 1,600, so it has little to do with 17,000-student Binghamton University. And I might have been tempted to explain that Harpur was extremely hard to get into, and that I was able to go there only because I'd earned a Regents Scholarship, which covered tuition, and that I worked in the cafeteria to earn spending money. But were I to say all that, it would sound defensive—because it is. Though I did not think it through at the time—I had only a few seconds to speak up before the conversation moved on—maybe I wanted to avoid calling attention to the fact that I had gone to a less prestigious college and, more significantly, had grown up in a lower socioeconomic class than the others. I have no reason to believe that they would have thought less of me. But no matter how they—or, for that matter, I—felt about this difference, we all shared the knowledge that there is more prestige associated with Wellesley, Barnard, or Bryn Mawr than with Harpur College.

But there is another reason that I didn't say anything, and I believe it is the more significant one. The comment "We all went to Seven Sisters schools" was meant in the spirit of connection, a sophisticated adult analogue to the preschool little girl who brightened and exclaimed, "The same?!" Had I spoken up, I would have introduced a discordant note into the conversation. It would have sounded like a rebuke—and, in a way, it would have been, by implying "Don't make assumptions that might not apply." Whatever the reason, I let the moment pass. Until that moment, I'd been feeling the same as—and therefore connected to—the other women at lunch. But hearing myself included, by implication, in a club I did not belong to made me suddenly feel different—and left out.

Alike in Our Likes

An eleven-year-old girl was explaining how her friendships develop. She said, "We say what we dislike and what we like so we know more about each other, and we become closer." And a nine-year-old, in telling me about one of her closest friends, said right off the bat that they both love cats. But she also told me that when they were in first grade, she and a classmate used their knowledge of each other's pet preferences as fodder for fights, and they pressured their classmates to take one's side or the other's. Since she loves cats and her then-nemesis loves dogs, "We went all over the playground at recess saying, 'You like cats' or 'You like dogs,' 'Which do you like better?' I think we wound up having about half and half. And then she was singing 'I hate cats, I hate cats.'" But of course the conflict wasn't about cats or dogs; it was about each other. The creatures they liked came to represent who they were.

Maybe it's not a coincidence that the word "like" means both "similar to" and "having affection for"—or that the action of showing approval online by clicking on the thumbs-up icon is identified by the same verb, "like." Sharing likes is only a step from being alike. "When I was younger," a woman remarked, "I used to always think, Why can't I find someone just like me to be my friend? Somebody who just likes what I like." On one level, this is practical: if a friend likes what you like, you can do things together and both get what you want. But there's a deeper satisfaction, too: if your friend shares your likes, and is just like you, it's a ratification not only of what you like to do but also of who you are.

Many colleges now allow incoming freshmen to select their room-mates by "meeting" other incoming freshmen on a website where each has answered a series of questions. Several high school students told me they paid particular attention to what other girls indicated they liked or disliked. For example, one said that she was drawn to the girl she eventu-ally selected in part by seeing that she named as her favorite book *The Things They Carried*—a book she herself also liked a lot.

A woman who immigrated to the United States from Guatemala met two of her good friends when they struck up conversations, having spot-ted each other—in one case at a bus stop, in the other on the subway—and guessed, correctly, that their backgrounds were similar. Friends may be drawn together by having similar family backgrounds—not only of the ethnic, class, or regional kind but any aspects of family. A woman who, from a young age, was in many ways like a parent to her parents de-scribed the comfort of a friend who'd taken a parallel role in her own family: "There is a kind of a solace in knowing that if I say this very per-sonal thing to her, she won't judge and she'll understand." A recent col-lege graduate, Carmen, explained a similar connection to a close friend: "Another great part of our friendship is we come from the same back-ground in that my parents are from El Salvador and Guatemala and so are hers. Our parents had similar backgrounds, too, in that they came to this country, worked really hard, struggled, obviously. And so we both connected on that level. That's what pushed us in our academics, like getting good grades in high school, getting into college, being first-generation college students. It was really awesome having someone to talk to about that."

Unalike

Sometimes, though, a friend with whom you share a background has experienced that background differently, so her assumption that you're the same can be distancing. Carmen was put off, rather than drawn in, when it became clear that a friend who shared her background had a different sense of what that background means. "We were both the first in our families to go to college," she recalls of this friend, "so we could relate to each other and encourage each other." But soon after college, her friend married, had a child, and decided to stay home. "You know Hispanics," the friend said, "our moms teach us that you have to depend on a man, and he goes out to work and you're the one that stays home and cooks and cleans and makes sure that the house looks good." Actually, Carmen did not know that. Listening to her friend, she thought, "I was never taught that! I was taught, you have to work! Wow! We're in such different spaces." They soon grew apart. Their shared ethnic heritage was no longer enough to bring them together, because their experiences of it—and, consequently, their lives—were so different.

Many others also told me of friendships that ended "because our lives are just very different." Sometimes this really did just mean "different," but it could also be a delicate way to express disapproval. For example, in telling me why she and a friend had grown apart, a woman said: "Our lives are completely different. She's always been very pampered and privileged and came from a family with a lot of money. She's worked, but she's never really had to learn the true value of a dollar." In recalling a high school friend she had distanced herself from, another woman recounted: "She'd want to go to the teen clubs and dance with everyone, and I'd be like, 'I don't want to dance with these guys; I don't know them.' I'd just sit there and go, 'No thank you, no thank you.' And she would be out there having a great time. We were just so different in that way." Dancing with one after another guy she doesn't know could come across as a rather unappealing behavior, especially in contrast to the speaker, who not only declines to dance with a string of strangers but does so politely: "No thank you, no thank you."

Yet difference can be appealing—so appealing that it can spark a friends-at-first-sight feeling. A woman recalled the first time she saw a fellow worker who would become a good friend: "I remember thinking she was very intriguing and interesting, funny, and just different than other people, and I wanted to be her friend." Maybe, too, someone who seems different might be easier to approach because whatever makes her different also makes her an outsider, so approaching her doesn't require breaking into a group, which can be daunting. A woman explained that, faced with such a group of mothers at her son's playground, she decided to approach the mother who seemed to be at a distance from the group— and who sported a prominent tattoo. She felt like it would be easier to talk to "the tattooed girl"—and also that someone who stood apart, and stood out as different, would be more interesting.

In telling me about friends, many women ticked off both similarities and differences, as if reading aloud two columns in their minds' eyes, tallying them to arrive at a total account of the friendship. For example, a woman from Guatemala mentioned a friend from Nicaragua, but added that both their husbands are from El Salvador. Another explained that her best friend's marriage paralleled hers, with slight differences: she is British and her husband American, while her friend is American with a British husband. Her husband and her friend grew up in the same American city, and she and her friend's husband grew up not far from each other in England. But these similarities are balanced by class differences: she and her friend had grown up middle class, both attending public schools, but their husbands had attended swankier private schools. Social class put her and her friend in the Similarities column, while their nationalities placed them under Differences, but their husbands' nationalities and class kept the two columns in balance.

I Can't Afford That

Sometimes women mentioned differences as a testament to how their friendship was able to transcend them, like the woman who told me that she cherishes a friend though one's father was a neurosurgeon and the other's a storekeeper. Some differences, such as which books you like, may seem significant in terms of assessing each other's interests or personalities, while other differences have implications for your time to-gether. A shared interest in clothes means you can enjoy shopping together, but if one has a lot more money to spend, it can affect where you shop, and where you have lunch. For some friends, the difference in their financial situations isn't a problem. They might go to a store to-gether and confer on the items that interest them, even though one finds her items on the sale rack while the other doesn't. And they can finesse where to have lunch as well.

At times, though, differences in finances can be a problem. A woman told me she was still close to a group of friends she had gone to high school with, but sometimes they'd arrange to go to a restaurant that she couldn't afford. She'd be faced with two equally unappealing options. She could say outright that the restaurant was out of her range, in hopes they'd switch to a more affordable spot. But that would call attention to her different financial circumstances, and she'd feel bad about making them change their plans. She could avoid all that by simply bowing out—and missing out. One time, a member of the group arranged a party in Miami. All the others were able to fly down for it; she alone didn't have the airfare. And then when they talked about it after, she was left out all over again.

Being left out in ways like that can make you feel bad about yourself, as if there is something about you that just isn't good enough. But it can also make you feel that you're better. A recent college graduate who lives on her own and is responsible for all her expenses said that some of her friends are living with parents who not only charge no rent but also pay for their gas, car insurance, and college loans. There's no way they can relate to her feeling financially strapped. But she admitted that though she envies them, she also feels superior in a way. There's a sense of moral satisfaction that comes with knowing she's managing on her own.

All these are ways that present challenges to the friend who is less well off financially. But the friend who has more money may also find the disparity challenging: should she offer to pay for a less affluent friend's ticket to a concert, or would that come across as condescending? And she may hesitate to complain about troubles she knows would strike her friend as frivolous, like having to decide among several vacation destinations. Maybe the most significant impact is the one that lies at the very heart of friendship: whether or not you feel understood. For example, a woman whose finances are tight told me that a friend whose family is well off doesn't understand the pressures she's under. If she says she's worried about money, her friend says, "You have to get better about saving." But how can she save if she doesn't have enough to meet expenses? Joyce Carol Oates describes similarly disconcerting conversations in her memoir *The Lost Landscape*. When she was in high school, an English teacher asked to see her stories, and Joyce gave her a two-hundred-page manuscript. All that work was lost forever: the teacher never returned the manuscript—and it had been her only copy. Friends, Oates writes, can't understand why she hadn't made carbon copies. It apparently never occurred to them that the cost of carbon paper—only twelve sheets per box—made that impossible.

Our Experiences Were Similar—or the Same

Finding someone who has lived through a happy or difficult experience similar to yours can relieve a sense of isolation. A middle school student had her life turned upside down when her mother became ill with cancer. Her group of friends, instead of offering support, abandoned her. She befriended a classmate whose mother had experienced a similar ordeal. It was a relief to be with someone who she felt understood what she was going through. It made her feel less alone. Understanding is also at the heart of friendship for a woman whose son has severe learning disabilities. Her closest friends are other mothers with children who are grappling with comparable challenges. Knowing that they understand what it's like to have a child like hers, she is more likely to talk to them about what's going on in her life. In other words, feeling understood can not only result from communication but also be a prerequisite for it. If you don't think someone will understand, you are far less likely to say what's on your mind—and anything not told weighs more heavily.

Having lived through similar circumstances can account for what might seem at first like surprising friendships. A newspaper article described such a friendship: between Republican and Democratic first ladies Laura Bush and Michelle Obama. Mrs. Obama is quoted as explaining, "It's hard to find people who know what you're going through, who understand the burdens and the fears and the challenges."

Especially cherished connections can be formed between friends whose experiences were not just similar but the same. Many women told me of friendships that endured because they had shared significant experiences, such as working at a difficult job, the intense years of college or graduate study, or being a member of a small expatriate community living abroad. One of the most dramatic examples I've encountered of a friendship formed by shared experience is the lifelong bond between two Austrian women. Born in 1920 and 1921, Grete Stern and Hella Fixel were two of very few survivors among five thousand Austrian Jews who were rounded up in Vienna in 1941 and deported to a ghetto in the Polish city of Lodz. In 1944, those who had not already died of starvation or disease in the ghetto, as had every member of Grete's and Hella's families, were moved to Auschwitz, from where an ever smaller number of still-surviving Austrians were later sent to Berlin for forced labor and to Ravensbrück for extermination. Grete and Hella met in the cattle wagon transporting them to Auschwitz, and stayed together until they were rescued, freed from a death march by the Soviet army in 1945. They eventually managed to return to Vienna—together.

There were many differences in these two women's lives and circumstances before and after the war: Hella grew up in Vienna, Grete in a small town; after the war, Grete married and had children, while Hella remained single; and in 1970 Grete moved with her husband and daughter to Israel. They differed as well in personality and temperament. Angelika Brechelmacher, who interviewed them in 2013, describes Grete as an "eloquent narrator, full of an almost indestructible optimism" and Hella as "serious" and "critically reflective." Whereas Grete was more than willing to talk about her experiences and did not want Brechelmacher to treat her with kid gloves, for Hella, recounting—and consequently reliving—that dreadful time was so upsetting that she'd be unable to sleep for many nights after the interviews. But these differences were insignificant beside the inconceivable hardships the two women had lived through together. Each found in the other the only person on earth who could truly understand what she had experienced. In Grete Stern's words, "No one can truly understand. It was an atmosphere that cannot be described. It is not something that can be filmed, or related." And in Hella Fixel's: "I can speak to people here of Lodz or what we went through, and I have the feeling that they do not understand at all." Using the affectionate form of her friend's name, she continued, "But with Gretl, it's been the same path. And that makes for a very strong bond."

You Just Don't Understand

If shared experience can create a bond, having an experience that your friends didn't share can make you feel distanced from them. A Guatemalan woman who left a small child at home when she came to the United States told me of her three close friends—from Mexico, Guatemala, and Nicaragua—who had also left children at home when they immigrated to the United States. Later in our conversation, she mentioned another friend whom she sees and talks to every day. I was surprised to be hearing so late in the conversation about a friend she sees so often. When I asked why she hadn't thought of her before, she explained that this friend didn't leave a child behind, so she doesn't understand. So much insight and meaning reside in the explanation "she doesn't understand"; the unspoken implication seemed to be "and therefore, no matter how often I see her, she can't be as close a friend."

A college student went through a hard time after returning from a semester abroad. She felt she had changed so much, it was disconcerting to be surrounded by friends who could not understand what she had experienced. She even felt alienated from some fellow students who had also spent the previous semester abroad—those who had been unhappy or had difficulties during their stays. She had loved her time in Italy, and had been happier there than at any other time of her life. So she felt completely differently about her time abroad, and about its coming to an end, than they did about theirs. It comes down, again, to understanding.

You don't have to travel, or to undergo a physical ordeal, to experience something that your friends don't understand. A woman who suffers from depression felt even more isolated when a friend told her, "Everyone is as happy as they make up their minds to be." That's about as helpful as telling someone with pneumonia, "Everyone is as healthy as they make up their minds to be." Feeling more isolated can also result if others display—or seem to seek—evidence that they are not going through, and hope never to go through, the same thing you are. A woman who was diagnosed with breast cancer felt hurt by, and alienated from, friends whose questions seemed designed to ward off a similar fate. Questions like "Did you breast-feed?" and "Is there cancer in your family?" sounded like attempts to reassure themselves, "I'm different from you, so I'm safe"—and, therefore, "You're alone in your cancer."

Feeling different can be so painful that it leads to avoiding a friend. A woman recalls that when she had her first child, a good friend cut her off. The friend was very up front about the reason: she longed to have a child but had been unable to conceive, so seeing someone else enjoying what she craved was just too painful. (Years later, the friend succeeded in becoming a mother, and she got back in touch; though they renewed the friendship, it was never quite the same.)

A woman who moved with her husband to a senior living complex spoke of the different levels of understanding—and hence of caring—between new and old friends. Referring not only to herself but to everyone living there, she explained that you can tell someone your child is getting divorced, and they might care—really care—but they don't know your child, so the depth of feeling can't be the same. And it saddens her that all the people she is surrounded by have known her husband only since dementia stole him. It makes her long for people who knew her husband when he was well—that is, knew him when he was him—and also therefore knew who she was when she was with him.

The evolving friendship between two college students illustrates how both similarities and differences can affect friends. Janet and Renee met during their freshman year when both were going through breakups with their high school boyfriends. The connection created by this shared experience became the foundation for a strong friendship, and they roomed together during junior year. A big part of Renee's life was a passionate commitment to political activism and social justice, a commitment that, through Renee, Janet came to share. Though Renee was a Black woman and Janet a white ally, their shared perspective on racism was one of many pillars on which their friendship stood. But during their senior year, events brought the difference in their races to the fore in a new and troubling way. The deaths of unarmed Black men Tamir Rice, Eric Garner, and Michael Brown at the hands of white police officers led to ever more urgency in the Black Lives Matter movement, and political activism became an ever larger focus of Renee's life. Janet began to feel that nothing in her life could compare in significance to Renee's concerns. In support of the movement, a demonstration, called a die-in, was planned: at a predetermined time, students gathered in a central location on campus and, like others taking part in similar demonstrations across the country, all lay down on the ground to represent and commemorate the innumerable Black men who had been killed as a result of their race. Janet took part in the die-in, and Renee told her that this meant a lot to her. But not long after, Janet saw that another of Renee's friends had posted an article on Facebook proclaiming that whites have no place in the Black Lives Matter movement and should not sully it by trying to take part. Janet didn't know whether Renee agreed with this article—it was on her friend's page, not Renee's; Renee hadn't "liked" it or left comments indicating that she did; and she wasn't tagged in it—but just knowing that Renee might share that view made Janet question whether she had done the right thing by attending the die-in. Janet began to feel that she no longer knew how to be a friend to Renee. She felt she had gone from being Renee's friend to being her white friend. A difference that before had seemed to make little difference, now made all the difference in the world.

The Cline of Person

I have long pondered why these questions remain so gripping: Are we similar or different? How similar? How different? How close? A partial answer lies in a concept developed by a linguist, A. L. Becker: "the cline of person." Becker proposed that human beings seek order by locating everything—people, things, ideas—on a continuum reflecting closeness or distance from ourselves. The pronouns "I" (close) and "you" (distant) are obvious starting points. Consider, as well, the linguistic pairs "this" (close) and "that" (distant); "here" (close) and "there" (distant); "now" (close) and "then" (distant). A similar pattern can be seen in many other categories. Animals can be pets (close) or wild (distant); people can be relatives (close) or strangers (distant).

Becker called this semantic dimension a "cline," or continuum, because—as everything we've seen so far about friends attests—"close" and "distant" are relative, not absolute. "Here" can refer to something in your hand, in the room, in the country you live in, or here on earth. "Now" can refer to this moment ("Do it now!"), this decade ("now that cellphones are widespread"), or this era ("dinosaurs are now extinct"). And nowhere is the relative nature of the cline of person more varied than in the ways we array people as close to or distant from us. We don't have just two categories, family members and strangers. We have members of our "immediate" or "extended" family. Family members are closer or farther depending on kinship—siblings are closer than cousins, first cousins closer than second or "distant" cousins—or on affinity: a particular cousin might be closer than a particular sibling. Those who are not relatives can be people we "know," people we "know of," or "total strangers." Or they can be friends—placed anywhere along the continuum that makes up the vast ground between family members and strangers.

The cline of person sheds light on why those whose family backgrounds are similar to yours, or whose experiences of family are similar to or complement yours, often become friends. But finding friends with similar backgrounds is especially hard if your background is unusual, or mixed. A woman whose parents were immigrants from Central America was raised alongside Anglo peers. So most others with Central American-born parents do not share the background in which she was raised, and peers who were raised in environments similar to hers do not share her family background. In college, she concluded, "I had to put away this notion that I could only relate to people who had a similar background to mine." She joined the Latino Student Alliance and made Hispanic friends with whom she shared aspects of her background, even though they did not share the circumstances in which she'd grown up. For example, she said of a new friend, "Her parents were also from Central America so we got to talk about that all the time, that connection of going back to our parents' native countries, interacting with our relatives, growing up bilingual." Another woman reached a similar conclusion: "We are all different," she said, so you'll be frustrated "until you grow up and realize you're never going to find anybody like you. Once you accept that we're not the same, and we avoid the subjects where we are different, hey! We're good!" These women's comments assume that friendship grows when conversation focuses on ways they're the same.

Friendship is a back-and-forth, a continual negotiation and renegotiation, of sameness and difference. Sameness makes you close, while difference drives you apart. Except sometimes difference makes you close. And sameness—for example, if you feel a friend shares qualities you'd like to suppress in yourself—can drive you apart. Yet the nuances, overlaps, and clashes of sameness and difference fail to account for the magic of friendship. Maybe all our explanations about why we are friends, including a catalog of how we're the same and how we're different, are just ways of trying to make sense of something that has nothing at all to do with reason. Maybe we can't really say why one friend remains from childhood, from summer camp, from college, from a former job or neighborhood, while others fall away. Mackenzie Price summed up, near the end of our interview, "It's really just about feeling connected with someone's spirit." She went on, "That connection can be strengthened or maybe facilitated by having things in common. But it's not just that. I think what makes a good friend is someone where you don't have to be doing something spectacular to have a good time. You can just be sitting quietly on a log and feel good and happy that you are with that person."

4

The Same—or Better?

Connection and Competition

Tracy and Sharon were having an amiable conversation when Sharon said something that caught Tracy up short: "You don't have the same sense of place that I have." Tracy winced. This felt like a put-down, and an unfounded one. Though she was disconcerted to hear herself being defensive, Tracy began rattling off the many ways she has a sense of place.

Why would a friend make such a statement? Conversation is a chain, each comment linked to, and taking meaning from, what was said before. We tend to think of our own remarks as responses to what others said, but are less likely to see others' comments as reactions to something we said. To figure out why Sharon might have made this remark, let's consider what led up to it. In the course of their conversation, Sharon had commented that she would love to go back to Barcelona, where she had spent a summer years before. Tracy had responded that she didn't feel that way; if she had a chance to travel, she'd want to go someplace new. It was then that Sharon said, "You don't have the same sense of place that I have." The discordant note might have been triggered by Tracy's claim to be different. Sharon could well have felt that Tracy's comment "I don't feel that way. If I had a chance to travel I'd want to go someplace new" implied "I'm more adventurous than you—more open to new experience, more forward-looking." Though it's unlikely Tracy meant it that way, intentions are no guarantee of interpretations. If Sharon heard Tracy's comment as a put-down—even a very subtle and very slight one—then her observation "You don't have the same sense of place that I have" could have been an attempt to defend or avenge herself. Having a sense of place puts a positive spin on the desire to return to a city she knows well. If it implies a deficit in Tracy, so much the better, to counter Tracy's implication of a deficit in her.

It's intriguing that both Sharon's and Tracy's remarks, which could be heard (though were probably not intended) as put-downs, were sparked by the other's saying, "I'm different." Any failure to say "I'm the same" risks being heard as implying "I'm better." "I'm the same" reinforces connection; "I'm better" reflects competition. At first glance, connection and competition seem incompatible, even opposite. But in conversation, the line between them may be blurry—or nonexistent. And this can be particularly tricky for women friends, given two equally important, but potentially conflicting, values: the special place that expressions of sameness have in their conversations, and the disapproval of any sign that someone thinks she's better.

Failure to Say "I Feel the Same Way"

The pursuit of sameness underlies the characteristic rejoinders, so common and so valued among women, "The same thing happened to me" and "I know, I feel the same way." But anything that is valued, even treasured, can become constricting if there seems to be no room for divergence. A woman told me that her women friends "don't let you be different." For example, she explained, if a friend says, "This is a problem for me," and she says, "It's not a problem for me," the friend might protest, "Stop putting me down." Another woman expressed a similar view: with women, she said, "If you express an opinion or a personal choice that's different from theirs, it's taken as criticism or as a value judgment." (In contrast, she added, "with men there's almost an expectation of difference.") These reactions illuminate why sameness is so highly valued among girls and women: it implies equality. People often say, "Not better or worse, just different," precisely to counteract the common assumption that if two things are different, one must be better and the other worse. In other words, "different" smacks of competition, and that violates the norm, tracing back to girls' same-sex play, that it's unacceptable to think you're better than your friends. That's the violation that incurs the labels "stuck up" and "snob" and the accusation "She thinks she's something."

In all conversations, and all relationships, we balance two intersecting and overlapping dynamics: on one hand, we seek connection, but at the same time, we can't avoid competition. If we both want to stand on the same spot, one of us will have to step aside. Anything we say can be judged by these two criteria: Does it bring us closer or push us farther apart? Does it put one of us in a one-up and the other in a one-down position? Research, including my own, has shown that girls and women tend to focus more on the closeness-distance dimension, whereas boys and men tend to focus more on who's up and who's down. The contrast is one of relative focus, not absolute. Though it's often said, and often attributed to me, that girls are cooperative and boys are competitive, in fact both girls and boys are both cooperative and competitive—or, to put it differently, they both seek connection as well as competition, though they may emphasize one or the other.

Recall the contrasting video clips of preschool boys and girls at play, which I described in the previous chapter. The boys' conversation began with one little boy boasting about how high he could hit a ball. Three other little boys, each in turn, found ways to top the ones who spoke before: "Mine's up to the sky"; "Mine's up to heaven"; "Mine's all the way up to God." Though these boys' talk is clearly competitive, it is also cooperative. They are cooperating in using competitive talk to connect with each other.

In the other clip, two little girls were sitting and drawing when one suddenly raised her head and announced that her babysitter wears contact lenses. After a moment's hesitation, the second girl said that her mom wears contact lenses, and her dad does, too. The first little girl then exclaimed, "The same?!" and laughed with delight. Though the girls connected by matching, emphasizing sameness, you could see an element of competition in their talk, too. The first girl spoke of one person, her babysitter, but the second talked about two: her mom and also her dad. You could say that she was being superenthusiastic in matching, or you could say that she wasn't just matching; she was topping.

Whether or not there was subtle competition in this little girl's rejoinder (for what it's worth, I'm inclined to think there wasn't), girls and women often compete at the same time that they are connecting. Take, for example, a group of women sharing experiences by matching personal stories. When one describes an experience, and another says that she's faced comparable circumstances, both can feel closer to each other and less alone in the world. But what if a listener's story subtly—or not so subtly—portrays her as superior? Like a wolf donning sheep's clothing, a friend can seem to be matching while actually topping.

Competition—Ouch!

A professor with three small children looked forward to getting together with other women faculty who also had young children at home. It would be a comfort to talk to colleagues who were grappling with challenges similar to hers. But when she found herself in a group of such women, though they did share stories, the experience was not what she'd hoped for. They didn't talk about the difficulty of raising young children while working at demanding jobs and continuing their research. Instead, the stories they told were "heroic" ones, like "I had my baby and three days later I was back in the classroom." When she heard stories like that, the last thing she was going to do was share her own.

The notion that competition precludes connection underlies one of the most persistent and stereotypical assumptions about women: that they compete for men. Though this catfight image is no doubt exaggerated, that type of competition does exist, and can threaten friendship. The journalist and memoirist Rosie Schaap recalls, in an essay, how competition for a man's affection affected her friendship with a woman. When she dropped out of high school to follow the Grateful Dead on their tours, Schaap became close friends with three other girls. With one of the three she "shared the attentions of the same tour-head bro . . ." One evening, the young man kissed her, but then, Schaap writes, he "shook his head and smiled at me apologetically. 'You're a cool girl,' he said, 'but Marla's so cute.'" Schaap comments, "I don't know if this is what precipitated the dissolution of my friendship with Marla. I'm sure it contributed to it."

Subtle competition can shadow just about any conversation. A woman who moved to a retirement community noticed this in the frequent conversations she heard about residents' children and grandchildren. On the surface, these conversations resembled the talk about family members that is common among women, a way of connecting by showing, and assuming, interest in each other's lives. But in the senior residence, talk about children and grandchildren often took on a subtle or not so subtle competitive edge. It seemed to address the underlying questions "How attentive are my relatives? And how successful?" Like Christmas letters, these conversations tended to include only boastable facts, neglecting to mention the problematic ones: my daughter has an important position at a top firm (but not that she was fired from her previous job); my grandson attends Harvard (but not that he had to take a term off because of psychological problems). Successful progeny enhance a resident's status. Status also accrues when a child or grandchild visits often or helps out by driving or buying needed items—evidence of connection that carries weight in an ongoing competition. The irony is that almost everyone can walk away from those conversations feeling diminished, as if the problems she and her family face are unusually unfortunate rather than the universal human condition.

Games are natural sites for connecting through competition, which can take many forms besides the basic competition to win. Edith regularly plays bridge with three other women, one of whom irritates the others by continually talking about rules she's read. Though all four women in the group are friends, Edith and another player suspect that the rule touter has been secretly studying about the game. To level the playing field, they decided to take private bridge lessons—secretly. There was no way they were going to let the rule expert join them, or even know that they were doing it. They didn't want her to get better at bridge, and they didn't want her to know that they were hoping to get better, because they didn't want to reinforce her conviction that she was superior.

Just about any conversation that can be about connection can also be about competition. Sheila enjoys going out with her friends, but hearing about their lives can make her feel that her own falls short. For example, when they talk about how their husbands cook and cohost gatherings in their homes, Sheila has to try hard not to feel bad that her own husband never enters the kitchen; if she invites people over, he acts more like another guest than a cohost. But still, she has a husband. The stress on friendships can reach a breaking point if the contrast is too painful: a woman who desperately wants to be married may lose patience with friends who complain about their husbands' minor failings—especially if they come across as humble brags, like "My husband gave me a dress for my birthday that I would never wear." And a woman who has been unable to conceive may find it too painful to be with friends who complain that their children are noisy or demanding. The line between connection and competition is not always clear. Zoe feels that she gets ideas from her friends that she can benefit from, like the excellent daycare center a friend's children attend. But when she tells her husband about what she's learned, he complains that she's comparing their lives in a competition that they lose, since they can't afford to send their children there.

In her memoir *The Lost Landscape,* Joyce Carol Oates recounts how a competition—a literal one—spelled the end of a friendship. When she was in seventh grade, Joyce began attending a Methodist church, and defining herself as Methodist, because she was thrilled to be invited to join by her friend Jean Grady. (Offering an explanation that could apply to many, if not all, girls that age, and many women of any age, Oates writes, "I was always eager to be included in virtually anything.") The reverend who led the church pressed both girls to enter a regional competition that required them to memorize about a hundred verses of the Gospel According to Saint John. Though they studied together, Jean, it turned out, wasn't very good at memorizing the verses, while Joyce turned out to be very good at it. She was the only contestant from their church to advance to the next level, and the next, until she was one of three winners. But Joyce's triumph did not please her friend. Jean's response was not to congratulate Joyce, but to hate her. "You think you're so smart!" Jean taunted, her "mouth twisted in resentment." Because she won the competition, Joyce lost her friend.

The taunt "You think you're so smart!" bears a family resemblance to the other criticisms that girls routinely hurl: "She's snobby!" "She's stuck up!" "She thinks she's something!" These damning assessments are almost inevitable when a girl stands out. How different from boys' routine and expected efforts to show that they're better—or best. Competition, taken for granted and encouraged among boys, is frowned on by girls. Any evidence that a girl is better, whether or not she does anything to display it and often despite her attempts to mask it, can unleash those accusations. A woman recalled, for example, that when she alone among her elementary school friends qualified for an accelerated junior high school class, those friends accused her of feeling superior—and rejected her. Another woman recounted that when she graduated from high school, her yearbook anointed her "Most Talented." She was also designated runner-up for "Most Conceited," even though she had spent her high school years, as she put it, "trying to be the nice girl to prove to everybody I wasn't stuck up." Looking back on this hurtful judgment decades later, she added, "I was a cheerleader. Maybe that didn't help." I'll bet it didn't. Being a cheerleader, in the past one of the few sports open to girls, conferred status but also violated the requirement that a girl not stand out.

Give Me Connection, Not Competition

Cheryl gave up her virginity to get closer to, and gain acceptance from, her best friend, Loraine. She sought connection, but had overlooked competition.

Loraine and Cheryl were best friends in high school, though Loraine was more sophisticated. She had learned to love classical music from her family; Cheryl had never heard music played in her home. Loraine's family vacationed every summer abroad; Cheryl's family's vacations, if they weren't spent visiting relatives, were car trips to American sites like Washington, D.C., and Williamsburg, Virginia. And there was another way that Loraine was more sophisticated: she began having sex with her boyfriend while Cheryl had not gotten anywhere near that stage with hers. Loraine lost no opportunity to remind Cheryl of that significant difference. She'd start to say something about sex, then stop and say, "You wouldn't understand. You've never done it." So it was with a sense of achievement that Cheryl finally made the leap from the innocent who'd never done it to Loraine's equal because she had. Now at last, Cheryl thought, she could hear the ends of those mysterious, tantalizing sentences; now she and Loraine would be even closer, sharing talk about sex. She eagerly anticipated Loraine's enthusiastic welcome into the club from which Cheryl had previously been excluded. But that's not what happened. To Cheryl's astonishment and disappointment, Loraine greeted her news with no interest at all. She expressed no congratulations, asked no questions, and quickly changed the subject.

Cheryl was stunned by Loraine's indifference. But her friend's lack of enthusiasm might have stemmed not from indifference but from a disappointment of her own: maybe she liked being the only one who had done it. Maybe it was satisfying to dangle an unfinished sentence, withholding the ending that Cheryl was unworthy to hear. Maybe Loraine hadn't longed for Cheryl to gain membership to her exclusive club, as Cheryl had longed to join it. Maybe for Loraine, no longer being able say "You wouldn't understand. You've never done it" was not the triumph of friendship that Cheryl thought it would be, but the loss of a triumph—her greater experience. Whereas Cheryl thought she was achieving connection, Loraine may have felt she was losing an advantage in a competition.

Three Cheers for Competition

It might seem at first that connection is always better than competition. But competition can coexist with connection among friends, as it often does among siblings. Women's friendships can be laced through with—and enhanced by—competition. That was true for a college student and her three closest friends. They were undergraduates when the Harry Potter books were being released to great fanfare, and the friends were swept up in the excitement. One of them recalls, "We used to compete to see who knew the most specific details about the Harry Potter universe."

I credit competition for the publication of my first book. Before I began graduate school in linguistics, I was teaching remedial writing and freshman composition at Lehman College of the City University of New York. I had a master's degree in English literature and had published two articles of literary criticism in academic journals. Based on those articles, and on my knowledge of modern Greek, I was given a contract to write a book about a modern Greek fiction writer, Lilika Nakos, for the Twayne's World Authors Series. Shortly after signing the contract, I left my teaching job and began graduate studies in linguistics at the University of California, Berkeley. I planned to spend the summer after my first year at

Berkeley in Greece working on the book about Nakos, ended up extending my stay to eight months, and returned to Berkeley with a rough draft of the book. But then I got immersed in taking linguistics classes and in writing and publishing in that field. The draft of my book about Nakos sat on the shelf.

Before leaving New York for California, I had told my Lehman College colleagues and friends about my plan to write a book for the Twayne's series. One of them, Carol Schoen, decided to contact Twayne and offer to write a book about the Jewish-American writer Anzia Yezierska. Carol, too, was given a contract. Since I was in California and Carol was in New York, I wasn't in constant touch with her. So it came as a surprise— I might say a shock—when I learned, several years later, that Carol had finished her book, and it was in press. My competitive flame was ignited. How could Carol's book be published before mine, when she'd gotten the idea to write a book for the series from me, and had begun writing it after I'd begun writing mine? I yanked my draft off the shelf and went into high gear, revising it and getting it into press. My book about Nakos was published a year after Carol's, but I have always been grateful to her for inspiring me to get it done. I needed competition for that inspiration. At the same time, it was my connection to Carol that fueled the competition. The steady stream of books published in the Twayne's series by authors I didn't know did not affect me in the same way; it did not affect me at all. Competition and connection were not mutually exclusive but inextricably intertwined.

The assumption that competition and connection are mutually exclusive underlies criticism directed at two German marathon runners at the 2016 Olympics in Rio. Anna and Lisa Hahner, identical twins who trained together, were criticized by German track and field officials because they crossed the finish line at the same moment, holding hands. The officials' anger had nothing to do with winning or losing: the sisters finished eighty-first and eighty-second. Their offense, as the sports director of the German Athletics Federation explained, was being insufficiently competitive: "Every athlete should be motivated to demonstrate his or her best performance and aim for the best possible result." He and his colleagues apparently felt that one or both runners had compromised their time in order to stay together—and to engineer their photo-op finish. But Anna explained that they hadn't planned to join hands. Unable to keep up with her sister's pace, she had fallen behind, but: "After forty kilometers there was a turning point, and I knew, 'Okay Anna, two kilometers to go to close the gap to Lisa. I invested all I had and three hundred meters before the finish line, I was next to Lisa. It was a magical moment that we could finish this marathon together." And the magic of that moment is what inspired them to spontaneously reach for each other's hands as they approached the finish line.

Another pair of identical twins crossed the finish line of the same race at precisely the same moment: North Korea's Kim Hye-song and Kim Hye-gyong came in tenth and eleventh. They were not chastised by their country's sports officials. Perhaps the Koreans did not share German assumptions about connection and competition. Or perhaps the difference that caught the attention and sparked the anger of the German officials was the Hahner twins' sealing and demonstrating their connection by holding hands—a gesture so different from the typical raised arms or pumping fists that characteristically celebrate triumph in a competition. That gesture may have been what gave the impression that connection had trumped competition. But Anna's account of how it came about made clear that competition had brought them to that final thrilling connection.

Connection or Competition?

Did Anna Hahner find the extra reserves to quicken her pace after running for five and a half hours because she wanted to catch up to her sister—connection!—or because she didn't want to let her sister finish the race ahead of her—competition! It's impossible to say, because the result is the same, and the motivation could be either or both.

It's not always clear whether a comment is meant to connect or compete—or, as when the little boys vied for how high they could hit a ball, to do both at once. And the way a comment is taken may not be the way it was intended. Nowhere is that confusion more dramatic, and more common, than with the archetypal women's conversational ritual, troubles talk. If one says, "I have this problem," and the other says, "I have a similar problem," the effect can be a feeling of comfort, assurance that you're not alone—connection. We've just seen that a response like "I don't have that problem" can be interpreted as a put-down—competition. But what if one says, "I have this problem," and the other says, "I have a similar problem—and it's worse than yours"? Is that connection or competition? Is the implication "Mine's worse" intended to make you feel better? If your problem isn't as bad as mine, then you shouldn't feel so bad about it. Or is it one-upmanship? If your problem isn't as bad as mine, then you have no right to feel bad about yours—or, even worse, Forget you! I'm the one who should be the center of attention here!

A college student recounted a conversation she had with a friend when they were both sophomores—a conversation that bothered her, because she felt she was trying to create connection and was met with competition. Their exchange sets in relief the inextricability of these motives.

It was the end of the term, that crazy time when final exams are under way and final papers are due. Helen and Brooke were studying together when Helen initiated a bit of troubles talk, much like similar complaints she had uttered and heard many times before. She said, "This is ridiculous. Everyone is getting to check things off, and I won't be done with a single class until next Thursday." Brooke's response was almost what Helen expected, but not quite. She said, "I would take that over my schedule! I have almost a hundred pages of papers to write by Monday. Please tell me how I'm supposed to not fail Chemistry!" The second part of Brooke's response was firmly in the connection camp: she, too, complained about end-of-term pressure. But the way she began

struck Helen as competitive—"I would take that over my schedule!"—
and implied that Brooke wasn't matching Helen's troubles but topping
them.

Though Brooke's remark made Helen uncomfortable, she nonetheless
tried to respond in a way that would provide comfort—and therefore
connection—by reassuring Brooke that her situation wasn't so bad; she
said, "At least it'll be over soon. Think about it. You'll have been home for
three days before I've taken a single exam. It'll be so nice when it's over."
Though Helen was certain her intention was to return to a spirit of
connection, she was pointing out that her situation was worse than
Brooke's—a perspective Brooke was not going to concede; she protested,
"Yeah but I literally have no time to study!" Declining to join the competition, Helen again responded in a way she thought would be reassuring:
"Yeah but you'll make it through. God, I'm so ready for finals to be over."
So it annoyed her that she saw Brooke as continuing to compete: "At
least you have the whole week to prepare!"

Helen felt certain that she meant her own comments to establish connection, whereas Brooke kept responding in a spirit of competition. But
to an outside observer, Helen's comments were indistinguishable from
what she regarded as Brooke's one-upmanship—or, more accurately, one-
downmanship. To comfort Brooke by pointing out the positive (Brooke's
ordeal would be over soon), Helen was saying that her situation was
worse (since her own ordeal would go on longer). There isn't any "real"
meaning here; the friends' comments aren't "really" about connection or
competition: the two are indistinguishable. Though I know how Helen
intended her comments and how she interpreted Brooke's, I can't know,
because I didn't talk to her, how Brooke intended her comments or interpreted Helen's. Both friends' words could be seen as either competition
or connection—or both at once. Given that inescapable ambiguity, it's
common for friends to feel, as Helen did, that their attempts to establish
connection were somehow twisted into competition. And it's common
for women to feel that competition is unpleasant and unseemly, especially if their intention was connection.

The Hierarchy of Age

Overt competition can seem distasteful or even unacceptable to girls and women because its goal is to establish—even worse, to display—superiority, a goal that girls' peer groups discourage. That's why girls and women typically expend a lot of effort to downplay differences in abilities or status. In seeking to understand how unequal status affects friendship, I thought about cultures in which the hierarchy of age—a universal of human relations, starting with families—plays a larger and more obvious role than it does in American culture. In many such societies, status associated with age cannot be forgotten, because it is built into language: the words speakers must use when addressing anyone older are different from the words they'd use when addressing someone of the same or a younger age. Korean is one of many such languages.

For her master's thesis in linguistics, Hanwool Choe studied messages exchanged over Kakao Talk, an instant messaging app, by five Korean women, friends who were attending American universities with Fulbright fellowships. (They had met at a gathering of Fulbright fellows.) One of the five is a year younger than the other four—and consequently addresses them with a word that reflects their age difference: *eon-ni*, pronounced "un-nee." (In Korean, address terms always reflect both relative age and gender; this is the term used by younger to older women.) Choe notes that Korean women use this term when addressing older friends or acquaintances, even if the older one has given them permission to forgo other ways of showing respect through language.

I asked Choe how the age difference affected the five-way friendship among the young women whose instant messages she studied, given the automatic, requisite, and ubiquitous linguistic reference to it. She explained that the four older friends did not have to think about their language, since they speak the same way to those who are of the same age and those who are younger. But the younger one had to be constantly on guard. Though her use of *eon-ni* would be automatic, she also had to show respect in other ways. For example, all the friends frequently responded to the others' messages by typing written equivalents of "mm-hmm" and "uh-huh," but the forms they used were slightly different. The year-older friends responded to each other's as well as to their younger friend's comments by writing *eung*, but the year-younger friend used a different word, *ne*, which showed not only appreciation of a comment but also respect to an elder. As a result, the younger one could never be quite as comfortable in the conversations—and the relationships—as the others.

I then asked Choe how the constant reminder of age hierarchy affects Korean friends' feelings for each other and their friendships generally. She, in turn, asked her high school friends how they feel toward their older women friends. Speaking in Korean, she used the Korean word for friend, *chin-gu*. However, though this is the word that is generally translated as "friend," in Korean it is used only for friends of the same age. So they could not understand her question. She clarified: "*chin-gus* who are older." They all then responded, "Older *chin-gus*? They aren't *chin-gus*. They are close *eon-nis*." In other words, in Korean, the unequal status conferred by age hierarchy fundamentally changes the relationship. People of different ages who know each other well and are close, Choe explained, can be friends, but not in the same way that those of the same age—that is, *chin-gus*—can be.

The role of language in reinforcing this sense of friendship is striking. Choe commented that her choice of the word "friends" to describe the relationships among all five of the Fulbright scholars despite the age difference of one, though partly a matter of convenience (since four of the five are the same age), also reflects American culture as well as the English language. Before coming to the United States for graduate study, she, too, did not think of her *eon-nis* as "friends"—that is, as *chin-gus*—but rather as "close *eon-nis*." But there is no English word that corresponds to *eon-ni*, so when she wrote up her study in English, she used the word "friend" for all the young women. That word then shaped her thinking about their relationships, and led her to use the Korean word for "friends," *chin-gus,* when asking her high school friends (her *chin-gus*) about their older women "friends." They had to remind her that in the Korean language—and therefore in Korean society—the age difference makes a difference: a "friend" who is older (*eon-ni*) is not a "friend" (*chin-gu*).

Age hierarchy is not competition. It is a type of status that is fixed, unalterable, and given, whereas relative status is up for grabs in a competition. Maybe that's why competition among siblings is so common: the age hierarchy is inescapable and constant (even identical twins are aware of which twin was born first), so it's tempting to strive for status in ways that are not. Among siblings, competition does not preclude connection; it can contribute to it, as when adult siblings enjoy recalling the ways they competed as kids. The same can apply to friends: connection is created in many ways, including competition.

Competing for Connection

Connection and competition are intertwined in another way, too. Connection can be the commodity for which girls and women compete. When high school girls post new pictures on their Facebook pages—and they are expected to change their pictures frequently—their friends will click "like" to show that they have seen and approved the new picture. But each "like" does far more than express approval. It's a public display of friendship. The more "likes" a girl's picture gets, the more friends she has, the higher her status: more friends mean more power. The same sense of power through connection results when girls post pictures of themselves at parties on Instagram: look how popular I am! Look how many friends I have! A high school student and her friends were angered when they generously included a newcomer in their parties, then saw that she had posted photos of herself at parties she had not told them about. They were pretty sure the new girl's thinking was: If your friends become my friends, and I make new friends that I don't share with you, then I have more friends! I win!

A high school student told me of a pattern she sees often: five girls form a clique, but among the five, three are the core. "And the three girls will want to show off," she said. Hearing "show off," I expected to hear about money, or clothes, or knowledge. But the end of the sentence wasn't about anything like that. They "will want to show off that they are closer. They will bring up that inside joke or something that happened when the other two were not there." It's competition, yes, but for connection. Describing a similar dynamic among adults, a woman who has several brothers observed that when the extended family gathers, her brothers' wives compete over which of them fits better into their husbands' family. They compete for inclusion—that is, for connection.

Competition for connection can come at unexpected times, in unexpected ways—and it can be very subtle. Chloe was hosting Sam, a former colleague who was paying a return visit to the company where he no longer worked but she still did. They were having lunch in the company cafeteria, and Chloe was filling him in about another former colleague, Chloe's close friend Ilene. Chloe was telling Sam about the tragic recurrence and metastasis of Ilene's cancer when another colleague who knew Sam spotted them and came over to greet him. Chloe mentioned that she had been telling Sam about Ilene. The newcomer to their conversation said, of yet another former colleague, "Jamie visited her." This seemingly insignificant remark got under Chloe's skin. She felt like blurting out, "Goody for Jamie! So she visited once! I've been in constant touch with Ilene since her cancer was first diagnosed! I have visited her far more times than I can count!" Chloe didn't say any of that. She simply said, "Yes, I heard it was a very good visit." Though this remark was gracious, it reaffirmed Chloe's place at the top of a hierarchy of closeness to Ilene by showing that she was in a position to know about Jamie's visit and to judge it. But that didn't end the conversation, or the competition. Jamie's spokesperson added, "She visits her whenever she's in town." This remark annoyed Chloe, too. How could Jamie's occasional visits be compared to her own continual involvement? But Chloe did not say this, either, because it felt shameful to be feeling competitive about who is closer to, and more devoted to, someone dying of cancer.

Shameful though her reaction seemed to Chloe, it is not unusual for women to feel competitive about who is closer to, or doing more for, a friend who is going through a difficult time, just as women may subtly compete for who knows more and sooner about what's going on in someone's life—or, even more troublingly, someone's death. A young woman had to tell others in her circle that a beloved mutual friend had died of a progressive illness. Among the many reasons this was one of the hardest things she'd ever done is that she knew they'd be doubly devastated. In addition to the terrible loss of a dear friend, they would be hurt that the friend had not told them she was sick, and was therefore not as close a friend as they'd thought she was.

Why Compete for Connection?

Why all this competition for connection? A clue emerged in a conversation reported to me by a nine-year-old girl. One of her friends, the girl told me, insisted that she answer the question "Who is your best friend other than me?" then followed up with "If you could either never see me again or never see her again, who would you choose never to see again?" What a revealing way to word that question. Not, Who do you love best? or Who is your really really best friend? But, Which of us is at greater risk of losing you? I suspect that that unspoken fear, probably unarticulated even to ourselves, is what underlies much of the competition among women for friends: fear of being left out, left stranded, left alone.

I was thirty when I quit my job teaching writing at Lehman College and moved to Berkeley to begin doctoral studies. Before making the move, I had a nightmare that I still vividly recall: in the dream, I had arrived at UC Berkeley and was walking down a wide staircase in the student center. To my horror, I saw the other students turn their backs on me, rushing to get away. No one would talk to me, because I was obviously too old to be a student. Though the specific basis for my fear—being older than my peers when I began doctoral studies—was particular to my circumstance at the time, the fear that turned my dream into a nightmare is, I believe, a common one among girls and women at every age: no one will be my friend; I'll be stranded. Many children's games play on this fear. It's embodied, for example, in the last line of the song children sing as they play the game the Farmer in the Dell: no one wants to be the cheese standing alone.

In her novel *You Are One of Them*, Elliott Holt portrays the ways that the children's games Hide-and-Seek and Marco Polo reflect this fear, and how a friendship can reflect—and reinforce—it as well. The protagonist, Sarah, is a plain, self-effacing girl who is miraculously befriended by a girl who lives across the street: the effervescent, ever-popular Jenny. This premise represents the way many of us feel that we are in some way unworthy of the love and attention our best friends provide, and therefore at risk of losing them. Sarah's home is a dark, lonely place, her mother eccentric and self-absorbed, while Jenny's home is opulent and welcoming, and her mother a glamorous, sociable baker of cookies. This, too, is a metaphor, for the impression that other families are ideal and happy, while ours doesn't measure up.

Sarah's fear of losing Jenny and her sense that she needs Jenny more than Jenny needs her are dramatized in an episode where the nine-year-old girls have ventured into the woods near their homes. Jenny suggests they play Hide-and-Seek, and offers to hide first. When Sarah opens her eyes and begins looking for Jenny, her friend is nowhere to be found. She goes searching for Jenny, pressing farther into the woods than feels safe, becoming ever more frightened. She can hear the fear in her own voice as she calls, repeatedly and in vain, "Jenny! Jenny!" Sarah's search becomes increasingly desperate as she begins to panic: Jenny must have been kidnapped! As darkness falls, Sarah gives up and only then realizes that she herself is in danger. When she finally manages to find her way out of the woods, she breaks into a run toward home, planning to enlist her mother's aid in finding Jenny. But that's not necessary. Jenny is blithely en-sconced on her front-porch swing, from which comfortable perch she calls out, "Slowpoke! It's seven-thirty. We've already had dinner."

Jenny had headed out of the woods the moment Sarah closed her eyes. That had been her plan when she suggested they play Hide-and-Seek: "I wanted to see how long it would take you to find me," she explains. Whereas Sarah was driven by worry that something bad had happened to her friend, a girl alone in the woods, Jenny had no corresponding worry about Sarah, who really was in that risky position, because Jenny had put her in it. And Jenny has no patience for Sarah's evident distress. "Jeez," she says, "it was only a test. Don't be so dramatic." And as if that weren't insult enough, she adds, "You're a nervous freak like your mom." Jenny took advantage of Sarah's loyalty to leave her stranded in the woods. Then she took advantage of her knowledge of Sarah's family to humiliate her. The game Hide-and-Seek gave her the means to do both. Just as thrillers embody adults' fears, then provide a catharsis when the hero miraculously escapes, the game Hide-and-Seek sets up a scenario that embodies the common children's fear of being stranded by losing their friends. The delight of finding them—when the game works as it should—provides a similar catharsis.

Later in the novel, Holt uses another children's game that plays on the same dynamics to represent Sarah's vexed relationship with Jenny. This game takes place in a dream that Sarah has when she is an adult. In the dream, she and Jenny are playing Marco Polo in Jenny's pool. (Of course Jenny's house had a pool, and Sarah's didn't.) By the rules of the game, one child must tag the other children, but with eyes closed. To locate them, the unseeing child calls out "Marco" and the others must reveal their locations by answering "Polo," but nothing stops them from im-mediately moving to a different location. Here again, Sarah is seeking an elusive Jenny.

My eyes were closed and I was groping around the shallow end, trying to find her. *Marco*, I called. *Polo*, she said, in a voice that barely suppressed a laugh. *Marco, Polo, Polo, Polo.* But the closer I moved to the voice, the farther away she was, and then I wasn't in a pool at all but in some kind of sludgy muck through which it was impossible to move. *Marco,* I called helplessly from the mire, but there was no answer . . .

This game, too, is a microcosm of the fear that shadows friendships: not only that you can lose the friend who has come to mean so much to you, but also that the friendship can mire you in "sludgy muck" from which you don't know how to extricate yourself. Or maybe you don't want to, because you don't want to lose the friendship.

In this novel, Holt portrays an extreme example of a child—and later a woman—clinging to a friendship that makes her feel more rather than less alone. We all put up with ways that a friend might annoy us because we don't want to lose the friendship. A woman told me that her mother complains of a friend who habitually calls her after ten at night, when her mother is about to go to bed, if she hasn't already fallen asleep. The daughter asked her mother the obvious question: why don't you tell her not to call so late? Her mother replied, "Because then she wouldn't call at all."

5

FOBLO, FOGKO, and the
Safe Embrace of Women in Groups

"A group of women is a scary thing unless you're really on the inside, really solidly in the group."

Audrey was telling me of a challenge that came with her second marriage: she and her husband socialized with a group of couples, her husband's longtime close friends and their wives. The couples regularly met for dinner at each other's homes, where, as the evening progressed, the men would end up in one room and the women in another. That's when Audrey's problems would set in. It wasn't anything about the individual women. One on one, she could have warm interactions with any of them, and often did. But with all the women together, she'd feel like the odd woman out. For one thing, since most of them don't work outside the home as she does, many of the topics they discuss don't interest her. Even more important is their shared history. Because they've known each other's children since they were in diapers, they refer to things they all know and she doesn't, so she can't take part in those conversations either. She would rather join the men, who talk about topics like politics and current events, which she can discuss as easily as they can. But she doesn't have that option.

Beyond all that, Audrey explained, there's something about women's groups as compared to men's that makes her feel she'll never quite fit in. "With a group of men," she said, "you can come and go. You can sit on the periphery. The boundary is permeable. It's an unstable group. With women, it's a stable hierarchy. Everyone knows what their role is in the group. The men are always jockeying for power and realigning status and relationships. For us, it's much more like we have it and it's fixed and that's it, period."

Several women told me they find groups of women impermeable and scary. One recalled that when she took her son to the playground, she'd see the other mothers gathered in a circle, and she'd feel her blood pressure rise. The prospect of having to break into that group reminded her of the "cliquish" high school scene she had found daunting. Imagine a line of skilled dancers who have danced together for years, so they know the rhythms, the steps, and the unique ways they string them together. Then imagine trying to join in. Even if you succeed in disengaging two people's hands to insert yourself in the line, and manage to pick up the beat, you'll have a hard time predicting the sequence in which the steps will come, and performing them with just the right twist. Your missteps will mess up the dance for everyone, and they will probably not hide their annoyance. They might well try to make you feel uncomfortable enough to step out of the line and go home. That challenge pretty much captures the way established groups of women can be scary.

But imagine, too, the glorious feeling of connection enjoyed by dancers who know the moves, the rhythms, and the sequences, and have danced them together so many times that they don't have to think about it; they just join hands, and their bodies take over. It's the visceral exhilaration that can come from *Keeping Together in Time,* as William McNeill demonstrates in his book by that title. McNeill coined the term "muscular bonding" for the unique sense of connection created by the coordinated movement of dance, military drills, religious rituals, and singing in unison. Though he writes of the literal coordination of movements, muscular bonding can be a metaphor for the more general drive to move together—to band together—in groups.

Group Support

I experienced the power of women in groups during the women's move-ment in the early 1970s, especially the part played by what were called consciousness-raising groups. During that period, a group of women gave me courage to do something I'd been unable to do, though I knew I had to. It wasn't even a group I belonged to, and I didn't know everyone in it. I was visiting my sister Mimi. Her women's group had a meeting scheduled during my visit, and she invited me to join them. When my turn came to speak, I told the group that I was going through a divorce, and mentioned something that had me stuck. I knew I had to stop wear-ing my wedding ring, but the prospect of taking it off and going forth in the world without it was so daunting that I just couldn't do it. The women in the group told me that they understood my reluctance, and what it represented: fear of facing the world as a single rather than a mar-ried woman. Then, with their encouragement and their expectant faces surrounding me, I screwed up my courage, pulled the ring off my finger, and threw it into the center of the circle—and everyone in the group ap-plauded. The experience was a physical embodiment of the spirit so many women told me their friends provide at difficult times: support.

At times of cataclysmic life events like divorce or grave illness, groups of friends can come through in ways that no individual can on her own. For example, when a woman who lived alone was diagnosed with cancer, her friends set up a website where they signed up to drive her to and from chemotherapy, deliver meals, and make sure her other needs were met. Her friends' cumulative help was far more comprehensive than would have been possible had they not coordinated their efforts as a group.

Friends don't have to be in the same location to come through as a group. Jeffrey Zaslow gives an example in *The Girls from Ames*, his book about a group of women who have maintained well into adulthood the friendship they established in high school. When one of them, Karla, suf-fered the worst tragedy imaginable—her teenage daughter was dying of leukemia—the friends, now scattered across the United States, joined together to come through: in addition to sending a steady stream of loving emails, they pooled their money and hired a service to clean Karla's house and another to deliver meals, since Karla was virtually living in her daughter's hospital room.

Friendships that have endured over many years are particularly inspiring. Lois is part of a group of four women who met in college and grad school (two were grad students, two undergrads) and are still friends, now that two are in their sixties and two in their seventies. Though they've lived distances apart, they stayed in touch and always marked major events together: successes and tragedies, births and deaths, graduations of children and grandchildren, and receipt of awards. And when someone suffers a loss, the others are there.

Lois's account of how this group of friends support each other has much in common with what filmmaker Iris Zaki observed in an Arab-owned hair salon in the Israeli city of Haifa. The double entendre of her film's title, *Women in Sink*, reflects what she depicts in the film: the Israeli Arab and Jewish women who frequent the salon form a community. A Jewish patron summarized how they function as a *mishpocha*, a large extended family: they celebrate occasions in each other's lives, and when someone has a problem, the others know about it and do what they can to help. The group spirit of the salon created friendships that reach across their ethnic and religious differences.

Hair salons are natural sites for group friendships because they bring women to the same place over time. But there are many other contexts for such groups to form. The consciousness-raising groups of the women's movement and the quilting bees of colonial times have been replaced by book groups, cooking groups, Bible study groups, and many other modern contexts in which women come together to accomplish tasks—and talk.

At the 2016 Olympics in Rio, the United States's "Women's Eight"—the eight-member women's rowing team—was in only third place halfway through the 2,000-meter race. The coxswain, who directs the team from the end of the shell, called out words of encouragement that, as later recalled by a team member, sent a "spark of electricity" through the rowers that powered the superhuman effort by which they pulled out ahead of the other shells and took the gold. What magic words had inspired the team to accomplish this Herculean task? The coxswain had said, through her headset, "This is the U.S. Women's Eight." She simply reminded the rowers that they were not individuals striving to do their best despite exhaustion and pain, but members of a team. The U.S. Women's Eight had not lost an international competition in ten years, but it wasn't the specter of breaking the team's winning streak that made it possible for them to continue it. That had to be "put aside," another team member commented later, because it was "overwhelming." The thought that inspired them was "Let's do this for each other."

In Good Company

Sometimes the appeal of a group is not just the chance to belong but the specific attributes of the group's members. Florence still regards her high school friendships as the most rewarding of her life. A shy girl to whom socializing did not come naturally, she prepared to enter an academically challenging Catholic girls' school by reading Dale Carnegie's *How to Win Friends and Influence People*. Once there, she consciously applied some of Carnegie's advice, and it worked. The friends she made were every bit as sophisticated, clever, and funny as she had expected. Florence recalls, "I had to keep on my toes and be sharp and funny to keep up with them, but the work paid off and I really loved them, and the relationships were deeply satisfying."

A woman who had an unusually successful career first as a journalist and then as a journalism professor at a prestigious university is certain that, had it not been for the group of friends she was part of in junior high and high school, she would have been a secretary. In junior high school, Dora joined a group of girls who lived in an affluent neighborhood adjacent to her own more modest one. When they finished junior high, her friends headed to an academic high school, but Dora did what her family expected: enrolled in a "professional" school where she'd prepare to be a secretary, and she took a job as one after graduation. But Dora remained in the group, spending time with her college-bound, then college-attending, friends on weekends and during summers, and when she moved with her family to California, she stayed in touch with them by writing. In California, Dora discovered that public colleges were virtually free, and she began taking classes at night, which set her on the course that shaped her career and her life. "Had I not become part of this group," she said, "I would have fit into the professional school group, and not set my sights any higher. Because of all my friends who were going off to college, and also because I won a scholarship, I then aimed for college."

In addition to support at extraordinary times, and inspiration to achieve beyond what would otherwise seem attainable, there is something precious that groups can provide in ordinary times and on a daily basis: company. Years ago, a friend remarked, "If we knew our friends would never marry, we wouldn't have to either." We were part of a group of friends, all single, who regularly socialized together. There is a word in Greek for such a group: *parea,* which is generally translated into English as "company." When I lived in Greece, I often heard Greeks say, in English, things like "I went on an excursion with my company." At the time, I thought that translation sounded odd, but now I think it's perfect, because that's what being part of a group ensures: that you'll have company. You never have to worry about what you'll do Saturday night or who will go with you to a movie you want to see. You'll be with your *parea.* If some in your *parea* have other plans, others will certainly be free.

Guaranteed company is a kind of protection that comes with group membership—protection against loneliness, or at least against isolation. And a group also affords protection against the dangers posed by members of other groups. Explaining why she joined a sorority in college, one woman said, "There are mean girls out there. You have your friends to protect you against that."

FOBLO

There is a carrot-and-stick aspect to groups, and both the carrot and the stick give the group power. Belonging to a group means feeling included, feeling connected to people you care about and who care about you, and the reassurance that comes with being similar. There are many ways that groups reinforce and display their connection—team colors, T-shirts or uniforms, mascots, or names they give themselves, like GNG for Game Night Gang, a group of middle school friends who got together to play Taboo and card games, or Hungry Girls, college students who set up a group text so anyone heading to lunch could meet up with others and no one would have to eat alone. That's the carrot—the warm comfort of belonging. But anything of value can be lost. And that's the stick: the threat of exclusion.

Young people speak of FOMO: Fear Of Missing Out. It's the reason they obsessively check their phones—first thing in the morning, last thing at night, and innumerable times in between, including when they're in conversation with others and even if they have to do it under the table at dinner. FOMO is not limited to youth. It's why I, like many of my peers, obsessively check email. But there's a related, maybe even stronger, force—one that is particular to girls and women. I call it FOBLO: Fear Of Being Left Out. With FOMO, you would have been welcome to attend a party but missed it because you didn't check your phone in time. With FOBLO, you fear there's a party that your friends deliberately did not tell you about. You didn't just miss out; you were left out.

The ubiquity of social media platforms where people post photographs of themselves beaming and mugging among joyful revelers means that people are constantly at risk of seeing a gathering they were not invited to, like a little match girl with her face pressed to a window, looking in on a happy world she can't enter. In the picture, everyone looks like they're having the time of their lives, intensifying the stabbing pain of being left out. The picture gives this impression even if the person who posted it was there only long enough to snap the photo or was miserable the whole time.

The same behavior that you delight in when you're part of a group can be off-putting if you're watching from the outside. A woman remarked that she avoids groups of women who "gather and giggle and have drinks and talk about golf." But elsewhere in our conversation she commented that she enjoys friends with whom she can be "goofy" and "giggle," as she could with her family growing up. The difference, I think, is the lovely feeling of connection that comes of laughing together—and the decidedly unlovely feeling that comes of watching others laughing over something you can't share.

FOBLO rears its head unbidden and can be puzzling even to the one who's suffering from it. Sandra, for example, feels snubbed by a group of women who are members of her synagogue. It bothers her—a lot—when they (ostentatiously, she thinks) turn their backs on her. And then it bothers her that she's bothered, because she doesn't actually like them! Groucho Marx said, famously, "I wouldn't want to join a club that would have me as a member." For Sandra, as for many women, it's more like "I wouldn't want to join a club that would not have me as a member, but I want to be invited to join." Being excluded can trigger FOBLO, regardless of how you feel about the group that's rejecting you.

Girls and women have good reason for FOBLO. Again, we can trace the source to children at play. When girls decide they don't like another girl, they lock her out. Think of little girls who express anger by threatening, "You can't come to my birthday!" Boys don't typically exclude boys they don't like; they let them play, though they might treat them badly. There are many reasons that girls are more likely than boys to ostracize a playmate they don't like or want to punish. One reason is the role of talk, especially secrets, in girls' friendships, in contrast to boys' focus on activities. If you're playing baseball or football, there's no reason a low-status boy can't be there; he might even be needed to round out the team. But if girls are telling secrets, only friends can be present; they can't let a girl hear their secrets if she's not, or they don't want her to be, a friend.

Little girls can be very creative in finding ways to exclude others, despite many schools' attempts to prevent hurt feelings by imposing the rule "You can't say, 'You can't play.'" A third grader recounted how a classmate circumvented that rule: when she tried to join two other girls at recess, one of them told her, "We're really not playing anything." Linguist Amy Sheldon observed similar creativity among preschool girls who managed to exclude a third girl without directly rejecting her. When they played house, they ostensibly included her but assigned her a role that precluded her participation: "You can be the baby brother, but you aren't born yet."

Trios

There is comfort in groups. There is comfort in threes. Three, the minimalist group, takes the pressure off each individual to carry the conversation. Three defuses the intensity of one-on-one conversation, with its expectation, for women and girls, of unbroken gaze between listener and speaker—the spotlight on you alone.

I have a friend whom I first saw socially as part of a trio. We'd meet for dinner and go places together, always the three of us. As we all got to know each other better, I began also doing things as a pair—with one of the three, but not the other. Whenever I suggested to the other friend that we get together, just us two, she would decline. Finally, I told her I was getting the impression that she didn't want to see me alone. She said I was right. But she assured me it wasn't anything about me personally: she just feels more comfortable in threes, where she can recede into the background if she feels like it. With just one other person, the pressure to be always on, to find things to say, to spend the entire evening in the foreground, was daunting. This changed as we got to know each other better, and no longer prevents us getting together, just two. But it helped me understand why many women, especially early in a friendship, prefer threes.

The intensity of twos—especially between new acquaintances—takes a special form among lesbians, because of the possibility of sexual attraction. As one young woman, drawing on her own experience, explained, "Lesbians definitely prefer group settings when they are hanging out with new friends; otherwise, the message of friendship can be unclear. It can be confusing if a girl asks to hang out one on one, even if she says it is just friends, because there is still that uncertainty. A third or a group helps prevent that." The way that threes can dispel that aspect of the intensity of twos apparently motivated Saint Augustine when he cautioned nuns in a convent to go to public baths in groups of three or more. But the involvement of a group presents other challenges. The young woman who said her lesbian friends prefer threes or groups at first went on to explain that groups entail risks as well: "If someone gets a crush on someone else and it is not reciprocated, the whole friend group ends up being involved in these awkward interactions. This happened with my group of five close friends. One girl got a crush on another and they both felt awkward, so then group interactions were awkward, too." Partly (though not only) because of that awkwardness, and because the rest of the group felt closer to the girl she had a crush on, they edged her out of the group. Enter FOBLO.

Alignment: Kin to FOBLO

Though three can be comforting by taking off some of the pressure of twos, threes also can intensify FOBLO, because of a phenomenon that is ubiquitous whenever more than two people interact: alignment.

When two people are talking to each other, the focus of attention is like a solid line connecting them. Though that connection may vary in strength and character, it can go only from one to the other (unless one or the other is distracted by a screen, but that is another story). As soon as there are more than two people, there are possibilities for more, and shifting, alignments. Like an expanding number of ways to connect an array of dots, the lines that connect some individuals may be stronger or clearer than those connecting others, and some dots—or people—may be left out entirely. Let's say three friends are talking. When the topic of high school comes up, the two who attended the same high school are aligned, as they share memories and observations about their high school years; the one who attended a different high school may simply stay silent or struggle to find a way of joining their conversation. When someone mentions that she is taking her children to Disney World, the friend who has been there begins to talk about her own trip, aligning those two and sidelining the third. At another point in the conversation, the topic switches to a party that two attended but one didn't, and the alignment switches yet again, connecting the two who went to the party and excluding the friend who missed it.

Alignment is a fundamental process in human communication. It describes how people are positioned with relation to each other, the way they focus their attention and emotional energy. It is always a powerful force in groups, but it is particularly noticeable in groups of three, because any alignment between two strands the third—and FOBLO becomes grounded in reality. Here is a physical analogue. If two people walk together, they automatically calibrate their steps so they are moving at the same pace. If one stops to tie a shoe and the other keeps walking, it's an error, a misfire. Add dogs, and the same thing happens. If one's dog stops to relieve himself, the other dog owner will stop, too, so their conversation can continue uninterrupted. But add a third person, and there's a built-in risk. One person is talking, and one is listening and nodding and offering timely mm-hmms. With this satisfying alignment between them, they may not notice when the third companion has been forced to stop, so they blithely walk on, leaving the third standing alone, tethered to her dog's leash.

Friends needn't be in the same physical space to feel the force of alignment. The experience of three friends bears this out. Dory, Miriam, and Jess formed a tight trio when they were juniors in college. After graduation, they headed for different cities and different lives, but their three-way friendship continued long distance. One year, Dory sent Jess a birthday present: a dozen cupcakes. When Miriam heard about it, she was mad; why hadn't Dory invited her to go in on the gift? Dory explained that her intention was to be considerate: she had a full-time job and therefore disposable income, while Miriam was in graduate school and, like most students, strapped for funds. Though this made sense, it didn't change Miriam's uncomfortable feeling that Dory's generous gesture would make Miriam look like a bad friend by comparison. Between friends, as between siblings, anything one does is likely to be viewed in comparison to the other. In the context of three, if only one friend gives a gift, the other becomes the friend who didn't give one.

Simply being aware of FOBLO can make threes tricky. Jennifer was a high school student whose parents made an exciting offer: the family would take a trip to Europe, and each of the children could bring one friend. But Jennifer faced a quandary: she had two close friends, and there was no way she could choose one over the other. The rejected friend would never forgive her, and she would never forgive herself for having caused her friend pain. So Jennifer ended up inviting a friend from a totally different context—one she wasn't as close to. She had no choice but to step outside the trio.

Maddy was made uncomfortable by an alignment in a trio when the other two didn't correct for FOBLO—or decided to exploit it. Maddy had allowed one of her two friends to stay in her home, a small house she owned, because Maddy was living with her boyfriend at the time. One day she got an SOS call from that friend: the toilet was broken; could Maddy come over and fix it? Since she's pretty handy, Maddy was happy to oblige. But she was less than happy to find, when she arrived, not just the friend who was staying in her house but also the third member of their trio. The two were merrily baking cookies together. Ouch! Whether displaying an alignment that left Maddy out was intentional or careless, this scenario dramatizes how threes set the stage for FOBLO.

Maddy doesn't know why the friend who was staying at her house failed to mention that their third friend was there. (Like many women, she tended to avoid confrontation, so she never said anything about it.) But another woman told me that when she was young, she often made friends with two girls, then deliberately set out to "divide and conquer." When I asked how she did that, she explained, "I would befriend each one alone, and make them feel closer to me. I probably gossiped about the other. Made one feel included, the other excluded." She used all the powers that girls and women have over friends: the competition for closeness, the ability to turn secrets into gossip, and the threat of being left out.

FOGKO

A young woman described an incident that occurred when she was in high school. Her group—about fifteen girls—had gone to a party together. At one point in the evening, one of them, Danielle, turned to her best friend, Abby, and said she wanted to leave. It was an agreed-upon obligation of friendship to leave a party when your friend wanted to. But Abby was there with her boyfriend, and wanted to stay. Danielle then turned to the rest of the group, who promptly fulfilled their obligation—and turned, en masse, against Abby, because she hadn't. Now that Abby was labeled a bad friend, any other girl who "had issues" with Abby voiced them, and for a month or so, when the group planned activities, Abby was not invited. She had no alternative but to migrate to a different group. After a period in purgatory, Abby was eased back in. Gradually, one or another of her former friends began to let her know when and where they were all hanging out. Girls in the clique who weren't all that angry at Abby in the first place jumped back into friend mode, and things returned to normal—except that the girls in Abby's new clique were hurt, because they were abandoned and reminded that they had been a stopgap, second-choice group.

If some of the girls hadn't been angry at Abby, and later found ways to re-integrate her in the group, why did they go along with excluding her in the first place? The answer, I suspect, is something that has a lot in common with FOBLO, but is a little different and a lot scarier—Fear Of Getting Kicked Out: FOGKO.

Among the worst instances of a group turning on and expelling one of its own are of proverbial "mean girls" at school. A woman told me how this happened to her. Gerry was in fifth grade when she changed elementary schools. By the end of that year, she was relieved and pleased to have fallen in with a group. At the start of sixth grade, her friends began bad-mouthing a girl named Katie: Katie is a know-it-all. Katie is mean. She's ugly. She thinks she has friends, but nobody likes her. She should die! Gerry didn't know Katie, so she didn't give this talk much thought—until one of the girls pulled her aside and said, "You know you're Katie, right?" Gerry recalls, "It shattered everything I had thought was going on, and thought about my life, and thought about my friendships." This devastating experience was no doubt in the back of Gerry's mind—or maybe the front—when she commented, later in our conversation, "In high school, there is this desperate need to stay in the lifeboat. Even if it means tossing people out in front of you, you just have to stay on it."

FOGKO is fear of being tossed out of the lifeboat, and it's fueled by knowledge that others may toss you out to ensure that they stay in. The way everyone in the lifeboat—that is, the group—goes along can be what's most hurtful to the one tossed out. Two stories I heard were poignant examples. Mona felt that her friend Kendall was collecting the girls and boys in their group around herself and isolating Mona. It came to a head when, in eighth grade, Mona was elected class president. She went home for lunch, since she lived close by, but Kendall and most of the others stayed at school. By the time Mona returned from lunch, she had been unelected. She was sure that Kendall had engineered this reversal, but Kendall could not have done it on her own. To unelect Mona, Kendall had gotten a majority, if not all, of the others to follow her lead.

Nicole, too, recalls an experience whereby a friend spearheaded a rebellion against her. Nicole was the leader of her high school drama group. She felt comfortable and safe in that role until, at a routine meeting, someone she thought was a close friend—one of two friends who were "like sisters" to her—suddenly turned on her. "You know, Nicole," she said, "we're having some problems with your leadership." At that, other members of the group chimed in with criticism, and not a single one stood up for her; they all either joined in or remained silent. I can only guess what those others were thinking or feeling—in Nicole's case as well as Mona's—but my guess is that at least some were feeling guilty about their silence but were, in Gerry's words, trying desperately to stay inside the lifeboat. I suspect this because many women told me of carrying just such guilt.

Being Popular, Being Disliked

Melanie, in her forties, is still haunted by regret and shame for having gone along with her middle school group when they banded together in high school to exclude a girl who had been Melanie's good friend. In ninth grade, Melanie explained, this girl "was like absolutely the queen bee. She was good at every sport and cute. And then we got to tenth grade, where she started hanging out with all the older kids. She didn't really do anything wrong, but the entire group of friends, which was probably seven or eight of us, turned on her. All of us. I went along with it. And we had been very, very close friends." The victimized friend was not blameless, Melanie explained: "She was being a snob. She was kind of dissing us. But she did not deserve everybody turning on her." Melanie feels this was one of the worst things she's done in her life. Though she wasn't the ringleader, she feels she should not have let it happen. I don't think there are many girls that age—or many individuals of any age—who have the courage to take a stand against a group. Had Melanie opposed her group, she could have been subjected to the same fate. That's exactly what happened to another woman, when she was in sixth grade: her group decided to expel one of their members, and she spoke up in the girl's defense. Rather than being persuaded to change their minds, the group expelled her, too. Just seeing a girl summarily ejected from the group is enough to dissuade others from risking their own isolation by standing up for her.

Melanie's account is revealing in many ways. I was intrigued by her saying that the ostracized girl had been a "queen bee" in middle school, a "snob" in high school, and "good at every sport and cute." Among boys, being handsome and excelling at sports would confer high status. But girls disapprove of peers who stand out. "Queen bee" and "snob" are two among many labels by which girls and women punish those who excel or appear to be better in any way. This may explain why her drama group turned on Nicole. She was talented—she went on to have a career in the theater—and regularly got leading roles in plays; that would be enough reason for the other girls to resent her and try to find ways to knock her off her perch.

Sociologist Donna Eder observed girls in middle school and came to the at first surprising conclusion that popular girls are widely disliked. Isn't that an oxymoron? Doesn't "popular" *mean,* by definition, being widely liked? Here's how it works. Girls get status by being close to high-status girls. So if a girl has high status—often because of her looks or her popularity with boys, but it could come from other factors as well—all the other girls want to be her friend. That's the sense in which she's popular. But she can't be friends with everyone, especially since girls tell secrets to friends, and only a small number of trusted friends can know her secrets. So she has to reject the overtures of most other girls, who, as a result, dislike her and brand her a snob. In the case of Melanie's ninth-grade friend, the opportunity to punish a girl who stood out by looking really good and excelling at sports must have been very tempting. That she further excelled in high school by winning the friendship of older girls would have been the last straw. Of course she deserved to be punished in the way that is usual among girls: being kicked out.

The danger of being ostracized results inevitably from the desire, the need, to be in a group. As members of a group jostle to get close to one another, they must distance themselves from those who are not group members. A microcosm of this scramble is roommate selection in college, especially if students live in suites that accommodate a set number of people. A sophomore at such a college described the dilemma this way: "Everyone has to choose roommates and also dorms, so they try to get close to other groups of friends. We tried to get near a group of guy friends—there are four of them in an apartment—but then other people took the apartment right next to them. So now we're next to my roommate from freshman year, which is very awkward. She was kind of friends with us, and thought we would all live together, but there are only four to an apartment and we had four without her." Not only did this unfortunate former roommate get left out of the second-year dorm arrangements but she had to be continually reminded by seeing the group that excluded her right next door. Awkward indeed! It's just the sort of suffering that gives rise to FOGKO.

Witches: The Fear of Women in Groups

A group member who is kicked out gets a crash course in how the power of groups can be turned inward as well as outward. And it is not only in the private sphere that women in groups can be scary. Think of the image of a witches' coven, that mythic notion that is so deeply rooted in our cultural imagination. This metaphoric embodiment of the fear of women in groups is the conceit at the heart of David Mamet's play *Oleanna*.

In the play's first act, a diffident and self-effacing student named Carol plaintively seeks guidance from John, a young professor on the cusp of academic success: he is about to receive tenure and buy a house. When Carol confesses that she can't understand the material John presents in class, he generously offers to help by meeting with her privately. In the second act, Carol is transformed: self-confident and belligerent, she has falsely accused John of sexual harassment. By the third act, Carol has upped her fabricated accusation to rape, and John has consequently been denied tenure—in academia, that means he's fired—and of course won't be able to buy the house, so his home life is wrecked as well. In justifying her behavior, Carol continually refers to an unnamed "group" she belongs to that set her on the path to destroy him.

How to make sense of Carol's transformation from the first act to the last? In my view, she is a modern-day witch, and her group a witches' coven. I'll borrow a definition of witches that appears in a book by Evelyn Fox Keller. It comes from another play, one written in the seventeenth century: *Ephesian Matron* by Walter Charleton. In that play, a soldier addresses witches who "allure us with the fairness of your skins; and when folly hath brought us within your reach, you leap upon us and devour us." That pretty much describes how Carol is portrayed in Mamet's play. Though it is her initial helplessness and vulnerability rather than her beauty that lure John into her trap, once she gets him to meet with her privately, Carol uses his proximity to "devour" him. Carol's power to ruin John by falsely accusing him of sexual harassment and rape is a modern version of a fear as old as the Bible story of Samson and Delilah: women have power to attract men, and can use that power to destroy them. I believe it's that fear which underlies the notion of witches, and the notion of a witches' coven reflects the attendant fear that individual women's destructive power is magnified many times over when women band together in groups.

Double, Double Toil and Trouble—Within Groups

A bunch of witches, like the three stirring a boiling cauldron in Shakespeare's *Macbeth*, is presumed to be stirring up trouble for others—a proverbial witches' brew, just as Carol's unnamed "group" in *Oleanna* cooks up a plot to destroy her poor professor. The witches in the coven and the women in Carol's group are assumed to be a harmonious unit, working cooperatively toward a common goal. Similarly, a group of girls or women, seen from the outside, often seems like a coherent unit. But the view from the inside may be very different. The roiling may well be more inside than out, quite apart from the danger of being left out or getting kicked out. Groups are subject to the strains that can complicate any close relationships. A college student commented that the closer and more coherent a group appears to be—like dance groups, sports teams, or members of a business cooperative—the more likely it is to be plagued by that bugbear of girls' and young women's friendships, drama!

A high school student explained that she and her soccer teammates experienced strains mostly within groups. "When you are on the field you respect each other," she said, "and you respect each other as teammates, but as soon as you get off the field every team I've been on has major cliques. When you go away for soccer tournaments you don't all hang out in one hotel room. It's always four or five girls in one hotel room and four or five girls in another. There is not usually much tension between the cliques unless you try to mesh them. But within the cliques there will be tension. Let's say one girl's name is Suzy. She'll become friends with Brittany and Stacy and bring them in. But her best friend is Erica, and Erica will bring in two other girls, too. And all those weird overlapping patterns make for a forced friend group. And within the clique there will always be talking behind each other's back when certain girls aren't there. In soccer a lot of it will be 'I don't know why she starts.' "

The dynamic of these high-school friend groups sounds a lot like a five-person friend group described by a woman, Fran, who had long been retired. Two of the women were Fran's good friends from church. Then one of them brought in a neighbor who was lonely, and the other brought in a childhood friend who moved to their town. Fran felt she had a lot in common with the original two friends, but less with the neighbor and even less with the new arrival. The result, she felt, was like mixing too many colors together while painting a picture.

Even if there are no overlapping or forced friendships within a group, there may well be tensions, hurt feelings, and any of the myriad stresses and misunderstandings that all conversations and relationships are heir to, and that can lead to extended discussions, negotiations, and rehashings among girls and women. Four women friends were enjoying a weekend vacation together when one of them, Leslie, offered to teach the others to play bridge. Her friends enthusiastically agreed. As Leslie began to explain the game, Kim began to ask questions—lots of questions, one after the other. Leslie felt more and more frustrated, till she burst out, "Stop asking so many questions. Let me tell you how it works!" Kim protested, "If I can't ask questions, how can I learn?" Then she began to cry, which was so humiliating that she retreated to her room and shut the door. Leslie went in after her but came out shortly, saying she had apologized, but it didn't make any difference. So another friend went into Kim's self-imposed isolation chamber; after she emerged, the third one followed suit. Finally, Kim rejoined the group, which did not resume the bridge lesson.

Why did it take so many visits to mollify Kim's hurt feelings? I don't know for sure, but I can surmise: unaware that she was getting on Leslie's nerves, Kim had probably been feeling safe in the group's embrace. So the sudden shattering of that feeling of safety, the distressing realization that someone in the group disliked her behavior and maybe even disliked her, may well have been what plunged Kim into misery. And why didn't Leslie's apology work? I don't know that for sure either, but if Leslie is like many others I do know, I suspect she may have tried to explain why she'd said what she did—that is, why Kim's questions were annoying— because she, too, would not want to be seen as a bad person. Just as Kim defended her behavior earlier ("If I can't ask questions, how can I learn?"), Leslie might have justified her reaction by saying something like, "If you keep asking questions, I can't get through the lesson." If she had, then it would have felt more like reaccusing Kim of being wrong—exactly what upset her in the first place.

I was struck by how similar these adult women friends' experience was to what happened at a twelve-year-old's birthday party. I had assigned my class the task of observing children's interactions, then describing and analyzing what they had seen. Ayana Hoffman took several classmates to her twelve-year-old cousin's birthday party. At one point, there was a commotion among the girls. One girl (I'll call her Whitney) was so hurt by the words of another girl (let's call her Val) that she retreated to the bathroom, crying. The other girls began going in and out of the bath-room, trying to find out why Whitney was upset and to comfort her. Whitney's best friend took a special role. She talked privately with Whit-ney as well as with the other girls, reported on Whitney's feelings, and talked privately with Val. Much like the adult friends trying to make peace between Kim and Leslie, the preteen girls pooled their negotiating skills to mollify the hurt feelings of a member of their group and bring her back into the fold. And in both cases, the wounded group member made sure they'd do this by physically withdrawing behind a closed door—a breach that demanded repair.

An Outsider on the Inside

Another way that the view from inside a group may be less rosy than it appears to outsiders is that not everyone in the group always feels like she belongs; people who seem to be on the inside often feel like outsiders. Betsy Lerner was fascinated by a group of women her mother had played bridge with weekly for as long as Betsy could remember. She wanted to understand what could keep these women returning week after week—for fifty-five years. So she learned to play bridge, joined the group, got to know each of the women separately, and wrote a book about her experi-ence. Though the group would look monolithic and coherent to an out-sider, Lerner explains in *The Bridge Ladies* that her mother always felt like an outsider in it—and continued to, into the sixth decade of her member-ship. Whereas the other women had been born and raised in the upscale New Haven community where Lerner had grown up, her mother had been born and raised in an immigrant neighborhood in Brooklyn. Lerner had assumed that her mother's sense of herself as an outsider traced to her embarrassment at her own mother's Russian accent and old-world ways, but ultimately Lerner concluded it was simply "because of how in-adequate she felt about herself." And that, I think, is the source of many, if not most, feelings of not-quite-fitting-in—and of FOBLO and FOGKO—

that lurk only slightly below the surface for many, if not all, members of any group: a fear that we don't measure up.

If longtime members can feel like outsiders, new members always do, because they are. A group that gets together over time develops habits and ways of talking that members come to understand. When a new member joins, she doesn't yet share that knowledge. For example, a group of friends—professional women—had developed the routine of celebrating each other's birthdays with an adult version of kids' pajama parties. They'd pamper the birthday celebrant by gathering at her home so she could be comfortable; in fact, she could be so comfortable as to attend in her pajamas. And to make her feel more at ease, the others would wear pajamas, too. After a few such celebrations, the women stopped actually wearing pajamas, but they kept "Come in your pajamas" on the email invitations, which were updated and recycled when each member's birthday rolled around. This all happened without anyone talking about it, so when a new member, Colleen, joined the group, no one thought to explain that "Come in your pajamas" was no longer meant literally. Colleen showed up in pajamas—and bunny slippers—and was mortified to see that everyone else was fully dressed in daytime clothes.

Shelley had the opposite experience, assuming that something was not meant literally when it was. She received an invitation to a luncheon that included the injunction to come wearing a hat. Shelley never wore hats, except for warmth in winter, and she doubted that a knitted woolen cap would be appropriate for the occasion. It also seemed to her unlikely that her host expected guests to buy hats, so she concluded that they must be optional and didn't wear one. But these assumptions turned out to be in error. As she sat down to lunch, she was embarrassed to be the only guest with nothing on her head but hair.

The power of a group to inspire insecurity can make people act in ways they otherwise wouldn't. Emma enjoys her friend Sylvia's company when they get together one on one, and she enjoys their conversations when they talk on the phone. But she does not enjoy Sylvia when they join a group of friends for dinner; in that context, Sylvia becomes a different person. She monopolizes the conversation, making it hard for Emma or anyone else to say much. And she seems to be driven to one-up whatever anyone says. Someone has been on a trip? Sylvia has been there. Someone mentions another person? Sylvia has known that person longer or her son went to school with them. There's nothing anyone can say that she doesn't already know, and know more about. Being in a group seems to make Sylvia feel she has to prove herself. In thinking about Emma's account, I wondered if Sylvia might have a particularly bad case of what many of us feel, to some extent, in groups: FOGKO.

Females (and Males) in Groups

For all these reasons, success in joining a group is no guarantee of being comfortable there. Florence, whose friendships at an elite Catholic girls' school were the most meaningful of her life, recalls that when her family moved and she found herself in a new school, she did manage to get into a clique, one with high status among the girls. But she never felt like she really belonged—and she didn't really like the other girls in it. When she finally graduated and started dating, she was astonished and relieved to discover how much easier it was to be friends with boys. For one thing, to get the notice of boys, she didn't have to do anything special. They were drawn to her just because she was a girl. That took off the pressure she'd always felt with girls—pressure to display an interesting personality to be liked. "Ironically," Florence said, "feeling that pressure gone made me feel I was being more interesting." Then she added, "And so it has been until this day, where I have felt more at ease, for the most part, with men, even as platonic friends."

These sentiments are similar to those expressed by Audrey, whose comments I quoted at the outset of this chapter: that she prefers groups of men because their boundaries are more permeable, and because men's positions in a group are constantly shifting, whereas the hierarchy in women's groups is stable. This doesn't mean that men have it easy. The need to jockey for power and position can be exhausting and unnerving, but there is possibility in it, too. Though women, Audrey went on to say, don't have to engage in that sort of competition, they also don't have the opportunity to change their positions in the group's hierarchy. As she put it: "For us, it's much more like we have it and it's fixed and that's it, period."

These contrasts between women's and men's groups sound eerily like what researchers have observed among nonhuman species. A wide range of mammals—including deer, elephants, lions, sperm whales, and orcas—have been found to live in groups with stable cores made up of females who never stray from the group into which they are born. Males, on the other hand, go in and out of different groups throughout their lives, and often spend time on their own as well. Most intriguing is research on the social lives of primates, humans' closest relatives in the animal world. In species as different as baboons, rhesus monkeys, vervets, and Japanese macaques, not only do females make up the core group from which they never stray but, in addition, their position in the group's hierarchy is, to borrow the phrase Audrey used to describe women's groups, "fixed and that's it, period." Females in these primate groups inherit their mothers' status. A daughter born to a high-status mother will have high status as she grows to adulthood, and one born to a low-status mother will have low status. That's it, period. Male infants, in contrast, don't inherit their mothers' status, and they don't generally remain with their mothers' group. When a male reaches adulthood, he typically leaves the group he was born into and joins a new one, where he will have to establish his position in aggressive competition with other males. His size and strength will significantly affect his chances, but the way he uses them will be up to him.

Regardless of the limitations imposed by the stability of status hierarchies among female mammals—or maybe because of it—the well-being and successful functioning of these primates and other mammals depends on the power and strength of their core female group. Among humans, too, strength and power can be found in women's groups, where connections are often based on bonds of friendship. This can be seen in the political as well as the personal world. History has benefited from political movements driven by groups of women, such as those who supported the abolition of slavery and women's suffrage. A modern example occurred in 2013, when a ruinous government shutdown was finally ended. Republican Senator John McCain and Democratic Senator Mark Pryor credited the breakthrough to the women in the Senate. And the women themselves explained how they accomplished that and, even more important, how they hoped to find a more long-term solution, thanks to their friendships. Minnesota Senator Amy Klobuchar said, "The twenty women in the Senate have formed such strong friendships of trust, even though we come from different places, that I'm very hopeful as we go forward.... Those relationships are going to make a difference as we get into what matters, which is the long-term budget."

Because we're human—and maybe also because we're mammals— women in groups can accomplish things that individual women could not, thanks, in large part, to the friendships among group members. Though groups also may be shadowed by FOBLO and FOGKO, they can wrap individuals in a warm embrace. And that is the promise and power of women in groups.

6

Too Close for Comfort

Cutoffs, Poaching, Drama!

In *The Prophet*, Kahlil Gibran wrote that romantic love "is for your growth" but also "for your pruning." The same is true of friendship. Friends can introduce you to worlds you would not otherwise have known, enrich your life, make you a better person. In these and countless other ways, they are for your growth. But friends can also be for your pruning. They may bring out sides of you that you'd sooner suppress; urge you to do things you shouldn't or discourage you from doing things you should; and hurt your feelings in specific ways or generally make you feel bad when you're around them.

A friend, even a very close one—especially a very close one—can be for your pruning simply because of her desire to keep a loved one near, when growth requires you to leave. In *The Social Sex*, Marilyn Yalom and Theresa Donovan Brown describe a friendship that developed between a mentor and her protégée in the early twelfth century. Hildegard of Bingen, a brilliant nun who founded and headed a convent, established a deep and close friendship with a much younger nun, Richardis of Stade. When Richardis was appointed abbess of a different monastery, Hildegard was distraught. To prevent the move, she sent pleading letters "to Richardis' mother, to archbishops, and even to the pope." Her efforts failed, and Richardis accepted the position. To convey the depth of Hildegard's pain, Yalom and Brown quote a letter she wrote to Richardis: "My sorrow is destroying the great confidence and consolation that I once had in mankind. . . . Why have you forsaken me? . . . Now, let all who have grief like me mourn with me, all who, in the love of god, have had such great love in their hearts and minds for a person—as I had for you—but who was snatched away from them in an instant, as you were from me." It is impossible not to be moved by Hildegard's suffering, yet I found myself cheering Richardis for not letting her mentor's love—and consequent need—prevent her from becoming an abbess in her own right. When she took the young Richardis under her wing and mentored her, Hildegard had been for her growth. But when she tried to prevent her protégée's advancement, Hildegard was for her pruning.

Friends can also be for your pruning by encouraging destructive behavior. Elena Dunkle nearly succumbed to anorexia nervosa as a teen. Years later she wrote a memoir about her experience together with her mother, Clare Dunkle. Speaking about the book on NPR's *The Diane Rehm Show*, Elena was asked if her mother had played a role in her developing anorexia. She replied that she was certain neither of her parents played any role at all. Rather, she got the idea of starving herself from other students at her all-girls' boarding school. Her mother was blameless, but her friends were not; they had been for her pruning—big-time.

Take That!

These examples of friends for your pruning were life-changing. Most of us experience pruning by friends in more mundane and subtle, even fleeting ways. A random, perhaps well-intentioned comment that would have been welcome in one context may be hurtful in another. For example, expressing empathy, which might seem at first to be an unalloyed good, isn't always. Ingrid was surprised when Gwen said, "I was shocked to see you weren't invited to that party. You certainly should have been."

Ingrid might have appreciated Gwen's taking her side if she'd known about the party and felt bad about being left out. But she hadn't known about it. So what made her feel bad about being left out of the party was Gwen's expression of support.

If you've suffered a loss, or someone you love is very sick, you might appreciate a friend asking how things are going so you know she cares. But other times, what really helps is finding respite from your sorrow and worries by encasing yourself in work. If you are in that buffered state when a friend approaches with a sad face and a voice thick with sympathy to ask how you're doing or how your ailing loved one is doing, your protective cocoon is shattered and you're plunged back into despair. The friend whose caring is for your growth has unwittingly been for your pruning.

It's easy to be hurt by seemingly insignificant remarks, or by the way a friend reacts to your remarks. You say something you think is a simple, unexceptional observation, and your friend responds, "What are you talking about?" in a tone that implies what you said was stupid. During a mah-jong game, another player says, "You need to put your wall out," and you wince. Had she said simply "Your wall" or "Your turn," you wouldn't have reacted that way; but the little phrase "you need to" implies you didn't know the most basic thing about the game. And the sting is intensified because the other players are witnesses. At a baby shower, you cheerfully say, in the party spirit, "Hey, when are you going to open your presents? We want to see them!" and another guest—one you thought was a friend—says, "It's not your party. Why are you in such a hurry?" Your party spirit is instantly soured, your enthusiasm reframed as selfish and rude, and your hurt compounded because you've been called out, exposed, in front of others—a public humiliation.

Rita and Nell, best friends in elementary school, had amazingly both settled in the same distant city and become prominent in the same field—real estate. One day they found themselves together on a panel at a professional development workshop. Rita spoke first. She began by mentioning that she and Nell had been friends pretty much their entire lives, and quipped that though they were in the same class in elementary school, she was younger! Rita felt sure it was self-evident that this opener was a good-natured gibe, since it was obvious that their age difference was a matter of months. When Nell got the floor, she gibed back: "You might be younger, but I'm thinner!" The audience gasped. If a woman is even a tiny bit overweight—indeed, in our weight-obsessed culture, even if her weight is normal—any reference to it is generally understood to be out of bounds.

Rita felt as if she'd been slugged, especially since the blow had been executed in public. The next day, she sent an email letting Nell know she'd been hurt by the remark. She expected what I think most women would expect in similar circumstances: an apology and expression of regret, something like "I'm so sorry. I meant it to tease but it came out wrong. I would never intentionally hurt you." Instead, Nell brushed it off, denying culpability: "Well, you started it! I just responded in kind." Perhaps Nell had felt justified because she'd been hurt by her old friend's quip about being younger. But Rita saw history in this standoff. There had always been an element of competition between her and Nell, and this latest zinger seemed like a move in that spirit. Though they were both on the panel—ostensibly peers—Rita was far more successful, the owner of her own agency, which bore her name. She felt that Nell had taken advantage of the opening to bring her down a peg.

My Friend the Thief

As I began reading a novel by Samantha Harvey about a friendship between two women, I was puzzled by the title: why, I wondered, would a book about friends be called *Dear Thief*? I had not read very far before I understood why: the friend in the novel had stolen something precious from the protagonist—her husband. Then I thought, Of course: a married man falling in love with his wife's friend. It happens. And the more I thought about it, the more I realized that friends can be like thieves.

Not a few women told me of friends who they felt had stolen from them—in most cases figuratively, but in a few cases, literally.

An Italian woman, Sofia, had an experience that felt like theft, although she gave the money willingly. In Italy, she explained, friendship is a more significant commitment than it is in the United States—a lifelong one. Friends become close to each other's parents and are a constant presence in each other's homes. When one is in need, there are no limits to what the other will do to help. Sofia had been close to Gianna since childhood. When Gianna became pregnant by a wealthy married man, and decided to have the baby, Sofia stood by her and became like a second mother to the baby. It struck her as odd, but understandable, when Gianna began asking Sofia for money—"for the baby." At first it was $100 here, then $200 there. Though Sofia was a student whose own finances were close to the bone, she always managed to give Gianna what she asked for. One day, Gianna made a request that was different in scale. She needed $5,000 for the baby. Sofia could only guess what dreadful circumstances could have led to such a need. Where would she find that much money? Still, a friend is a friend, and her friendship with Gianna went back to their childhood, so Sofia scraped the money together by borrowing from relatives and other friends, and handed it over. Not long after, Sofia's mother stopped by a high-end clothing store whose owner she knew. She and the store owner were amiably chatting when a customer came in to pick up $4,500 worth of clothing she had purchased from the store. It was Sofia's friend Gianna. Now her former friend.

Several women told me of friends who literally stole, or tried to. One was Isabel. Her friend Maria was visiting when Isabel excused herself to go to the bathroom. Then, remembering something she wanted to say, Isabel turned on her heel and returned almost immediately—and found Maria standing over Isabel's open purse! Mortified to have been caught, Maria muttered something about seeing the purse open (it hadn't been) and going to close it. Isabel had prevented the theft by her surprise appearance. A high school student, Adrienne, discovered that her friend Judy had succeeded in stealing her clothes—more than once. One time

Judy borrowed a skirt from Adrienne, then gave back a different skirt. Another time Adrienne and Judy were hanging out in Judy's room. At one point, Judy opened her closet to take out a sweater, and Adrienne spotted a very familiar sweater hanging right next to it—one of her own, which she'd been missing for several months. The pain of theft is intensified when the thief is a friend: you've been robbed of something more valuable and irreplaceable than money and property—trust in a friend, and in your judgment for having mistakenly placed that trust.

Too Close for Comfort

How easy it is for a friend to steal: you let her into your home, your life. Yet finding a friend literally stealing is mercifully rare. But figuratively? That's surprisingly common. A cartoon on BuzzFeed portrays some mundane ways that a friend can feel like a thief. The cartoon is in two frames. The first, titled "When Your Friend Comes Over," shows two young women embracing as they greet each other with broad smiles: "Hey," says one; "So good to see you," says the other. The second frame is titled "When Your Best Friend Comes Over." Here the host doesn't bother to take her eyes off her phone. Without looking up, she calls out, "Hey loser," greeting her friend with a playful insult. The visiting friend walks right past her, saying, "I'll be in the kitchen eating your food and stealing the love of your pets." The cartoonist, Rubyetc, captured a paradox about the closeness of women friends. Imagine you are the hosting friend in the cartoon. In the first frame you focus attention on a visiting friend. No surprises there. But in the second, you pay scant attention to a "best" friend—someone you're really close to. And that friend is like a thief who helps herself to food—your food—and plays with your pets so often that they treat her like family. Seeing your dog licking her face or your cat purring in her lap can give you a stab: how come your pet loves her more than you? That feels like theft, too.

There are many minor, almost metaphoric, ways that friends can seem to be stealing, not money or objects but more intangible and maybe more precious possessions, like your style, your taste, your identity. Haley was genuinely fond of and close to Alexa, but there was one habit of Alexa's that she found disconcerting. When Haley wore something nifty, Alexa often noticed and admired it, a common way that women express approval and caring. But then Alexa would ask, "Where did you get it?" And it wouldn't be long before she'd turn up wearing the same thing. It was so small an incursion, and so understandable, Haley would tell herself: if you see something you admire, it's natural to buy the same thing for yourself; it's a form of flattery. And, after all, Alexa had as much right to shop in that store as Haley did. So Haley felt it would be churlish to say anything. Yet it gnawed at her, making Haley feel, in an odd sort of way, that her friend had stolen from her—not the clothing, but her taste in clothing, and therefore her personal style and her sense of identity.

Shannon experienced a similar yet deeper incursion. Her friend Tory, who lived in a distant state, was having a hard time, so Shannon invited her to visit. At first, she felt fine about helping Tory out in this way, but she started feeling uncomfortable when Tory seemed to be not only sharing Shannon's life but appropriating it. Tory went to Shannon's hair salon—and got exactly the same haircut. Then she started seeing Shannon's therapist. Shannon had been happy to recommend him, since she thought he was good, and Tory was so obviously hurting. But Shannon's feelings changed when Tory reported that she was going to take LSD under his supervision. (This was back in the sixties.) Shannon would never have wanted to take LSD, but it bothered her that Tory was going to share this intimate experience with her therapist.

Because closeness is typically a goal in women's friendships—the barometer by which women tend to measure relationships—there is always a risk that a friend will get too close for comfort. It is the flip side of the search for sameness. This, too, is reflected in the video clip of two little girls that I described in Chapter 3. In the video, one little girl announces that her babysitter, Amber, wears contact lenses, and the second responds that her mom wears contacts and her dad does, too. This display of similarity seems to please them both. But then the first girl exclaims, "The same?!" and bursts into gleeful laughter, then leans with a sudden lurch toward her playmate. The second girl does not receive this gesture with matching delight. Instead, she visibly recoils, looking away as she hunches her shoulder toward her ear as if to ward off her playmate's nuzzle. Evidently, though she was happy to provide the requisite verbal expression of sameness, this little girl was not thrilled with her playmate's intrusion into her physical space. Maybe the feeling that a friend is stealing your style is analogous to that recoil: sameness is great, to a point. But it can go too far and begin to feel like what one woman called "impingy"—or even like theft.

Copying

Children often experience the same things adults do, in distilled form. Telling me about stresses that had arisen with friends, several girls mentioned "copying." In one case, two girls, both new to their middle school, became friends. When Amanda announced that she would invite a friend from her previous school to a dance, Cathy said she would do the same. Amanda protested, "You're copying me!" Cathy didn't think she was. How do you know, when a friend does the same thing as you, whether she's independently responding to the same impulse in the same way, or is imitating you? It's tricky because the former—liking the same things, having similar interests and inclinations—can be the basis for friendship, but the latter—achieving similarity by imitating—can feel like a violation, taking advantage of, or overdoing, closeness. It's copying.

A nine-year-old girl, Jessica, described how copying caused trouble in two of her friendships. One friend has a habit of repeating exactly what Jessica just said, and Jessica doesn't like it. Another friend repeats word for word what she's heard from others, and insists that Jessica do the same. Jessica doesn't like copying but doesn't want to upset her friend, so she changes some little thing. But her friend always notices the change, and gets mad. She wants it to be an exact copy. In this small struggle is a microcosm of the drive to sameness as a token of friendship, as well as the drive to resist sameness when it gets to be too much.

Many years ago, I experienced discomfort with a friend's "copying," though I didn't think of it in those terms. During college, I shared an apartment with a friend. One evening, my roommate and I were cleaning up after dinner. I had recently bought a frying pan that had a beautiful enamel coating: gray on the inside, orange on the outside. While drying this frying pan, I made a remark that I was proud of in the way that very young people can be proud of finding their verbal style, their sense of irony or humor. I said, while running the dish towel over the pan's richly colored surface, "I wouldn't have thought a person could be in love with an object, but I'm in love with this frying pan." Not long after, my room- mate and I were again cleaning up after dinner. She picked up this frying pan to dry and said, "You wouldn't think anyone could be in love with an object, but I'm in love with this frying pan." Nothing about the way she said it gave any hint that she'd heard this observation before, let alone that she'd heard it from me. I was stunned. I felt robbed—of my clever thought, my wry humor, my voice. I said nothing about it, but I still re- member, more than half a century later, how dismayed I was. And I still wonder what led her to repeat my words: did she forget she'd heard them from me and think she had originated them? Did she think I'd appreci- ate her saying it precisely because it was something I myself had said? (We're still friends, so I asked her. She doesn't recall, because, not surpris- ingly, she doesn't recall having said it. The only reason I remember is my emotional reaction—and my silence about it.)

These struggles over copying, though seemingly trivial, reflect our deep sense that how we act or speak reflects who we are—and the threat inherent in closeness. When a friend acts or speaks just like us, or shops at the same website or picks up our taste in art, it can feel like a ratifica- tion of who we are and a reassurance of the rightness of our friendship. But it can also feel like an invasion, a theft. This conundrum underlies the double meaning of the word "bond": the bond of a close bond can morph into the bond of bondage. Navigating between the two can be a delicate balance, especially for women, who both seek out this bond and bristle more easily at its limits. A high school student, Caitlin, recalls how she handled such a challenge when she admired her friend Julie's new backpack but was hesitant to say outright that she wanted to buy one just like it. Caitlin simply said, "Where did you get your backpack?" Julie replied with enthusiasm, "Oh, this awesome store, I'll take you there sometime." Caitlin responded, "Oh cool," but Julie said, "You should totally get the same one; we could be twinning. You should get this color; it's going to be awesome." When the girls were in elementary school, at least one of them had found "copying" to be an infringement. But now the prospect of becoming closer by similarity, "twinning," had appeal, perhaps because they were older, or perhaps because they attended different middle schools and having the same backpack could lessen the gap that distance now placed between them. And perhaps it was simply the pleasure of being similar, and in appreciation of the compliment: "I like your taste—and you—enough to want the same thing."

No Poaching

When my parents were in their eighties, they moved to a retirement community where they made new friends through playing bridge. My mother was particularly taken—I could say she was smitten—by a woman named Mary Green. Whenever I talked to my mother, I heard a lot about Mary Green. My mother began inviting Mary and her husband to get together with her and my father as couples, and she included Mary when she socialized with her closest friend, her sister-in-law Mildred. One day my mother called me, very upset. Mildred had invited Mary to a luncheon and had not invited my mother. Then Mildred began mentioning things to which Mary had invited her and not my mother. These slights caused my mother genuine heartache, even tears. My mother couldn't get over not only the hurt but also the injustice. Mary was *her* friend; it was only thanks to her that Mildred knew Mary. My mother had one consolation, though, which she would tell me about with great satisfaction: Mildred could not play bridge. That, at least, was a domain where my mother still had sole dominion over Mary—a protected preserve where Mildred could not poach.

Poaching provokes a kind of aggravated FOBLO. Whenever there are three friends, there is Fear Of Being Left Out. But the hurt can be greater, and compounded by a sense of injustice, when the two people who are leaving you out know each other only because you introduced them. And the source of hurt isn't limited to being left out of face-to-face gatherings. Evidence of poaching can also come from realizing that your friend revealed personal information to the mutual friend before she told you. Because girls and women tend to regard knowing secrets as evidence of closeness, and closeness is the pot of gold at the end of the relationship rainbow, learning that a friend knows something that you don't about someone you introduced her to, can feel like a betrayal—or a theft.

Taylor and Casey met through their mutual friend Pat. When they realized that they both like to run, which Pat did not, they began running together regularly. And when they ran, they talked. It was natural for Taylor to mention, in the course of a morning run, an upcoming date. And it was natural for Casey to mention Taylor's date to Pat, since news about mutual friends is a common and expected topic of conversation. But there was nothing natural, from Pat's point of view, about hearing this important news from Casey rather than from Taylor herself. The next time she and Taylor were together, Pat brought it up. "So you and Casey are getting pretty close now," she said. "I didn't even know about your date, but she did." Then Pat added: "I hope you don't feel like I've been a bad friend. I still want to hear things." Two dynamics that are typical of women's friendships are evident here. One is the importance of keeping friends apprised of what's going on in your life. The other is the tendency to compare: if one friend does something that shows she's a good friend, the other can feel that she appears to be a bad friend in comparison. And it feels particularly unfair to be shown up by someone you yourself introduced to your friend.

Knowing how hurtful it is to be left out by people who met through you, some women feel it is simply unacceptable: if I introduced you to my friend Natalie, you cannot make plans to see Natalie without me. For others, there is an unwritten rule: the first time you invite Natalie to something, you must also invite me. After that, you and Natalie are officially friends, so you can go ahead and get together without me. Some women manage the threat by asking permission of the friend who introduced them: "Would it be weird if I hung out with Natalie? Would that be okay?" And some women feel, even if I say it's okay, I still maintain priority as Natalie's number one friend. You two can be friends so long as you are not better friends with each other than you are with me.

And where is Natalie in all this? She might be flattered to be fought over, or she might feel uncomfortable caught between her two friends. And she might resent the implication that her first friend owns her. The very concept of poaching implies that a friend is a possession, a notion that some people resist and resent. That's the reason why, a high school student, Ali, told me, it makes her uncomfortable when someone says she wants to be her best friend—and wants others to know she is. Putting it out that Ali has a best friend would discourage others from trying to be her friend, too. The concept of poaching helped me understand Ali's point of view. In a way, if someone were to make it known that Ali is her best friend, it would be like hanging a sign on her saying, "Keep off. No poaching."

This dynamic, too, can be more explicit and exaggerated among girls. A fourth grader, Nina, told me that she and her friend Elisa had had a feud that lasted a year because each thought the other had stolen a third friend, Riki. Nina explained how the feud ended: "We decided to call a truce and say we don't have to be best friends, but we can't always be fighting." They agreed that neither really stole Riki from the other. When I asked why that impression had arisen in the first place, Nina said, "In the beginning of first grade, and maybe to the middle, they were fighting over me. Then that changed. Then Riki felt like it was cool to have two people fighting over her. And then it kept going in second grade." This analysis made me wonder whether Riki herself had instigated the dynamic by appropriating—you might say stealing from Nina—the role of fought-over friend.

My Friend the Schnorrer

"You never know how many friends you have until you have a beach house." This adage (which I saw on the wall of a beach house) captures a more general dilemma: how do you know if someone wants to be your friend for you yourself or for something she can get from being your friend? It's probably impossible to know for sure, and the person seeking your friendship may not know for sure either, though sometimes she does. In *The Bridge Ladies*, Betsy Lerner quotes a now-elderly woman, Bette, who recalls that in high school she deliberately befriended a girl whose grandfather owned a Connecticut theater where Broadway-bound musicals routinely opened first. Already seriously studying drama and determined to have a career in theater, Bette felt guilty about her ulterior motive, but, she told Lerner, the friendship afforded her the happiest hours of her life, enthralled by the shows she would otherwise never have seen.

The widely touted concept of networking replicates the way friends can be of use. Befriending people, or making sure to keep friends, because they can advance your career is not cynical if it's mutual and aboveboard. And it's not gender specific. A real estate agent, for example, commented that even when she's on vacation, she keeps an eye on Facebook and makes sure to "'like' people's things because I want to stay in their mind. I want to be seen as someone who is supportive, friendly, open, because I want them to use me when they want to sell their house. And I have definitely gotten business from people who know from Facebook that I'm a realtor." The result of her behaving like a friend on Facebook is a win-win situation. She gets business, and the Facebook friends who use her as a realtor also benefit: their task of finding a realtor is facilitated, and they have the added benefit of feeling comfortable with the realtor they hire, knowing she is a friend.

Networking can be unsettling, though, when viewed as a perversion of friendship, and women seem to have a developed kind of radar for this. I see just such a perversion in the way a Yiddish word, *schmooze,* has come to be used in American English. In Yiddish, *schmooze* means something like "shooting the breeze": casually talking about this and that. If you come upon two people talking and ask, "Am I interrupting?" the answer might be "Not at all. We were just schmoozing." Unfortunately (in my view), the word has come to mean chatting people up to gain something. In other words, the meaning of "schmoozing" has morphed from something done among friends to something hypocritical: acting like a friend in order to gain benefit for yourself. The word "thief" might be an overstatement as a description of this activity, but another Yiddish word—*schnorrer*—might not be. A schnorrer is a sponger or freeloader, someone who tries to get something without paying for it. In the context of friendship, it's someone who wants the benefits of friendship—like the use of your beach house—without actually being a friend.

Leah felt that Joanne was using her as a pawn. Joanne would adopt Leah's friends, then leave Leah out. Even worse, if Leah included Joanne with a couple, and if Joanne took a liking to the husband, she'd begin playing to him, ignoring or even putting down not only Leah but also the wife. One year Leah and Joanne attended their college reunion together. Joanne ignored Leah there, too, unless Leah was talking to someone really interesting. Then Joanne would magically materialize at Leah's side, using their friendship as a pretext for joining the conversation. But if Leah saw Joanne talking to someone interesting, Joanne made it clear, by her body language and refusal to glance up, that Leah was not to intrude. Joanne's approach to her friendship with Leah seemed to be "What's yours is mine and what's mine is mine."

Leah's experience with Joanne sounded very similar to the way a high school student, Kira, described a friend who made a habit of posting pictures of herself with friends she had met through Kira or Kira's crowd—at parties Kira and her crowd weren't invited to. "She was just mooching off all our friends," Kira said, "and left us in the dust." Why did Kira hold the moocher (that is, the schnorrer), and not the mutual friends who had invited Kira and not her, responsible for leaving her out of those posted parties? She explained that those friends would have assumed that the friend Kira had introduced them to would have told Kira about it. In other words, they'd assume she'd follow the unwritten rule that if friend A introduced you to friend B, you won't get together with friend B without telling friend A.

Invest in a Friend

When I asked women if they'd experienced poaching, some immediately recognized the concept and gave me examples. That's how I learned of the various ways the practice can be viewed. But others seemed not to know what I was talking about, even to find the idea repugnant. Why would anyone feel she owns a friend?

The notion that a friend is a possession that can be stolen may seem like an unacceptable view of a human relationship. Yet it's common to hear people speak of friendship as an investment, even using that term. For example, a woman told me of a friend who complained that she "didn't invest enough in the friendship," because she didn't call frequently and didn't "do stuff" with her. When two college students were discussing friendship, one observed, "It's not okay to drop a friend when you get a boyfriend. It's disrespectful of the time you put in." The other picked up the implication of her comment: "Do you think friendship is a kind of investment? Then you lose that return when they get rid of you?" The first one acknowledged, "Maybe it is. It's more meaningful if both people are investing emotionally."

On one level, "investing emotionally" is just a metaphoric way to indicate a level of commitment that can deepen a relationship. But there are layers of meaning in the word "invest": a financial investment is premised on the assumption that you will get back more than you put in. That's the "return on investment" that you lose if a friend drops you, or initiates less than you do. The first student remarked that how much she minds if a friend fails to follow through on vague promises to get together depends on "how much I invest" in the friendship.

Thinking of friendship as an investment may simply be a way of acknowledging that friendship takes time. It takes work. A woman confessed that when one of her friends moved to Florida, she felt a sense of relief; it was one less burden. I don't think it's a coincidence that this woman described herself as "a very, very strong introvert." This has been one of my biggest surprises in writing this book: the distinction between introverts and extraverts did not come up in any of my previous books about relationships, but it emerged early on as a significant factor in this one. Those who told me they have or need few friends tended to describe themselves as introverts. And it was often introverts who commented that friendship takes work and can be burdensome. But women who seemed to be extraverts (no one used that term to describe herself) also mentioned that friendship is a burden as well as a gift. Recalling how, when she was younger, she talked to her close friends every day, a woman commented, "I can't imagine putting that burden on myself today."

If the time and effort devoted to a friendship is an investment, then both partners should invest equally. If two friends live some distance from each other, that would mean evenly splitting the investment of travel time: either they take turns traveling to the other's home, or they meet in the middle. But it doesn't always work out that way. A woman, Dawn, who lives in San Francisco, told me of a longtime friend, Toby, who lives a bit more than an hour's drive away, in San Jose. However, Dawn commented wryly, the distance from San Jose to San Francisco seems to be longer than the distance from San Francisco to San Jose, since somehow Toby never makes the drive; that investment of time always falls to Dawn.

Finding a Balance

Less tangibly but maybe even more importantly, women told me that an investment that should be shared more or less equally is care and listening. That assumption accounts for the concept of a friend who is "needy." One woman put it this way: "I have a thing about needy people. I'm a compassionate person, but I also don't want to be friends with somebody who doesn't fully show up as well. Where I have to take care of them all the time." It's the imbalance that she regarded as unacceptable: with a needy friend you have to take care of her, but she doesn't take care of you, doesn't "fully show up." In other words, the investment of giving is not repaid in receiving.

Sometimes the imbalance is simply in the apportionment of talking and listening. Joan describes a typical two-hour Skype conversation with a friend: "It's an hour and forty-five minutes of 'Look how awful my life is' and then 'But how are you?' with fifteen minutes left. It's like, 'Quick summary!' She gets things off her chest, and I feel a little exhausted. I don't feel I get much other than the exhaustion." In the end, Joan feels less like a friend than like a cut-rate therapist. Another woman described a conversationalist who doesn't even give her fifteen minutes: "She just goes on and on. It's all about her. And finally she'll say, 'Everything all right with you?' and I say, 'Yes,' and she'll say, 'Okay, I gotta go now.' And she hangs up."

The asymmetry may be not in how much a friend listens, but in how much she seems to care about what she hears—how much attention she pays. Lillian and Peggy had a long phone conversation during which they worked out a disagreement that had arisen between them. In addition, in the spirit of catching up, Lillian told her friend that she'd had a recurrence of the sciatica pain that had kept her out of work for weeks in the past. In addition to being in very bad pain, she was worried about how her boss would react if she had to miss that much work again. At the end of their conversation, in the spirit of wrapping things up, Peggy said, "All's well that ends well." Lillian understood that Peggy was referring to their having settled their disagreement, but all was far from well regarding her health. Had their roles been reversed, Lillian would have ended the conversation by saying she hoped her friend's sciatica would improve, her pain would subside, and her job would not be imperiled. And she would have called the next day to find out how her friend was doing, something she knew Peggy was not likely to do.

Another woman told of a far more egregious and explicit failure to respond with expected caring. When she confided to a friend that she was having a problem with her husband, the friend responded, "You have two kids, you have a husband, you have a house. What the hell do you have to complain about?" I suspect it may be that sort of envy—the conviction that your friend has it all while you are deprived—that might explain how friends justify to themselves the "borrowing" of money, clothes, and people—not only other friends but even, sometimes, spouses—that amounts to theft.

When are a friend's lapses so egregious that she really isn't a friend? Roberta ended a friendship because of a lapse which reinforced her mounting impression that the investment was going one way. Her college friend Bonnie had long since settled into a routine of spending a week each year as a houseguest with Roberta and her husband at their summer home by a lake. One year, Roberta's husband fell ill; when Bonnie left, he was still in the hospital. Yet Bonnie never called to find out how he was doing. In fact, Roberta didn't hear from her until the next summer rolled around and Bonnie called to arrange her yearly visit. Roberta informed her there weren't going to be any more. Weeklong visits were for friends; Bonnie's failure to show concern for Roberta's husband proved that she wasn't one.

My Friend the Tyrant

Penny met Jade through a third friend, Vera, but neither of them sees Vera anymore. In fact, their friendship crystallized when each confessed to feeling mistreated by Vera—something they both had been reluctant to mention, each thinking that the other was Vera's good friend and therefore must experience her differently. One day Penny confessed to Jade that she'd been upset by something Vera had done, and "it was like the floodgates opened. She basically felt like a battered woman. We both were afraid to say something and finally one of us did and then it all came out. We were so happy, we bonded over it. It made us realize we totally loved each other, because we had the same exact reaction to how we were being treated. It's validating. If you experience the same thing in the same way, you are kindred spirits."

Penny and Jade bonded when they realized they both felt they'd been treated badly by their mutual friend. But why did they both put up with that treatment until Penny opened the "floodgates" by speaking of it? Why did they both consider Vera a friend, despite feeling mistreated by her? Playwright Caleen Sinnette Jennings uses the word "tyrant" for friends who make you feel like you have to do what they say even though you don't want to. In her autobiographical play *Queens Girl in the World,* Jennings introduces a high school classmate, Jane, who was such a friend. When Jackie, the protagonist of the play, who is based on Jennings, goes for a sleepover to Jane's house, Jane keeps her up all night, replicating the torture tactic of sleep deprivation. Among the activities she pressures Jackie to take part in, Jane raids her parents' liquor cabinet and insists that Jackie drink a whole glass of sickeningly sweet and dizzying crème de menthe. She also makes prank phone calls to strangers, then thinks it hysterically funny when they become angry. Jennings recalls, "The sun is coming up, I'm woozy, my head hurts. I don't know why I couldn't say to her, 'I don't want to do this. No! Leave me alone!' I just couldn't." Perhaps the reason she couldn't was that openly opposing someone is not something most young women are taught to do. But perhaps also the prospect of losing a friend—even one you don't like—taps into the fear of being friendless, and can keep us in friendships long after we've sensed that they are for our pruning.

Friends whose company you enjoy can also be for your pruning if they get you into situations that are awkward or downright dangerous. Laura recalls that Alex would get her into such situations when they were growing up. For example, Alex would say, "If your mom can drop us off at the movies, my mom can pick us up." Fair enough. Laura's mother would drive the girls to the movie, but when it ended, Alex's mother was nowhere in sight. Alex had never asked her to come. They'd have to walk home (cellphones had not yet been invented), which meant walking through a park where boys hung out—something that delighted Alex but frightened Laura. Laura recounted numerous ways that Alex drew her into situations that made her uncomfortable, and numerous ways she tried to distance herself from Alex, but, she said, Alex would always "reel me back in." This metaphor captures the feeling that a friend has the power to control you, while you, like a fish caught at the end of a line, have no power to get away.

A girl whose friend habitually and continually tears her down is the ten-year-old protagonist in Joy Williams's short story "Train." Danica and Jane (yes, Williams's character has the same name as Jennings') are traveling by train to Florida, where they both live, having spent the summer at Jane's family's vacation home in Maine. Right on the first page, Jane looks at a postcard Danica has just written and says, "That is real messy writing. It's all scrunched together." This is only the first of a nonstop stream of criticism that Jane heaps on Danica. When Danica says she is going to collect postcards, Jane says, "I've been through that phase. It's just a phase. I don't think you're much of a correspondent." Jane's insults can be even less subtle, such as "What is a clod like yourself doing on this fabulous journey!" Jane also talks to strangers and makes things up. Approaching a couple in the dining car, she announces, "My name is Crystal, and this is my twin sister, Clara." The author comments, representing Danica's thoughts, "Jane was always inventing drab names for her." The irony is clear: Jane is the one with a drab name, compared to Danica, whose real name is exotic.

Part of the satisfaction in reading this story is getting to see Danica finally stand up for herself. Jane is recounting a dream, and Danica comments, about someone in the dream, "It was probably the cleaning lady." Jane responds as we have come to expect: "Cleaning lady! Cleaning lady, for god's sake. What do you know about cleaning ladies!" This time Danica responds in a way we have not seen before. She "realized she was mad, madder than she'd been all summer, for all summer she'd only felt humiliated when Jane was nasty to her." This time Danica says, "Listen up. Don't talk to me like that anymore." At that, she gets up and walks away.

In Joy Williams's story, there are hints as to why these two girls have taken the roles they have in relation to each other. Jane's parents are at war, her mother relentlessly criticizing and humiliating her father. When Jane does the same to her friend, we can surmise she is mimicking that model. And why does Danica put up with it? For one thing, she has been Jane's guest for the summer. But this fact has resulted from a more damaging one: Danica is neglected. Her mother has sent her away because she recently remarried, and her new husband has little interest in her child. It is rarely so obvious, in our lives, why people behave the way they do, though we can surmise, or guess. As a ten-year-old, Danica isn't likely to figure out why Jane continually puts her down. What matters is that something inside her rebels, and she finds the strength to protest and walk away. Such a simple move: get up and walk away. Yet it can feel just about impossible when you are in the midst of a conversation or relationship with a friend you experience as a tyrant.

Sheer Spite

Shari grew up on a farm. As a small child, she had a friend, Adele, who lived down the road. Shari wasn't allowed to go to Adele's home because Adele's parents were alcoholic, her brothers were wild, and her dilapidated house was guarded by a ferocious German shepherd. But Adele spent time in Shari's home, where they played together and helped Shari's mother cook. When the time came for Shari to start school, she was scared. Arriving at the one-room schoolhouse on the first day of first grade, she felt lost. She didn't know anyone. So she was relieved to spot Adele among the welter of kids clambering up the steps. At the same moment, Shari also spied a fuzzy orange caterpillar on the steps, and was terrified for it: the beautiful creature might be inadvertently trampled by a child heading up the stairs. Just as Shari was seized by this fear, Adele caught her eye. Shari recalls, "Without changing her expression, she deliberately stomped on the end of the caterpillar, causing all of its insides to squoosh out the other end." For years afterward, Shari had nightmares of crushed caterpillars. And she struggled to understand why her friend did that. "Much later," she said, "I came to understand that she was jealous of me and my sheltered, happy home; that this moment was her chance to make me understand the world she lived in, the world where she was the caterpillar." Shari now thinks it was Adele's way of saying, "Get used to it, Shari. You can't worry about a stupid caterpillar when life is going to squash you."

In a way, Adele represented the wide world of school that Shari, like all children, feared: strangers who can do you harm. So it was ironic, and shattering, that Shari was harmed not by a stranger but by the one child she knew, her one friend. And it was because Adele knew her that she intuited what Shari was thinking when she spotted the caterpillar. It was because of their friendship that Adele knew she could hurt Shari by hurting the caterpillar.

There is something universal about this story—a child destroying something a friend cares about to spite the friend. A similar impulse leads to the climax of another short story, "They Were All to Be Pitied," by a Greek writer, Elli Alexiou. The protagonist is a child whose unhappy parents vie for her affection by buying her expensive gifts. Eventually her mother is so miserable in the marriage that she leaves, abandoning her young daughter. The bereft child becomes deeply attached to a remarkable doll that her father had ordered from Germany. Gorgeously dressed, the doll has eyelids that open and close; it has a music box inside that, when wound up, plays a sweet song as the doll's hand moves up and down across a harp she's holding; and, when tipped, the doll says "Mama." One day, the child is playing with another little girl, the daughter of the family's driver. She shows her playmate the doll, tantalizing her by winding it up so it plays the harp and tipping it so it says "Mama." Transfixed, her playmate reaches to touch the magical doll. The child taunts, "Do you like it?" "Is it pretty?"—and hurls her beloved doll to the floor and stomps on it, just as Shari's friend Adele stomped on the caterpillar to upset her.

The child in this story pays a price for her spite. The doll that had consoled her never again calls her "Mama," a loss so painful that she can't bear to listen to its music anymore either. Like Shari's real-life encounter, this story involves children from families with very different economic circumstances, the poorer one joining the wealthier one in her far more comfortable home. But whereas Adele destroyed something Shari cared about, perhaps out of resentment for her better fortune, the child who lashes out in Alexiou's story is the wealthier one. But in another way, she is poorer: her playmate has two parents, an advantage that could surely spark envy in a child whose mother abandoned her. Whatever the motivation, so strong is her impulse to prevent her playmate from enjoying something she admires that she destroys something she herself loves. What better way to prove that the doll is her property than to destroy it?

Cutoffs

A psychologist might surmise that the protagonist of Elli Alexiou's story believed she must have done something to drive her mother away: if her mother didn't love her, she must be unlovable. Similar self-doubt can creep in when someone is abandoned by a spouse, a lover, or a friend.

Among the most painful stories I heard were of friendships precipitously ended. When someone you've been close to, who has been part of your life, suddenly refuses to see you or speak to you, her departure leaves a hole in your life and your heart, and can leave you wondering what you did to cause your abandonment. You may suspect that you harbor within yourself a fatal flaw that renders you unfit for friendship. I know I did.

I grew up in Brooklyn but went to high school in Manhattan. (For those who know New York, it was Hunter College High School.) No one else from my neighborhood or my junior high went to that high school, so I had to make new friends there. I soon made two: Marlene, Susan, and I ate lunch together every day and spent a lot of time together outside of school, sometimes all three, often in twos. We were frequent visitors in each other's homes and knew each other's parents and siblings. We were constant companions—until Susan, for reasons she did not disclose, stopped speaking to me and refused to have anything more to do with me. Marlene tried to stay friends with both of us, but she continued to have lunch with Susan, and that meant I was effectively cut off from her, too, at least at school, because I could no longer join them. I was devastated.

In retrospect, I can say I ended up okay, maybe even better off. Marlene, Susan, and I had all entered Hunter High in tenth grade, but most of the girls in our year had been at the school since seventh grade, and they were intimidating: they knew their way around; they seemed to have known each other forever; and they had long since settled into friendships and cliques. When I found myself stranded, I was more open to conversations and interactions with some of those girls, and became best friends with one who went to the same college I did and was my roommate the first year. But the experience of being suddenly cut off by a close friend, someone I loved who was integral to my daily life, was shattering. It was an introduction to a calamity that is not uncommon among girls and women: cutoffs.

I Never Spoke to Her Again

Women who told me they had been cut off always said they'd been devastated, as I had been—and, also like me, almost always said they didn't know why they had been cut off. But women who told me they had cut off a friend could always tell me why. Ellen, for example, explained how she came to cut off her friend Amelia. When the man Amelia had been living with ended their relationship, Ellen's heart went out to her. Ellen knew what it was like when days that had previously been filled with someone's company now loomed like a limitless expanse of gaping time; she knew that being deprived of a voice and a presence that had become like the air you breathe felt like gasping for breath. So no matter how busy Ellen was, she made time when Amelia needed company, or someone to talk to—for as long as Amelia needed to talk. Amelia was still in a bad state when Ellen moved across the country, so she continued to make herself available to talk by phone, even though the three-hour time difference meant that Amelia's evening was now well past Ellen's bedtime.

One evening Ellen was already asleep when the phone woke her; it was Amelia, needing to talk. Ellen would not have considered telling her that it wasn't a good time; she did her best to listen and to offer comforting words. But something Ellen said struck Amelia the wrong way, and she reacted with outrage. "What a terrible thing to say!" Amelia exploded. "I can't believe you said that!" She went on in that vein until they hung up. Amelia's anger seemed as outrageous to Ellen as her ill-chosen words had apparently seemed to Amelia. No, Ellen was sure it was more outrageous. After all she had done, all the effort she had made to stick by Amelia when she needed a friend, the innumerable ways she had put Amelia's needs ahead of her own (and maybe that was part of the problem, she later thought—maybe she went a bit overboard putting her friend's needs ahead of her own)—how could all that count for nothing, because of one false move? Ellen never spoke to Amelia again.

"I never spoke to her again." Those words capped many stories I heard of cutoffs. Roz used them in telling me why she ended her friendship with Doreen. Doreen's roommate had moved out, and she couldn't afford the rent on her own, so Roz invited Doreen to stay with her. Though her apartment was small, Roz spent quite a bit of time, including many nights, at her boyfriend's. As the length of Doreen's stay expanded, Roz realized that she was spending more and more time at her boyfriend's apartment because she no longer felt comfortable in her own: it had begun to feel like it wasn't hers anymore, but Doreen's—and Doreen treated it that way. Finally, Roz felt she had to ask her friend to leave. Rather than thanking Roz for having provided her a home rent-free for months, Doreen became angry and began yelling. Among the accusations she hurled was that if Roz's boyfriend ever moved in with her, Roz would no doubt kick him out after a few months, too. Roz, who not only didn't kick her boyfriend out but eventually married him, told me that she never spoke to Doreen again.

Roz's and Ellen's reasons for cutting off their friends had something in common: an outburst of anger that seemed unjust both in itself and, even worse, in view of past generosity. The effect of Doreen's, like Amelia's, verbal attack was like the line from a poem by T. S. Eliot: "After such knowledge, what forgiveness?" The knowledge that their friends could turn on them would lurk around any conversations that Roz and Ellen might have had after that.

Even if a cutoff can be traced to a single moment—a cruel thing said or outrageous thing done—that supremely tellable violation usually is the climax to frustrations and disappointments that had been building over time. College students Erin and Angie had been inseparable in ninth grade, but now it seemed to Erin that Angie never lost an opportunity to let her know that other friends were more special to her. The preferred friend might be a girl Angie had known since childhood, or the third girl in their trio, or, worst of all, a popular girl who seemed to pay her no mind. It came to a head when Erin made a point of traveling from where she attended college to their hometown in order to celebrate Angie's birthday, only to discover that Angie had made plans for her birthday that left Erin out. That was the last straw. Erin cut her off.

It's How I Feel When I'm with You

"I love you not for who you are but for who I am when I am with you." This line, which is often quoted and variously attributed, can apply not only to romantic partners but also to friends. Many women said as much: "When I am with her I can be who I am"; "When I'm with them I feel clever and funny." A variation on that line can explain cutoffs that occur not because of a single crowning offense but because of a mounting sense that a friendship is for your pruning: "I dislike you not for who you are but for who I am when I am with you." In explaining friendships that ended, women told me of friends who made them feel bad about themselves: "She made me feel inadequate and intimidated, correcting my grammar and always having done one better"; she "did a number on me, made me feel inadequate, awkward, unattractive"; "She made me feel inadequate and depressed." The word that appears in all these descriptions is "inadequate"—that fundamental and probably universal fear that we are just not good enough.

A college student, Libby, recalled a high school friendship that she "hard-stop ended." Her friend Celia "was great and funny and just a riot. She was a hoot, and great to be around." But Celia's joking, which made her so much fun to be around, could also make Libby feel terrible. For example, one time Libby and Celia and another friend were driving home from a shopping trip when Libby mentioned something personal that was troubling her. Celia quipped, "What are you gonna do? Cry about it?" That's exactly what Libby did, as a result not of the problem but of her friend's flippant response. Her tears were welling as she stepped out of the car. Though Libby truly believed that Celia had intended this, like many other similar quips, as a joke, it made her feel bad, though she didn't say anything—until one day she did. When Celia posted an insensitive response on Facebook, Libby texted, "When you do these things, it makes me feel like shit." Celia texted back, "I must be a really bad friend." To that, Libby recalls, "I just didn't reply and that was the hard-stop to our friendship"—not because of that one Facebook post but because "it just kind of built up after a while. I didn't want to keep enduring it."

A friend who makes you feel bad when you're with her sounds like the definition of "frenemy," but I think it's more complicated than that. A psychologist I spoke to observed, "Every relationship is an ambivalent one." Since friendship is a relationship, being hurt at some point, in some way, is probably inevitable with all friends. It's only when you seem to be hurt more than you're helped, when you consistently don't like how you feel—who you are—when you are with a friend that you start to realize you'd be better off without that friend: you distance yourself—or cut her off.

To Tell or Not to Tell

In explaining why she "hard-stopped" her friendship with Celia, Libby emphasized that until she sent that final text message, she had said nothing about how Celia was making her feel. She couldn't help wondering whether things might have turned out differently if she had spoken up sooner. The first verse of a poem by William Blake suggests that they might have:

> I was angry with my friend;
> I told my wrath, my wrath did end.
> I was angry with my foe:
> I told it not, my wrath did grow.

I have often wondered why I said nothing when my college roommate echoed my words about loving a frying pan. Silence can come across as acceptance or even encouragement; she had no way of knowing that her words bothered me. Why didn't I just say, "Hey, that's exactly what I said last week!" I'll never know what would have happened if I had.

Haley, whose friend Alexa had a habit of admiring Haley's clothes then buying the same thing, also never said anything to her friend about it. But Haley had a chance to observe what a difference speaking up could make. Once she and Alexa were together at a party when Alexa, as usual, complimented Haley on the dress she was wearing, then reached up to look at the label. Haley felt her blood pressure rise, as she knew Alexa was planning to buy one just like it. But that time, Haley's husband was standing by. "Don't you buy that dress!" he said to Alexa. "Let Haley have her own style!" It was as simple as that. Not only did Alexa not buy that dress, but she stopped turning up in clothes just like Haley's. And Haley realized that she, too, could have stopped Alexa's annoying habit by speaking up.

In some cases, though, telling a friend you're not happy with something she said or did does not end well. Cindy, for example, had a new friend who accused Cindy of "flaking" on her. Though Cindy apologized and explained herself, she made a mental note to be cautious about this friend. One concern was "Is this person too fragile?" The other was "I don't want this aggression." These two concerns might seem, on the surface, paradoxical: isn't being fragile the opposite of being aggressive? But in truth, feeling hurt can spark anger, so someone who is easily hurt can also be quick to attack, and an accusation is, after all, a kind of attack. Registering a complaint can become a cause for complaint in itself. Agnes complained to Lucy, "Why did you tell Marian that you gave birth before you told me?" On hearing this complaint, Lucy lost patience with Agnes. There was a good reason why Marian was the first to know: she was the one who watched Lucy's older child when Lucy went into labor and headed for the hospital. The complaint seemed out of line. Agnes's registering it didn't inspire contrition or an apology; it inspired Lucy to distance herself from Agnes.

Part of true friendship is telling a friend something she needs to hear when no one else will. But there might be a reason why no one else tells her: she doesn't want to hear it. Often it involves a boyfriend or husband: he was cheating on her, or for other reasons wasn't good for her. If you try to be a true friend by telling her, she may thank you—or never talk to you again. Maxine lost a friend by trying to help her, though in a different way. Maxine's friend Celeste was suffering because of an ongoing conflict with her daughter. Maxine felt she could help by orchestrating a rapprochement. She could see exactly what Celeste was doing to upset her daughter, and how simple it would be to act differently and get her daughter back. But when Maxine tried to explain this to her, Celeste got angry; she thought Maxine was taking her daughter's side. It felt to her less like being enlightened and helped than like being ganged up on.

Many women are acutely aware that registering a complaint can be risky, so they avoid it, much as they tend to avoid anything that resembles conflict. Yet not saying anything can itself spark conflict. When women told me of times their friends disappointed or angered them, it often seemed that the offense might have resulted from the friend's desire to avoid confrontation. Marjorie, for example, was hurt by a close college friend. She recalls, "We were supposed to go to my aunt's house for a holiday dinner an hour drive away, and when I went to find her to leave, she was hiding from me. She didn't want to go." Physically hiding is an unusually concrete way to avoid following through on a commitment you've come to regret—or, as often happens, you didn't really want to make in the first place. The quandary is common: you don't want to disappoint a friend by saying no, and it's even harder to renege after you've said yes. But avoiding confrontation can create more problems down the line—certainly in the way Marjorie's friend handled it, but also, potentially, if she'd kept her promise despite not wanting to go. The extreme result would be a cutoff, the ultimate paradoxical way to avoid confrontation. Someone who simply cannot oppose a friend may build up a store of resentment that finally becomes unsustainable: the only way out she can see is exiting the friendship and closing the door behind her.

What Did I Do? Nothing!

Women who told me of cutting friends off always told me why they did it, but I don't know whether they explained their reasons to the friends they rejected. I am chagrined to admit that when I cut friends off (I recall two such times), I did it precipitously, without explanation. I think that's because explaining my reasons would have kept the conversation—and the friendship—going, the opposite of what I had made up my mind to do. But switching to the perspective of the one who is cut off—as I was in high school by my friend Susan—I can see that it is especially upsetting if the one cut off doesn't know what she did to cause it. In some cases, an answer may not exist, because it wasn't anything she did.

A woman who'd been hurt by a cutoff was relieved when—decades later—the friend who had cut her off reconnected and explained that she had been having a tough time back then and had cut everyone off. Another woman recalled her own habit, when she was younger, of cutting friends off: she'd pursue a friendship with enthusiastic determination, then would feel overwhelmed by the closeness she'd created—and would flee. This can explain the bewildering experience where someone at first seems to yearn for your friendship then suddenly backs off. It could be not despite but because of her eagerness: she had set up expectations of so much mutual confession and constant companionship that they became more than she felt she could handle.

Another circumstance that can lead to being cut off through no fault of your own is when the decision wasn't made by the friend herself. When children or young adults still live with parents or guardians, it is not unusual for the adults to demand a cutoff, because they disapprove of a friend or—though they probably don't think of it that way—because they envy their child's attachment to the friend and feel displaced by it. Long after writing this paragraph, I discovered that this is exactly why my high school friend Susan cut me off.

In the many decades since high school, I had frequently thought of contacting Susan and asking her why she stopped speaking to me. I periodically tried to find her, but, as often happens with women who marry and change their names, she couldn't be found. When the Internet came along, I tried again, but again had no luck. From the moment I decided to write this book, I knew I wanted to solve this mystery once and for all. When the book was pretty much done, and I'd still failed in my own attempts, I enlisted the aid of a friend who has a gift for finding people online. Within a day, Paul had found the record of Susan's arrival in the United States at the age of seven, with her parents and three much older siblings, from their native Iraq. Luckily, her siblings included a brother whose email address Paul was able to locate online. Within another day—fifty-four years after our last conversation—I was talking to Susan on the phone. The very first thing she said to me was that it was her older brother—not the one I'd emailed, but a different one—who had insisted she stop seeing me, because I had too much influence over her. But looking back, she said, she thinks he was just jealous. And it broke her heart at the same time that it broke mine.

Sometimes friendships end for reasons that are entirely outside anyone's control, such as political developments. An Israeli woman who was living in Egypt had formed a close friendship with an Egyptian woman. When a crisis erupted between their countries, Israelis living in Egypt were evacuated, and the friendship was summarily ended.

The forced ending of that friendship was a loss, but it wasn't tragic, since the friendship had been fairly new. In a book about the turmoil that followed the 2011 political upheaval in the Middle East, Robert Worth describes the demise of a friendship that does feel tragic. Two Syrian women, Aliaa and Noura, had been inseparable best friends since high school, oblivious of their religious differences: Aliaa's family was Alawi, like the Syrian president, Bashar al-Assad, while Noura's was Sunni. Worth, a journalist who met and talked to both women, describes them walking to the university arm in arm and lying side by side on Aliaa's bed as Noura debated whether to accept a marriage proposal. She decided against it in large part because of her suitor's animus against Alawis, which she didn't share and couldn't understand. But political developments in Syria eventually led Noura to share that animus, and inspired in Aliaa a parallel hatred of Sunnis. By the end of Worth's chapter about this failed friendship, Noura is a refugee in Turkey married to a man "whose Facebook page was full of jihadi symbols and warlike slogans," and Aliaa is still living in Syria. The two women had not only ended their friendship but convinced themselves that the other and her family were guilty of offenses and intentions that Worth finds preposterous. To explain the reframing of her former best friend as an enemy, each told Worth of comments the other had made years before that had seemed meaningless at the time but that she now saw as evidence to support her demonization.

The post hoc reinterpretation of words caught my attention in this heartbreaking account. This cutoff is extreme in its particulars because the circumstances that led to it were extreme. But the tendency to recall things said by a former friend and reinterpret them as evidence of perfidy is not uncommon in the process of cutting off a friendship, especially one that was highly valued and an integral part of one's life. It is almost as if evidence of outsize offenses is necessary to justify so great a loss.

Drama!

A woman said of a friend, "We told each other our secrets, we trusted each other, we could depend on each other, we were together a great deal of the time." This brief description hits many, if not most, of the elements of women's friendship. And many of the reasons women gave for feeling disappointed or frustrated by friends were violations of one or another of these requisites: she kept something from me; she repeated something I told her or brought it up to me later; she let me down when I needed her; she didn't spend enough time with me. If these violations were serious enough, they might lead to a cutoff. Trying instead to tackle them can be a valued element of friendship. One woman mentioned "being able to talk things through" as part of her definition of friendship. But sometimes talking things through becomes part of what is disparaged as "drama." And drama itself can be a source of frustration and disappointment, and can lead to cutoffs.

Many girls and women told me that they don't like drama—and that they associate it with others of their sex, especially in groups. A high school senior said, "Ever since all the middle school stuff I sort of actively try to stay away from the drama of the girl groups. It just baffles me." A college student bemoaned all the "gossip and drama" that had characterized her high school friends. Yet another sounded a similar note: "I have a lot of good friends who are guys because I don't like drama." The essence of drama is the experience of emotional upheaval—someone is hurt or gets mad or both, things are said, sleep is lost—followed by talking about it. It's the extended, intensive talking that makes many girls and women susceptible to drama. In a way, drama is just human relations. If you are close to someone, if your lives intersect, there's a pretty good chance that at some point feelings will be hurt. Talking it over to figure out what caused the trouble and how to repair it can be healing. But talking about it—to the person responsible or to others who know you both—can stir up emotions, too, and cause new wounds. So can learning that you've been talked about.

Angela was concerned because her good friend Maggie didn't call on her birthday as she usually did. She wasn't eager to confront Maggie, because she didn't want drama, especially since there might have been another, more benign reason for the oversight. So she asked a mutual friend if Maggie was angry at her and was relieved when the friend said no. But her relief was short-lived. The friend reported Angela's concern to Maggie, who was upset to learn that Angela had been talking about her. Maggie registered her complaint with Angela, who therefore found herself embroiled in what she had wanted to avoid: drama!

People have different levels of tolerance for the talk about hurt feelings and complications of relationships that make up drama: some avoid it at all costs, some take part in it when necessary, some seem to seek and glory in it. And sometimes too much drama—or a feeling that the relationship doesn't merit the emotional investment of drama—leads to distancing from or even cutting off friends. Though this can be very difficult—for both people involved—the freedom to end a relationship that you feel is more for your pruning than for your growth is one of many ways that you have more agency, choice, and control with friends than with family members. You might say that, ironically, while poaching, drama, and the danger of being hurt or even cut off are among the risks of friendship, the option of cutting off someone you feel is for your pruning is among its gifts.

7

"Like" It or Not

Women, Friendship, and Social Media

We use social media to do many things that people have always done: make plans or cancel plans; let someone know we'll be late; check in to find out how a friend is doing; have fights, make up, tell jokes. But social media have also fundamentally changed communication and, even more deeply, ways of being in the world. In the past, a person was in active communication only with those present. That could change if another person showed up and, to a lesser degree, if a letter arrived. The invention of the telephone meant that an absent person could be present by calling or being called. But the default case was that when no one else was present, each person was alone—psychologically as well as physically. For many people, social media mean being in an open state of communication all the time. Others can initiate communication at any moment just as surely as if they were in the same room, so they are like constant shadow presences. Psychologically, a person with a digital device turned on is not alone. Having become accustomed to this default state, many people panic if they find themselves without a working phone. To recapture a sense of solitude, some seek out and savor rare moments or vacations in which they are out of cellphone contact. What used to be the default case of consciousness is now a temporary exotic adventure.

Whenever anyone initiates communication, there is potential for both connection and intrusion. A telephone call could be a welcome connection or a distracting intrusion. The same is true if someone knocks on the door, or joins a conversation taking place face to face. Intrusion, after all, is simply an unwelcome bid for connection. Or perhaps it's the reverse: connection is a welcome intrusion. The addition of ubiquitous social media recapitulates and amplifies this ambiguity. When a distant person appears on a screen, it can be a precious connection or an intrusive distraction. Just knowing that someone—anyone—might appear at any moment creates the same ambiguity: it makes you feel less alone (in the room and in the world) and also leaves you perennially open to intrusion and distraction. It protects you from loneliness or robs you of solitude—or both. The difference between soul-searing loneliness and soul-salving solitude is a conundrum at the heart of social media—and of women's friendship. The ability—the requirement—for girls and women to be in constant communication with friends makes social media particularly engaging, given the role of talk in maintaining girls' and women's friendships. But it can also be exhausting, and can aggravate the liability that is particularly potent for women: FOBLO—Fear Of Being Left Out.

Seeing Where You're Not

Sitting up in bed, about to lie down and go to sleep, Meghan picks up her phone and opens Snapchat to scroll through the stories—photographs and videos that remain visible for twenty-four hours—posted by her friends since the last time she checked the app. She smiles to herself as the images roll by: a party she went to, a friend's visit to relatives in a distant city, pets' antics. Then her heart skips a beat, and a lump of misery lands on her chest. She's faced with photos of a party where several of her friends are grinning and mugging, their heads pressed together to fit in the frame. Meghan didn't know about that party; she wasn't invited.

Before social media, Meghan wouldn't have known what her friends were doing without her unless she was told—and even then, she'd only hear about it; she wouldn't see it. A woman who is just old enough to have missed growing up with social media told me she is grateful because: "I was a bookworm in middle school, happy to be alone reading. Had I known all the things I was missing out on, I might not have been a bookworm. Or I might have felt bad about being one, instead of just loving reading." Today, people are far more likely to know what they're missing—and to see it in living color. Social media give you a view—a literal view, a photograph or video—of people you aren't with in places where they are and you're not. The emotions these pictures can arouse are as vast and as varied as human experience, from heartwarming connection to heart-piercing pangs at being left out. And for better or worse, these images can spring up before your eyes no matter where you are, including in your home and even in your bed. Before social media, kids might be bullied or neglected at school, and adults might be upset by people at work, but when they got home and closed the door behind them, they were temporarily safe. Now voices and views from the outside world—both friendly and unfriendly—slip into your house as easily as an intruder with a key to your front door.

At every moment, everyone you know who is not with you is doing something without you. And FOBLO is always lurking, a universal human frailty, but one that has special power for girls and women, because their peers tend to punish those they don't like or are mad at by locking them out. These two circumstances needn't intersect if you don't know about and can't see what others are up to. But if you are active on social media, now you often do. When FOBLO and social media collude, hurt feelings are sure to result. And that's a problem not only for the ones who were left out but also for those who were there—again, especially women and girls, not only because they are particularly sensitive to being left out, but also because they often worry as much about others' feelings as about their own (and sometimes they worry more about hurting others' feelings than about having their own feelings hurt).

Lizzie, for example, spent an evening with friends—nothing special, no big deal. But one of those friends posted photos on Facebook, where they were seen by Lizzie's friend Madeleine, who had recently moved to another city and was feeling lonely. Madeleine texted Lizzie, upset: "You went out with Em and Jocelyn! You wore such a pretty dress!" Lizzie knew she'd done nothing wrong; she understood that the hurt and resentment in her friend's tone were mostly about her isolation as a newcomer to a strange city. Nonetheless Lizzie felt bad to be their immediate cause. If it weren't for Facebook, a friend in another city wouldn't know what Lizzie was doing back home. And even if Lizzie or another friend told her, it wouldn't be as hurtful as actually *seeing* Lizzie, dressed up and smiling, out on the town with other friends, and not with her.

Women of any age face similar dilemmas. It's always been challenging, when organizing an event—a small dinner, a large party, or a huge reception—to decide where to draw the line that must be drawn: whom to invite, whom to leave out. There was always a risk that people who weren't invited might find out and be angry or hurt, but for the most part, most people are circumspect about mentioning an event to those they didn't see there or weren't sure had been invited. Now anyone who was there may post a photo or refer to the event on social media, where anyone not invited may see it. And pictures in particular can cause hurt feelings and consequent anger. Aubrey, for example, decided to keep the celebration of her fifty-second birthday—not a major round number—low key: she and her husband simply went out for dinner with another couple. And who could fault the woman of that couple for sharing her own news on Facebook: "Celebrated Aubrey's birthday!" Aubrey could—because it sparked a protest from another friend: "Hey, how come you celebrated your birthday with her and not me?!"

The feeling of being left out can be an unintended consequence of photo sharing, or an intended one. "At the beginning of college," a freshman told me, everyone creates and sends a Snapchat story at every party they go to "because you want to show, 'I'm having a better time at college than all my friends back in high school.'" Photos have particular power because they're vivid and seem real—so real, there's a saying: "Pics or it didn't happen." Yet photos can be misleading. For example, a high school student told me, "I'll get a phone call from one of my friends saying that she had a terrible time at this party and wishes she hadn't gone. Then I'll get off the phone and check Instagram and I'll see a picture of her smiling and having fun at the party which if I didn't just have that conversation with her I would think I was missing the party of the year." Photos can be misleading in others ways, too. A young woman was shocked that her boyfriend got angry after seeing a photo she posted of herself at a party. He'd spotted a boy he particularly disliked standing behind her—a boy she hadn't even spoken to at the party!

Social media can trigger FOBLO in person, too. If a small group of friends are together and two become engrossed in a private conversation, it can be off-putting to the others. But add a phone to the scene, and the two friends are not just talking to each other but huddled close together, hunched over a screen, conferring and smiling over something that the others cannot see, publicly proclaiming that, in that moment, the others don't count.

More or Less

Teenage girls used to spend hours talking to their friends on the telephone. Karen, now in her sixties, recalls that she and her best friend would take the long way home from school so they'd have more time to talk, and then when they arrived and retreated to their separate homes, they'd call each other to continue the conversation. It wasn't unusual for families who could afford it to get a second telephone line, because the first one was always tied up if a teenage daughter was home. Women of all ages told me about having one- or two-hour phone conversations with friends. Because of social media, many girls and women today have more and less communication with friends: more in that they exchange more frequent messages and photos, in many cases throughout the day; less in that they spend fewer hours in extended voice-to-voice conversation. Is this a difference that makes a difference? Karen, for example, commented that she no longer has time for the long telephone conversations that she used to have with her friends. I asked if email is a substitute. Yes and no, she said. Email does maintain contact but it's a bit like Christmas letters: it can keep friends informed of major developments in your life, but it doesn't allow for exploring and sharing the feelings and nuances that go with those major developments, or the recounting of day-to-day details that make up a life—certainly not regularly, day after day.

Many women I spoke to expressed the worry that social media have changed not only the nature of communication but the nature of friendship. Someone who has hundreds of friends on Facebook, they fear, might lose sight of what true friendship is. I don't share that concern. Even the most avid users of Facebook know the difference between a Facebook friend and a close friend. For example, a college student on a semester abroad changed her Facebook status from "in a relationship" to "single." Messages flowed in expressing sympathy and concern. But none were from her closest friends. They did not learn of her heartbreak on Facebook. By the time she made it known in that public way, she had already told them privately, and they'd expressed their concern—at length—privately, too.

A professor noticed a pattern: when she returned home after attending a conference, she'd see a flurry of friend requests on Facebook. At first it felt odd to accept them, since she barely knew the people who'd sent them. But then she realized that a Facebook friend request is not a false claim of friendship but a gesture toward it, a way of saying, "I would like to get to know you better." She came to think of such requests as pre-friendship friendships.

It's unfortunate that Facebook and other networking sites use the word "friend" for contacts made on their platforms, but it's not surprising. The practice began in 2002 with the name of one of the first social networking websites, Friendster. It was a natural choice because "friend" is the most common way to characterize a human connection that is not a family relationship. Social media didn't invent those kinds of connections, but they have made them possible among more people and people farther away, in addition to amplifying and reshaping the relationships of those who would have been friends without them.

A fourteen-year-old girl visiting relatives in London refused to leave the house after 3:00 P.M. because from that time on, her friends back in Sri Lanka became active on the instant messaging app WhatsApp, and she could not bear to miss out on their conversations. FOMO and FOBLO were keeping her inside—inside the house and inside her circle of friends—but cut off from London and from her mother and aunt, who did go out (a separation that might have its own appeal for a teenager). WhatsApp kept her connected to friends at home, who were physically distant, but it also placed distance between her and the people and places that were physically close. Is this more connection or less? That's hard to say; it's both.

Keeping—and Comparing—Friends

In years past, moving usually meant losing touch with friends. Today it's common to stay in touch through social media. A college student explained, "I had two best friends in high school. I talk to them—if not daily, every other day, over Facebook. We have a group chat just the three of us. And we talk about everything from schoolwork to family to boys to bitching about roommates. We talk all the time." For her, maintaining nearly daily contact with friends from home is the norm; it's expected. If it doesn't happen, it's a disappointment. With another friend from high school, she said, "We would text each other maybe once a month at the beginning of the school year like, 'Oh hey we haven't talked in so long, what's up stranger?' But the conversation would never go past two or three texts." She regarded this lapse, this loss of a friendship, as "strange"; it made her feel neglected.

Facebook can not only keep up connections with former high school classmates; it can rekindle them. A woman in her fifties told me she had lost touch with her high school friends soon after graduating, because their interests and values seemed very different from hers. Years later, they found each other through Facebook and began exchanging messages and catching up. Soon they were clicking "like" in response to each other's postings and photos, and adding comments like "Your kids are so beautiful," "Congrats on that job," even the much-maligned "Happy birthday." Facebook, she explained, provides an "ideal distance" to keep in touch with high school friends: "It's like a holiday card on steroids." And since they'd married at similar ages, their children were of similar ages and going through similar stages. Facebook brought into focus the things they have in common.

Perhaps it was the passage of time that allowed Facebook to bring out these similarities. But it can also have the opposite effect. A college student, Claire, noticed a striking difference between how her college and high school friends used Facebook. Her college friends' postings were about current events and social justice, while her high school friends' Facebook pages featured pictures and messages that struck her as frivolous. One of those friends made it clear that those choices were intentional, and that Claire's politically engaged postings baffled her. "I don't understand," she objected. "Facebook should be for life updates, posting pictures of yourself, and videos of cats."

Even without such obviously contrasting assumptions about how it should be used, Facebook creates problems precisely because it so vastly expands connections. A woman explained one such problem this way: "Facebook is like being in a room with people you know from different parts of your life, so you can't figure out which self to be." It's true: you tell different people different things, and if you tell them the same thing, you talk about it differently. You wouldn't talk the same way to your grandmother, father, best friend, boss, and someone you just met—or never met. Though Facebook provides options for privacy settings that give users control over who can see which material they post, there is always the chance that a setting will be misused or confused, and there is always some material that everyone can see. No matter what privacy settings you choose, some of those who see what you post may not be the audience you had in mind when you wrote it. And there will always be differences among friends from different times and corners of your life.

Who Wants to Know?

A typical high school or college student uses at least some and often many or all of the platforms: texting, iMessage, Instagram, Snapchat, WeChat, GroupMe, Facebook, WhatsApp, Yik Yak, email, Tinder, Twitter, FaceTime, Skype, Pinterest, and Spotify. And more and more, these media are used not only, and not mostly, to send word messages but also to send pictures and videos. The pictures girls send are often of themselves, and often include friends. It can seem at times that activities are engineered just for the picture. A high school senior described the elaborate preparations for prom night—and they seemed to be a series of setups for photos. Two friends got ready at the house of one, but then split so each could join another group of friends to take pictures. Two other friends got ready together, after which they, too, joined other groups, but not until one had made sure that her boyfriend came to take their picture.

Some women I spoke to expressed the view that pictures posted or sent are often trivial and self-centered. Special scorn was reserved for the literal self-focus of selfies—and the practice of sending pictures of insignificant daily events and objects, especially food. "I don't care what somebody had for dinner," one woman complained. "All this stuff out there that nobody needs to know." But think of everyday conversation, especially the how-was-your-day exchange of details that women prize. If we all spoke only on a need-to-know basis, most of our conversations would be ruled out of bounds. Everyday talk is less about needing to know information and more about needing to maintain connections with other people. And that is a need that photo sharing on social media is extremely well suited to fulfill.

In a paper written for my class, Corinne Counsell explained how her friends' use of Instagram creates connection. Corinne and her friends post pictures of themselves and their surroundings, with the goal of garnering as many "likes" as possible. To do this they make creative use of Instagram's features—tagging, adding locations, and captioning—to display and reinforce their connections to friends. Tagging links a picture to others' Instagram accounts, thereby identifying others and notifying them that their pictures are posted; adding a location and captioning allows (or allowed at the time Corinne was in my class) the poster to add a word message to a picture. For example, when her younger sister visited, Corinne posted pictures of herself and her sister engaged in various activities then "tagged" her sister, thereby bringing her into the circle of Corinne's friends. She also added a caption—"Counsell girls take DC"—and an emoji of two identical figures of girls dancing, highlighting her connection to her sister and their similarity. She further emphasized and reinforced the connection to her sister by using the location feature (which at the time allowed users to write anything they wanted in that slot), not to tag their location but to provide a second caption: "why is she my height?" referring to the irony that her six-years-younger sister is as tall as she is.

Another of Corinne's examples is a picture of objects on a table: bowls of food and liquid-filled wineglasses surrounding sheets of paper topped by a pen. The picture was taken at an "Oscar party," and the sheets of paper are Oscar ballots. Corinne's friend Sydney, who had posted the photo, tagged their housemates and friends who were at the party, though they don't appear in the photo. She captioned the photo, "and the Oscar goes to . . ." and added the location "Main Street" to complete the caption. (One of the tagged friends completed the caption in the same way, by leaving a comment consisting of the address where the party took place: "123 Main Street!!!!!") Corinne explained that whereas "the image on its own might, at first glance, scream 'Look at me and this cool party I had,'" it actually stresses the group cohesion among the friends who attended the party: since each one contributed food or drink, posting the photos of what they brought, plus tagging and thereby naming them, was a way to thank them for helping to make the party a success and to remind them of their shared evening. In all these ways, Corinne and her friends adapted Instagram's features to extend the connections among them, just as girls and women tended to do through conversation before social media.

Since girls and women tend to frown on self-promotion, many have developed a code of selfie etiquette. A student in my class, Serena Gleklen, laid out the rules that the young women in her cohort tend to observe: a girl who posts a picture of herself on Instagram must show that she doesn't take herself too seriously, either by mugging or with a self-deprecating or humorous caption or, preferably, both. The location tag should not be accurate but rather should contribute to the humor, and captions should be lighthearted, as reflected in spelling errors, lack of punctuation, and addition of emojis and hashtags. All these elements send a metamessage, "I'm not making myself the center of attention here," even as, by posting pictures of themselves, they are doing just that.

Absent Presence: There While Not There

Sending pictures, even selfies, can be the opposite of self-focused by creating a sense of shared presence despite absence. People who are together in physical space are looking at the same surroundings, and that common perspective contributes to the closeness that shared presence can create. When two people are apart, that aspect of consciousness is different for each, and that's a big part of the separation that distance creates. Sending pictures spans that gulf: it brings people into your space (virtually), allowing them to see the world as you are seeing it at that moment. No wonder that taking and sending pictures so quickly overtook the sending of typed-word messages, and that word messages often include pictures or begin with them. A student in my class, Kaley Palanjian, examined thirty text messages that she and two friends sent. She found that more than half began with a photo. Pictures are handy for starting conversations on social media, just as you might comment on something in your surroundings to start a conversation face to face. A woman in her twenties, describing her digital conversations with friends, said, "There's a lot of pictures of something and then you talk about the picture and then from that it's, 'Oh hey what else is going on?'"

Here's another example that Kaley Palanjian analyzed; it shows how a single picture can carry layers of meaning and create connection. Kaley's friend and roommate Denise sent her a photo of the back of her hand with the caption "The tomfoolery cannot be erased." Her hand? Why would anyone send a picture of that? If you look closely, you see some blurry print. The night before, Kaley and Denise had gone to a bar where their hands were stamped when they entered. By showing Kaley that traces of the stamp were still visible, Denise reminded her of their shared experience, and added humor by characterizing their outing as "tomfoolery." Kaley pointed out that because they live in the same house, Denise would not have had to wait very long to show Kaley her hand in person. But sending the photo accomplished something very different and very special: it reminded Kaley that not only do she and Denise spend much of their time together but they are connected even when apart. You might say they are virtually present in each other's lives all the time, thanks to social media. It's the very trivialness, the day-to-dayness, of the photograph that re-creates the experience of being together and sends a metamessage about how close they are.

It might seem at first that living in the same house would mean less need for friends to text each other. But Kaley explained why becoming roommates led to more frequent texting: "We felt this need to continue the sense of always being together. If we were together and saw a guy we thought was cute, we'd talk about it. So if we saw a cute guy and weren't together, we'd text about it." The point wasn't the message—whatever they were saying about the guy—but the metamessage: we're so connected that we share these fleeting impressions. Texting creates a sense of being together even when you're not.

An activity that has massively shifted from in person to online is shopping. For many women, shopping together was something they did with friends (and with mothers, daughters, or sisters), so this shift could be a loss to those relationships. Yet many have found ways to use shopping as the basis for connecting through social media. For example, a woman told me how she does this with two close friends: "If I haven't talked to one of them in a while, haven't connected with them for lunch or drinks and haven't seen them at a school event, I will send a photo of something, like a picture of something online, and just for fun I will say, 'frumpy or fabulous? I'm going to think about buying this.' I'm probably not going to buy it, but it's just to get their attention, and say, 'Hi, I'm here,' and remind them of our shared interest in clothing. And it just takes two seconds, and they send me something comical, and it reminds us of our common interest." Sending a photo with the question "frumpy or fabulous?" creates a connection without taking a big chunk of time.

What if someone is genuinely considering whether or not to buy something online? Friends can shop together virtually by exchanging links to retail websites. Two friends, for example, used iMessage to collaborate on a gift for a mutual friend by sending each other links and discussing the pros and cons of the various options. Texting can also bring a friend along virtually if you're shopping in a store without her. A woman who had just bought a pair of earrings snapped a photo of one in her ear and texted it to her friend, who responded:

> OMG!!!!! THEY ARE SOSOSOSOSO GORGEOUS!!!!!!!!!!
> just so YOU and so perfect!!!!!! Absolutely beautiful!!!!!!!

Her friend used the capabilities of a smart phone keyboard to dramatize the enthusiasm that's expected, even required, among girls and women. The CAPS, repetition ("SOSOSOSOSO"), and multiple exclamation points all conveyed the sense of excitement that she would have shown by facial expressions, body language, and vocal features such as intonation, pitch, and drawn-out vowels, had she been physically present. Actually, her typed emphasis was exaggerated, to make up for the fact that she wasn't there—and to be humorous. Incidentally, the sender was not a teenager but a woman in her fifties—a physician—being playful, just as women of all ages cherish friends they can be silly with.

Texting: Written Conversation

When women told me they "talk" to a friend every day, they might mean they talk voice to voice, in person, or by phone, or they might mean they text. A high school student told me if she or a friend lets too much time pass before responding to a text, the other will call on the phone and say, "Answer the text please!" They don't expect the answer to be given over the phone; the phone call is a prompt to continue the conversation by text. For them, as for many others, texting is conversation and conversation is texting.

Texting can be both more and less intrusive than communication over other digital platforms. A text message intrudes on your consciousness, demanding attention *now* regardless of what you are doing when it arrives. But it breaks concentration less because it's short and stands alone, and the one who receives it can put off replying. Email is less intrusive if your phone is not set to notify you when new mail arrives, but if you go to your in-box to see one message, you can't avoid seeing others that are there, too; the tantalizing bold typeface that announces an unopened message can be irresistible, because of FOMO or just the allure of something new and unexamined, a small mystery. Before you know it, you're opening and reading one and then another and another, till your attention is pulled thoroughly away from whatever you were doing before you stopped for what you thought would be a quick interruption. Though a text is more intrusive because it comes unbidden, it is less so because it comes solo.

Texting provides new ways of watching out for friends. A college student wanted to avoid a young man she had dated briefly, because running into him was awkward. As (bad) luck would have it, that very young man took a work-study job checking the IDs of students entering her dorm. If her friends saw him down there, they'd text: "Don't go downstairs right now." But using the immediacy of texting to watch out for a friend can have unintended consequences, because of the way it can interact with other platforms, like Facebook. A student in my class, Natasha, described how a serious but brief flurry of anxiety among a small number of friends mushroomed into a Facebook spectacle involving more than sixty-five people.

Following a late-night party at a Georgetown nightclub, a senior, Paige, disappeared. Her worried friends began frantically calling and texting everyone they knew to ask if anyone knew where Paige was. After about four hours, they learned that she had gone home with friends who had graduated the year before, and fallen asleep at their house. That settled the matter—or would have, were it not for Facebook. Natasha had gone to sleep before all this happened, but when she awoke the next morning, her Facebook News Feed was ablast with this event. Once they knew that Paige was safe, her friends had taken screen shots of the frantic text messages they had received and posted them on her Facebook page where they could be seen by anyone who could see the page— together with wry and humorous comments. In one case, forty-seven people "liked" the screen shots (indicating not that they literally "liked" them, as in "fond of," but that they had taken note of them) and four wrote out comments. As much as twenty-four hours later, at least one friend was still unsure of the status of those texts and posted her concern: "Paige, with all the stuff I've been seeing I feel obligated to ask if you are 1) alive 2) know where you are and 3) safe."

Though the sixty-five people who participated in this Facebook drama included both women and men, their levels and types of participation were different. Young men had done most of the "liking," that is, registering their involvement in a minimalist way, whereas young women had written out most of the comments: extended verbal interactions replete with generous sprinklings of ??????s, !!!!!!!!!!!!!!!s, and emoticons. This pattern is not surprising, not only because it was a young woman who had disappeared but because they were showing their concern through talk, and displaying the depth of their caring through digital expressions of enthusiasm—exactly what girls and women expect of their friends in conversation.

Searching for a missing friend could easily have been accomplished through phone calls rather than typed messages, and the friends could have talked about what happened the next day, voice to voice. But what expanded the disappearance to include so many people and to extend into the next day was the ability to take screen shots and post them on Facebook. That ability, and the knowledge that others have it, means that nothing on a screen is really private. This is a liability but also an opportunity. If you are telling a friend about something that happened, you often report what was said. If the conversation you're reporting was spoken, you probably won't remember the exact words, and even if you did, you couldn't re-create the tone of voice and inflections with which they were said—and you have no way of proving that your account is accurate. But if what you're reporting was "said" in print—in a text, or a Facebook, Instagram, or email message—you can show it in exactly the form you received it. A young woman was telling her friend why she was upset: a man who had professed eternal love was now showing no interest in her at all. To support her point, she took a screen shot of a text he had sent her only a few months before—"You are the love of my life," he had written. "You are the best thing that ever happened to me. I know we are forever!"—followed by several lines of red hearts. Anyone who has been told by a friend, "Maybe you got the wrong impression; maybe he didn't mean it that way," can appreciate the satisfaction of being able to show a friend exactly what was said, knowing she will then understand and not second-guess your feelings.

Finding Your Footing on Shifting Ground

Social media platforms are so many, so varied, and so rapidly changing that assumptions about right and wrong ways to use them vary as well. Even women friends the same age can have different assumptions about media platforms: what's appropriate, what's expected, what's right. There have always been ways that infidelity could be uncovered: letters discovered, telltale traces let slip. Modern variations on that theme often involve digital media: an email message left open on a screen, or a text message that pops up on a phone lying faceup on a table. A young woman got an unexpected chance to view her boyfriend's Facebook page when he opened it on her cellphone and neglected to log out. After he'd left, a name appeared on her phone's screen with a heart beside it. Recognizing the name as his former girlfriend's, she had a moment's hesitation: the message was intended for him, not her, so she shouldn't open it. But it was, after all, her phone, so she went ahead and clicked. Boom! Before her were romantic messages with date stamps spanning the entire time she'd been seeing him. All her friends understood her decision to end the relationship, but some of them found more fault with her for clicking on his message than with him for cheating on her.

Even best friends can differ in their ideas about appropriate ways to use social media. Lara and Connie had been close friends in college, and they stayed in touch after graduation, often having long telephone conversations catching up and keeping up. After a number of years, however, they began communicating through texting. This meant more frequent conversations—often daily or even multiple times a day. So Lara was surprised when Connie registered a complaint: she'd been telling Lara about problems she was having, and felt that Lara's responses hadn't shown real concern: they were too casual and cryptic. Connie missed her caring, emotionally supportive friend. They traced the trouble to different assumptions about texting. To Lara, comforting closeness resided in the frequency of their exchanges. To Connie, frequency didn't substitute for the expression of feeling and extended troubles talk that they'd shared in the past—a kind of conversation that Lara didn't feel could or should take place through texting.

What Does It Mean?

Because talk plays such a large role in most women's friendships, knowing which platforms your friends use and how they use them becomes essential. Some friends will answer texts but not emails. Others don't regularly check their phones so you can't rely on texting to reach them. The proliferation of platforms means more options to exploit but also more opportunities for messages to be misinterpreted. How quickly does a particular friend usually reply to a text or email? What does the lack of a response mean? Silence in conversation can be an eloquent, often negative, communication. But what constitutes silence in a digital conversation? A woman told me that when she transferred from one college to another, her roommate from the first one stopped talking to her. She explained, "She'd text me back two days later." A two-day delay was tantamount to not talking at all.

Even a brief delay in responding to a text can feel like deliberate silence, and sometimes it is. A woman said of a text she received from a friend, "I was so annoyed, I'm just not responding. I just didn't answer." Yet in other cases, silence doesn't mean anything at all; it results from circumstances, like being busy or misplacing a phone. And what if a response is quick but cryptic? That, too, can mean that a friend is annoyed or even angry. But then again it might not. Rebecca received a text from a friend canceling a lunch date the same day because she had to help her daughter complete an assignment. Rebecca texted back, "OK no problem!" To that she received a concerned response: "uh-oh you sound annoyed. I hope you're not, but I'm worried. I just tried to call you and you didn't answer, which worries me more! I'll try again later! And please forgive me if my last minute copout caused any trouble." Rebecca replied, "Goodness, no, I'm not annoyed. My message was short because I was stopped at a red light. I completely understand, and hope the assignment turns out well." Rebecca's message was brief because of the situation she was in when she received the text, but it set off alarms because it lacked the extra words that women typically add to reassure friends of their goodwill and positive disposition.

Metamessages—intended or unintended—can reside in just about any aspect of digital communication, even something as minor and automatic as listing recipients' names. Whenever you send an email to more than one person, if you enter the addresses on the "to" or the "cc" line, everyone who receives it can see who else is getting the same message, and what order you put the names in. This can lead to strong feelings, as two women, Vivian and Gabby, explained: "You feel special when you're the first one on there," Vivian said. Gabby agreed: "You do. And you feel not special when you're the last one." Vivian concurred: "Because if you're dead last, it's like they were thinking, Who am I forgetting?" To avoid offending those whose names come later or last, you can put recipients' email addresses on the bcc line. But that is what people do when sending a message to a long list of recipients, so "It looks like you're inviting all of Northwest Washington!" Software developers aware of this dilemma came up with a solution: a program that puts each recipient's name at the head of the list on the message that goes to them. Gabby received an email at work and thought, Ooh, my name is first. Then she happened to see the same email on a colleague's screen and was surprised, and amused, to see that the version her colleague received had her own name first. That was a case of intentionally misleading metamessages.

Read Receipts

A feature with vast opportunities for creativity, but also for miscommunication, is "read receipts," whereby senders are alerted when their messages have been opened and, presumably, read. Read receipts can be reassuring, since electronic messages sometimes fall into a black hole: you don't know if they've arrived or if the recipient saw them. But read receipts can also be misleading, and can be used to communicate a range of meanings, as my student Holly DiClemente pointed out in a paper written for my class. Some people keep the feature on, so someone they're mad at will see that they read their message and are intentionally not responding—a visual virtual snub. But it doesn't always mean that. Someone may open a message and read it, but put off replying until she has the time to write a thoughtful response. The person who sent the message can't know the recipient's motive, so she might feel snubbed, getting the mistaken impression that her friend intends not to reply—and to make that intention known.

If the phone or platform she's using allows it, someone can turn off the read receipts feature to avoid such misinterpretations. But if she doesn't have that option, or doesn't want to use it, she can resort to "ghost reading": reading a message without opening it, so the sender won't know it was read. That way, for example, if someone sends a message asking a friend if she wants to hang out, and the receiver doesn't want to but doesn't want to hurt her friend's feelings, she can open the message later and say, "I'm so sorry, I just got this." It's also possible to open a message and not read it, which might happen if someone sees it's long and doesn't have time to read a long message just then. In this case, too, the "read receipt" function is misleading. It should really be called "opened" not "read." Though everyone who uses this feature knows these possibilities, many still feel hurt or annoyed if they get a read receipt to a message but no reply. What they get is an image of a friend blowing them off, and an invitation to imagine any number of reasons why she isn't replying, none of which might be true. This can—and does—happen to men as well as women, but it has special resonance for girls and women, because they are particularly sensitive to implications of being left out or pushed away—and particularly eager to avoid hurting the feelings of friends who, they know, have similar sensitivities.

Kaley Palanjian described how she and her friend Denise made creative use of this and other features to resolve a conflict. It wasn't actually a fight, but Kaley had been genuinely upset by something Denise said—upset enough to walk out. They then resolved the situation and reestablished harmony by using the capabilities of social media to reframe the conflict as play: "She texted me 'please don't be mad' and I sent her the words 'read receipt.' If I had not replied, it would have shown that I saw it and just didn't respond. So saying 'read receipt' was acknowledging that it was passive-aggressive, because that's the association with read receipts, but not actually being passive-aggressive because this was play fighting." Kaley and her friend also used GIFs—very short video clips that repeat in a loop: "We texted about it after but through GIFs that were angry or upset or 'I'm not talking to you,' but because it was a GIF you knew it was a joke. So I didn't have to surrender, and Denise was apologizing but not in a serious way. She was sending me these GIFs of cats dancing through a field, 'we're best friends.' And then I would send like Urkel saying, 'I'm over you.' You know it was a joke because it was ridiculous that I was sending a picture image but the words were conflict, as if we were having a serious conversation." The message, conflict, was overridden by the metamessage of humor, and therefore goodwill, that was communicated by putting the words into the voice and image of a popular TV sitcom character. And it all started with the phrase "read receipt."

Age Matters

Most friendships, including most women's, are among people of the same age, so friendships across generations can feel special. Age differences can bring different perspectives and assumptions that both friends value. But habits and assumptions regarding social media can make conversations between friends of different ages like cross-cultural communication. In a way, younger women are native speakers of social media, while older ones can be like second-language learners—and their odd usages can lead to misunderstanding.

A young woman texts about being unhappy, and her older friend writes words of comfort, then closes with LOL. She thinks these letters mean "lots of love," but to her young friend, they mean "laughing out loud"—not quite the sentiment intended. Then there's punctuation. A young woman texts exciting news to an older friend, and receives the response "Wow . . ." The friend, like many of her generation, uses three dots to mean, "and so on, more and more." But to younger people three dots undercut what came before. "Wow!" needs an exclamation point to feel celebratory. "Wow . . ." with three dots sounds sarcastic, as if to imply, "Couldn't you do better than that?" Even the simple period, which many older people automatically place at the ends of sentences, is likely to be interpreted negatively by younger ones, who wouldn't use a period unless they were angry. This happened when a college student received a text asking, "Talk in 30?" and replied "I'm free now and in 3 hours." The response—"Now."—made her think she was in for a tongue lashing, so she was relieved, and surprised, to make the call and find herself having a routine friendly conversation. The period after "Now" had not been intended to express anger, as it would have had a peer used it in that way.

Women friends of different ages can get the impression that the other is rude when they're actually being considerate in different ways. An older friend feels snubbed when her young friend checks her phone while they're together, but she's only doing what's expected among her same-age friends—responding to a text in a timely way. Doing otherwise would constitute rudeness to the friend who texted. Knowing that, her peers wouldn't be offended, so long as the time she takes to respond to a text is relatively brief. Both women are honoring codes that require attention to friends, but the young friend's generation has evolved new norms to accommodate the omnipresence of friends on social media, while the older one is still applying norms from before, when the only significant presence was physical.

To many women, attention to a screen can go beyond rude: as one woman put it, "Devices can ruin a friendship." I've heard of several instances where they did. In one case a woman who took a trip to Europe with an old friend from college said she'd never travel with that friend again because she spent the whole time emailing and texting. Another told me of a friend whose company she'd enjoyed for years, "until iPhones came." Then: "You will talk and she's not really listening. When my husband does that, I can say, 'I'll wait.' But I can't say that to a friend." Instead, she gave up the friendship. Yet another woman said that just putting a phone on the table is reason enough to give up a friend, because doing that shows she isn't really there; she's more interested in someone who might pop up on her screen. All these practices, anathema to many in one generation, are a normal part of life to many in another.

A college student, Felice, mentioned "two women that I communicate with back home, and they're older—thirty-five and forty-fiveish—women that I grew up with who I think now would consider me a friend." These older friends communicate with Felice through Facebook Messenger, but they use it—and expect her to use it—in a way that she and her peers would not. They assume that whenever Felice has Facebook open, she's available to talk through Messenger. In fact, Felice explained, "I could be on my phone just scrolling and not wanting to chitchat, or I could have it up in the background while I'm in class and they'll try and talk to me while I'm in class." (This couldn't happen in my class, because I don't allow laptops or other devices!) "I am never sitting at my computer long enough to type out long messages," Felice said, which is probably why she and her same-age friends tend to chat by texting instead.

Conversational Style—in Writing

Girls and women tend to text more often and to send longer texts, and they are more likely to exchange personal information that way, as compared to boys and men. (The same is true on social networking sites and apps like Facebook and Instagram.) They also tend to use more exclamation points, emoticons, emojis, capitalization, and repetition of words ("SOSOSOSOSO GORGEOUS"), punctuation (?????), and letters ("soooooo sorry," "a verrrrry long time"). All these are ways to do through typing what they would do in speech by changes in pitch and intonation and drawing out sounds: show enthusiasm. These expressions of enthusiasm are so common among girls and women that they are expected; not using them comes across as cold or angry. The greeting "Hi" is typically written as "Hiiiii" or "Haii" because "Hi" with one "i" feels frosty.

A student in my class, Jonice Jackson, noticed an irony. During their first year of college, she and her two close friends from high school stayed in touch. When they made plans to get together during spring break, the messages they exchanged either used no exclamation points or used just one:

> i'm so excited to see y'all though! Miss you so much
> Me too! Super super excited

But after another year passed, their new lives and new friends became their focus in college, and they'd grown apart. Jonice noticed that their GroupMe exchange now used more exclamation points as well as heart emojis:

> I know it's been forever but I miss y'all!! {red heart} {red heart}
> Aww! i miss you guys too!!

Jonice pointed out that they used the extra punctuation and bright red heart emojis to make up for that distance.

These ways of writing conversation reflect patterns that typify women's and girls' ways of talking to friends. Boys and men, who are less likely to just sit and talk when they get together with friends, tend to use texting to send jokes and make plans but not for extended conversation. I was intrigued that lesbians I interviewed mentioned differences they'd observed between masculine-presenting and feminine-presenting lesbian friends. Someone I interviewed, Halle, who self-identifies as queer, contrasted two friends' preferences with regard to texting as compared to phone conversation. With the "more masculine" lesbian friend, Halle said, they text only to make plans. The more feminine friend likes to call. "I don't really like talking on the phone," Halle said—unless, of course, they're in a relationship.

There are parallel gender differences among women and men having digital conversations with friends in all cultures where this has been studied. For example, Fathiya Al Rashdi compared messages that were exchanged among an all-female group and an all-male group of Omani friends and relatives using WhatsApp. She found that both women and men frequently used a thumbs-up emoji to show approval, but the women often intensified their approval by adding other emojis, such as smiling faces, whereas the men, with only one exception, used the thumbs-up icon alone. This pattern parallels American women's routine displays of enthusiasm by repeating letters, adding multiple exclamation points, and capitalizing words—to avoid giving the opposite impression.

Al Rashdi also noticed that certain emojis were used by friends of one gender but not the other. The men in her study sometimes used the thumbs-down emoji to show disapproval, something the women in her study never did. An emoji that the women used, and the men didn't, was an ear. They used it to mean "I'm listening" or "I'm paying attention." This is in line with the valuing of talk—and listening—that is pervasive in girls' and women's relationships, in contrast to the focus on doing things together that is more common among boys and men. The focus on action is also reflected in another pattern Al Rashdi observed: the men in her study often ended WhatsApp conversations with a pair of emojis representing action: a man running and a cloud of dust. In contrast, the women's standard way of closing was a kissing emoji—a face with a little heart on its cheek, representing a kiss. While kissing is also an action, the substitution of a heart in place of the face doing the kissing emphasized the attitude or emotion that goes with the action—affection.

What's Real, What's Fake?

Keeping friends up to date on what's going on in your life is a requirement for women and girls: friends expect to be informed and may be hurt or even angry if they're not. Facebook and other social media can be a boon in this regard, by making it easier to keep more people up to date. But that blessing is mixed, because women can also be hurt to learn of important developments in a friend's life through that public medium: they perceive a metamessage, "You're not a close enough friend for me to tell you personally." And friends can have very different ideas about what medium is appropriate for what kinds of news.

When Courtney's sister didn't give birth by her due date, and the past-due days piled up, her sister kept family and friends apprised of and involved in the dramatic waiting game by posting frequently on Facebook. In response, even casual friends responded with encouragement and well wishes, such as "I was late, too, and I turned out pretty well!" Courtney felt that these postings sent her sister a precious metamessage—many people love her and care about her pregnancy—strengthening her network of support. Were it not for Facebook, many of these friends (and more distant relatives) would have been keeping abreast of the pregnancy through others, and her sister would have been unaware of their caring. Courtney was surprised to learn that her roommate had a very different view. She told Courtney that she would have been offended to be kept up to date about a friend's pregnancy by Facebook; she would think, "Geez, why didn't you call?" Her roommate reasoned that posting on Facebook is so easy that it means nothing. A phone conversation reflects and creates a meaningful relationship, whereas Facebook creates a false sense of intimacy, not a real relationship.

The impression that posting on Facebook is insincere because it's too easy sounds a lot like why a friend told me (on email) she dislikes "THAT DRAT 'xoxo,' which means nothing, just keys to hit." I replied that I kind of like those letters, because they fill a need: a more affectionate way to close than "Best" but not as fervent as "Love," which, in any case, some people don't feel comfortable using with friends, though some do. She further explained that "xoxo" strikes her as "rushed, unthinking, impersonal," and added, "It's a cop-out. It's so much easier to type the meaningless symbols than to think about how one wants to sign off—what degree of warmth or affection one wants to express." This perspective—if something is too easy it's meaningless or insincere—makes sense. Taking time sends a metamessage of caring. But why is it easier to type "xoxo" than to type "love"? I think it comes down to expectations and associations. The word "love" feels like the real thing because that's what the word means. Maybe "xoxo" can seem fake because it's a substitution, standing for "hugs and kisses" but not denoting it. Or maybe "xoxo" just seems too cutesy, given its traditional association with the handwritten letters of teenage girls.

Intrigued by this difference of opinion, I kept an eye out for x's and o's in emails I received. I noticed these letters in a brief exchange I had with someone I didn't know well but had had a particularly warm interaction with. She signed her first email to me "With affection." I signed my reply "Warmly." She closed her next email "Xo." I took this as intending to move our connection a notch closer, so I ended my reply to that message "xoxo." By accepting the shift from words to the informal letters, I was accepting the invitation to closeness. By doubling them, I was saying, "I meet your move and I up it." The metamessage of x's and o's was increasing familiarity, getting closer. I began to admire the flexibility of these two simple letters to negotiate closeness in digital conversations, a negotiation that plays such a large role in girls' and women's friendships.

Switching to x's and o's can also be a way to wind down an exchange.

Sometimes it's hard to know which email should go unanswered, ending the thread. You give me information I asked for, and I thank you. Is that the end of it, or do you have to come back with "You're welcome"? You write me a complimentary email and I respond in kind; does our exchange end there, or are you supposed to respond to my compliment with a thank-you? And if you do, should I respond to that? Someone with whom I had a mutually complimentary exchange used the magic letters to respond to my response without prolonging the email thread. Her reply to my reply to her email was "Xoxoxoxoxoxo!" I found this stand-alone expression of goodwill charming, so I acknowledged it with a virtual smile—":)". That ended the thread. The metamessage of her "Xoxoxoxoxoxo!" was "This isn't an actual message you have to respond to, but I want you to know I'm feeling positive toward you." My reply matched hers by using an emoticon rather than words, mirroring her positive intent, while the brevity of a two-keystroke missive signaled a closing to our exchange.

Clearly I like the creativity and flexibility of x's, o's, and emoticons. But I know that others find them insincere, even fake. All communication raises the question: how do you judge whether speakers or writers really mean and feel what they say, or if they are only trying to have a desired effect? Distinguishing what's real and what's fake, something we do all the time in any exchange, is particularly challenging in digital communication, because norms and expectations change so quickly and can differ so much from one person to another.

Finstagram: The Real Fake Thing

Many young women post pictures of themselves on the photo-sharing site Instagram. In recent years, they have taken to posting entirely different pictures of themselves in addition—photos they allow only a small number of friends to see. These alternate Instagram accounts are referred to as finstagram, or finsta—and, as with Instagram itself, a majority of users are young women. Reading a *New York Times* article about it, I was struck that everything said about how young people use finstagram is resonant of dynamics and challenges more generally associated with women's friendships. Start with the name and its striking irony: the letter "f" means "fake," yet we are told that finstagram's fake accounts allow users to "present truer versions of themselves" than is possible on Instagram. Discerning what is true and what is fake is a challenge that comes with friendship. A comment I heard often is that a true friend is someone with whom you can be your true self. I also heard of a corresponding disappointment that comes from learning that a friend was not the person you thought her to be—in other words, she had not been showing her true self.

Inextricable from the fake-real conundrum is the way that social media, like the Internet, have obscured, confused, and transformed our notion of public and private—a challenge that is fundamental to girls' and women's friendships, because of the special role played by exchanging secrets and the risk that secrets, by definition private, will be repeated to others—that is, made public. As a young finstagram user put it, "If you're going to post embarrassing things, you have to trust that group of people to not share it out." Inevitably, as with secrets told in conversation, sometimes that trust turns out to be misplaced. Much as secrets exchanged among supposed friends can turn up as rumors or gossip, high school students' compromising finstagram photos have found their way to school administrators. To lessen this risk, an eighteen-year-old is quoted as saying, "Finstas are private accounts that you only let your closest friends follow." Then it turns out she has about 50 finstagram followers. Fifty closest friends? Well, yes, in contrast with her 2,700 followers on Instagram. The proportions of this teen's numbers are similar to those of others quoted in the article. For example, another says that on finstagram, "You tend to follow your best friends," and notes that she has 33 on hers, compared to 370 on her Instagram account.

The plot thickens. What do young women post on finstagram? "Things you wouldn't want anyone but your closest friends to see, like unattractive pictures, random stories about your day and drunk pictures from parties." If the pictures are unattractive, why post them at all? Maybe to show you are unaffected and willing to let your friends see you with your hair, figuratively or literally, down. This, too, was a sign of close friendship that women often mentioned. Random stories about your day? That's typical of women's conversations with those they are close to.

If finstagram is about your true self rather than the made-for-public-consumption self that Instagram encourages, it is confusing to read of the teen who "took on an alter ego on her fake account, filling it with images and captions meant to portray her as a right-wing 'trophy wife'"—a "character" that was so far from who she really is that her friends would know it was a joke. Yet presenting yourself as completely different from your true self as a sign of true friendship isn't as odd as it may sound. A woman told me, as evidence of how close she and a friend were, that they had taken on fake roles: they wangled their way into a construction site in their neighborhood by pretending to be members of the architectural review committee. Many women said that they valued in close friends the ability to be silly together, and even more women mentioned humor—being able to laugh together—as a key to friendship. The idea that portraying yourself as other than you are is something you do only with your closest friends makes sense in a similar way.

Enforced Overhearing

During spring break, Alicia visited her sister Jan in New York City. She posted on Instagram a picture of herself and her sister in front of a Broadway theater and Geotagged the location. On returning to her college town at the end of spring break, she was walking toward her house pulling her roller bag behind her when she saw Heather coming toward her. As they passed, Heather said, "Hey, Alicia. How was New York? Did you have a nice time with Jan?" Alicia replied, "It was good, thanks," and kept walking. A pleasant, insignificant exchange, right? Far from it. The chance encounter left Alicia feeling hurt and upset. She and Heather had been roommates and very good friends the year before. Though they had moved on to different living arrangements, Alicia had assumed they'd remain friends, but that didn't happen. Heather never accepted Alicia's offers to get together and never initiated any, so Alicia backed off. Heather had obviously decided not to continue their friendship. So the way she greeted Alicia when they passed on the street was a hurtful reminder of their past friendship—and it was thanks to social media.

That Alicia had spent the weekend in New York was information available to anyone who followed her on Instagram. By posting and Geotagging the photo, she had made that information public. But that the person with her in the photo was her sister, and that her sister was named Jan—Heather knew those things only because of their former friendship. Had Heather asked simply "How was New York?" she would have been drawing on public information, in keeping with the distance of their current relationship. But by asking if she had a nice time with Jan, Heather was reminding Alicia that they'd once been good friends—and that she'd been following her on Instagram but didn't care enough even to "like" the photo, the minimal response possible. All in all, the metamessage of Heather's greeting was that Alicia was now just a social media presence to someone who had once been a friend.

Painful reminders that a former close friend no longer is can occur not only because of but on social media. Imagine you're in a stall in a restroom behind a closed door when you hear familiar voices. With a sense of horror you realize you're overhearing former friends talking in ways they wouldn't if they knew you were there. This unsettling experience, relatively uncommon in face-to-face life, is a frequent occurrence and perennial risk with digital communication, especially when messages are sent to more than one person at the same time. This is one of many ironies of social media conversation: on one hand, technologies that make it possible to communicate with all members of a group at once can enhance feelings of connection. But, on the other hand, they can spotlight a lack of connection, as happened when a college student sent an email to her four close friends from high school. Just as Alicia winced because her former friend Heather's greeting reminded her of their lost friendship, one of the friends who received this group email objected loudly. The student who told me about this exchange called it email drama.

The five girls, who had formed a friend group in high school, ended up at three colleges: two at one, two at another, and the fifth by herself at a third. In their first year of college, all five maintained their sense of solidarity by participating in group "life update" emails that went to everyone. But as their college years progressed, each pair of girls who attended the same college experienced a falling-out, until, in their senior year, they had virtually stopped talking to each other. The digital drama was touched off when the fifth friend, who was still on good terms with all four of the others, decided to send a "life update" email to all of them. First one and then a second of those recipients objected on the grounds that addressing the group as if they were still all friends was—as Alicia had labeled Heather's greeting—"inauthentic," reflecting once again the fake-real dilemma.

The first to object was Calley. With apologies for introducing a contentious tone, she pointed out that she and the second member of their high school group who goes to the same college have seen each other "like three times" all year, so it was hurtful to read about grad school acceptances and decisions she had not been told about, and a boyfriend she had not been introduced to. Explaining that she didn't want to "pretend" that nothing had changed and they all still loved each other, Calley asked to be removed from the group email. Then Margaret, one of the two attending the other college who no longer spoke, emailed her agreement: it's "insincere," she said, to send emails to everyone "like everything is normal, just like it was in high school." Both Calley and Margaret said they'd be happy to hear from any of the others individually; it was only the group emails they objected to. They wanted to receive messages addressed to them personally; they did not want to read messages containing information that would not otherwise be said to them. They were seeking to avoid an inadvertent aspect of digital communication to multiple recipients: overhearing.

Sending messages to multiple recipients often leads to less significant but nonetheless awkward interactions. A group I was part of regularly exchanged emails about a project we were involved in. In one such email, a member of our group expressed well wishes to another about a medical condition, after which all the others chimed in, echoing the expressions of concern. I was puzzled. I didn't know whether this flurry of well wishes was related to the medical challenge I knew this group member had been experiencing or whether there had been a new and dangerous development I didn't know about. I did not want to ask the person in question, or the original well-wisher, because I did not want to reveal ignorance of something everyone else seemed to know. Instead, I asked another group member. She said she was not aware of any new developments either but wanted to express her general support for our ailing friend. Since I try to use the "reply-all" function sparingly, I sent my own well wishes but cc'd only the one who had first expressed concern. But as soon as I did that, I worried that the others would think me callous and uncaring, assuming I'd opted out of the group's choral support. I rather regretted having foregone the option of allowing—or forcing—everyone to overhear my well wishes.

There are instances in which enforced overhearing can be used strategically. Simone, for example, used that aspect of Facebook to communicate news that made her look good without bragging, which was unacceptable among her peers, as it is for most girls and women. The graduating seniors at her highly competitive high school all knew which colleges the others had applied to. As college acceptances and rejections began arriving, seniors typically used Facebook statuses to announce they'd been accepted at their first-choice schools. A status might read, "GEORGETOWN CLASS OF 2019!!!!" That was approved and expected because it announced a senior's plans. That it also announced her acceptance by a prestigious college was communicated indirectly. Someone who got into Georgetown but wasn't planning to go there wouldn't announce, "ACCEPTED AT GEORGETOWN!" That would be bragging. Following these customs, Simone couldn't let her peers know that she'd been accepted by a number of prestigious colleges, because she wasn't yet certain which one she would actually attend. But posting no college-related status would give the impression that she hadn't been accepted by any, since others' new statuses made it known that those colleges had sent out their decisions. Simone solved this dilemma by having her sister post messages on her Facebook page where any of her Facebook friends could see it: "Congrats on UVA acceptance! So proud of you!" That way Simone hadn't bragged; her peers learned of her acceptances by over-hearing.

Hard Times

Keeping friends informed of what's going on in your life is a requirement of women's friendships generally, but it becomes particularly urgent when what's going on is unfortunate. During hard times, troubles talk, which plays a large part in women's friendships under any circumstances, becomes especially important, but also challenging. Websites make it possible to keep friends and family informed and involved when some-one is facing a medical crisis, and to express condolences and grief when someone has died. And email makes possible communication that would not have happened, or would not have been as effective, by other means. Many people are able to "say" in writing—email, text, or other digital media—what they can't quite say by voice. This can also apply to positive communication. For example, a woman noticed that a friend who seemed never able to utter a compliment when they were talking in person freely offered them on email. Positive and emotional expressions become pre-cious at a time of personal tragedy. A woman who lost her husband told me (on email), "I've gotten hundreds and hundreds of emails and they've been wonderfully comforting." And these messages were comforting in specific ways that email made possible: "I feel no obligation to respond," she explained, "and in general they're more feeling and less stilted than what people write on cards."

Email gave me connection to a college friend—as it happened, a guy—who was diagnosed with metastatic lung cancer. Learning of his fatal illness was deeply upsetting; I thought of him continually. But I did not feel we were close enough friends to warrant calling him regularly on the phone. Email gave me a path along which I could walk beside him on his final journey. In the last year and a half of his life, we "talked" regularly on email, and not only about his health; we had expansive conversations like the ones we'd had in college, moving seamlessly from light topics to heavy ones, from funny to philosophical ones. The last message he sent me, two days before he died, ended with his goodbye: "I will miss our emails, deb, it was great being your friend, and I will always remain so." That message was precious to me—it still is—as was his friendship. And for the privilege of having received it, and of being able to talk to him so close to the end of his life, I am indebted to email.

My two sisters and I spent the twelfth anniversary of our mother's death together—virtually. Though we live in different states, we carried on a three-way conversation throughout the day—actually, two parallel three-way conversations: one by text and another by email. In keeping with Jewish tradition, we each lit a twenty-four-hour memorial candle, and, in keeping with our sisterly tradition, placed the candles beside photographs of our mother. Each of us took a photo of our candle and sent it by text to the others. We then used texting to talk about the photos we'd chosen and went on to discuss plans to visit the cemetery where our parents are buried—and plans for the ends of our own lives. A different conversation took place over email, where we talked at greater length about our memories of the days surrounding our mother's death, burial, and funeral, and also our father's. Had we talked to each other in a three-way phone conversation, it would have been comforting, but short-lived. The seemingly more distant digital media, texting and email, had allowed our conversations to continue, and allowed us to feel each other's company, across the entire day.

Connection to friends can be lifesaving when tragedy strikes. A woman whose husband died suddenly said, "One of the reasons I was able to get through my husband's death—I didn't get through it that well, but one thing that really helped me get through it—I have wonderful women friends." The same is true when dealing with serious illness. But the desire—the need—to keep friends informed can also be challenging when time is in short supply. The ability to send updates to friends and relatives with a single keystroke can be like a lifesaver, too. Calling or emailing each one separately would be emotionally and physically exhausting if not downright impossible.

Group texting can work in a similar way, but it comes with a liability. Though it's a relief to send one message to all at once, many or all might reply—and that can quickly create message overload, especially onerous if the messages arrive as texts. A woman whose husband had been hospitalized sent this text to family and friends:

> Going home today!
> Probably late
> Afternoon. Yea!!!! No
> need to reply. Too
> many texts ** I know
> you are all happy as
> we are.

Without that second sentence, she might have received a slew of "YAY"s and "SO HAPPY"s, each one's arrival announced by an intrusive ping or buzz.

For Better or Worse

It's not only in times of trouble that continual pings, buzzes, and rings can be crazy-making. Increasingly, that's a challenge under normal circumstances, especially as media platforms tend to evolve in ways that multiply the number of recipients. This tendency fits with women's and girls' inclination to not leave friends out (except of course when they want to). Snapchat, a mobile app through which users can send pictures, short videos and messages that disappear as soon as they are viewed, began as a type of instant messaging sent to a single recipient. It soon evolved to include stories, which both remain visible for twenty-four hours and also go to everyone on the sender's friend list. Sending messages to multiple recipients is the purpose of the app GroupMe, by which messages go to all in the group. It's common to set up GroupMe groups for all kinds of social units or joint activities. One woman told me that a group she's part of has three separate GroupMe groups: "one for random talk, one for social events, and one official one, for business stuff." She was also included in a GroupMe group for the women who were about to become her roommates later that month; another for a shared apartment planned for the following year; and one more for the work she'd be doing over the summer. In addition, she said, "I was a field manager for the Fund for the Public Interest, working on behalf of the Human Rights Campaign, and someone asked, 'Should we have a GroupMe?' Absolutely not! But they did." She commented, "I love everybody but sometimes I have to mute my phone because it drives me crazy, buzzing all the time."

Being able to send a message to many people at once is a great benefit if you're the sender, but when you're on the receiving end, the benefit is also a liability: the ease of sending messages increases exponentially the number of messages you receive. And the sheer number of messages is only the start. Like all the affordances and burdens of social media that I've described in this chapter—like all the affordances and burdens of women's friendships—gifts of connection can be wrapped in ribbons that sometimes get tied in knots and require effort and time to untangle. Often for better and sometimes for worse, social media are now a large part, and for many a constant part, of communication, which has always been at the heart of women's friendships.

My Friend, My Sister, My Self

What It Means to Be Close

"My friends are the sisters I was meant to have."

"My friends are more precious than my sisters because they remember things from my past that my sisters don't and can't, since they weren't there."

"I don't enjoy her company all that much, but it's beside the point. She's family."

In talking to women about their friendships, I was struck by how often I heard that one or another friend is "like family," and by how often I heard women friends compared to sisters—or sisters praised for also being friends. These comments, and how the women explained them, shed light on the nature of women's friendships, the nature of family, and something that lies at the heart of both: what it means to be close.

"He's Like My Brother"

When women told me about their best friends, in most cases those friends were also women. But sometimes they were men, and in most of those cases, they were gay men. My own best friend is a gay man. And our friendship is very much like the friendships that women described to me when they told me of their best friends, and of friends who are like family.

I often say of Karl, "He's like my brother." What I typically say next—"He's been my best friend since I was fifteen"—zeros in on one way that friends can be like family: longevity. Karl and I met at summer camp when we were both "work campers": we served meals to the younger campers. The seeds of closeness were planted during one of those wondrous extended self-revealing conversations that are a revelation to teenagers, when we began to talk after dinner behind the dining hall—and didn't stop until it got dark. After the summer ended, our friendship continued and deepened as we exchanged long letters that traversed the distance between our homes in Brooklyn and the Bronx. We also had long telephone conversations—often enough that I still remember his phone number. (I hear it in my mind now as I said it to myself then, starting with the letters "SY," for the exchange Sycamore, which I pronounced "sigh.") The only other phone number I recall that begins with letters was my own.

Karl and I often saw each other on weekends, as part of a small group of friends from camp. We kept in touch through college, and began spending more and more of our free time together when we were home during summers. After graduation, when we were both living in New York City, it was almost all our time. Several years later, he was living in England and France, and I was living in Greece, and again our friendship was carried out on paper: those flimsy blue self-folding airmail letters. Still more years later, we were both back in the States, and both living in Berkeley, where I was going to graduate school and he was teaching piano—and again we were constant companions. Karl is the star of my doctoral dissertation and first book, an analysis of the conversation during Thanksgiving dinner at his house in 1978. The next year I took up my position at Georgetown University in Washington, D.C., and once again our friendship was long distance. Nearly two decades later, we were traveling together when I showed him the photograph of a man I'd just met, saying, "It's crazy but I keep thinking I'm going to marry him"—and I did, with Karl as the master of ceremonies at our wedding.

We were there at key moments in each other's lives. Karl was the one I called at 2:00 A.M. when I made a last-minute decision not to join the Peace Corps, though I was all packed and had a ticket to fly to Hawaii for training—the next morning. I was there when Karl dropped out of college to study music and, years later, when he came out as gay. He knew my parents, my cousins, my first husband, and the other friends who have been important in my life, as I knew and know his. In the last years of her life, I visited his mother in a nursing home just as I'd have visited my own, had she lived in one. We can refer to anything and anyone in our pasts without having to explain—and sometimes one refers to something in the other's past that the other had forgotten. If either of us is upset about something, we call the other. I trust Karl's judgment, though I might not always follow his advice. When my husband and I spent a year in Palo Alto, California, Karl greeted our arrival as I knew my parents would have, had they been alive, and my sisters would have, had they lived nearby. As soon as we arrived, he and his partner, Richard, drove over from Berkeley. The fanfare with which they greeted the house we had rented—bringing flowers and little vases to put them in as a house-warming gift, touring the rooms and exclaiming about them—made the rented house feel like a new home.

Maybe most of all, Karl is like family because of how I feel when I'm around him: completely and unself-consciously myself.

Come Closer

All the elements that make Karl like my brother were threaded through the accounts of women who told me about their own best friends. The word they used most often to explain those special friendships was "close," and it could be emphasized by repetition: "close close friend" or "very very very very close friend."

For friends, as for family, "close" is the holy grail of relationships, especially for women. In both contexts I often heard "I wish we were closer" but never "I wish we weren't so close." But what people meant by "close" could be very different. It could mean they talk about anything; or that they see each other often; or that, though they don't see each other often, when they do, it's as though no time has passed: they just pick up where they left off. And sometimes "close" meant none of the above, but that they have a special connection, a connection of the heart.

There were also differences in what people had in mind when they said, "We can talk about anything." Paradoxically, it could be either very important, very personal topics or insignificant details. A woman said of one friend, "We're not that close; we wouldn't talk about problems in our kids' lives," but, of another, "We're not that close; we wouldn't talk about what we're having for dinner."

Why would talking about what you're having for dinner mean that you're close, or make you so? Years ago I was reminded of why when my great-aunt Mary, long widowed and living alone in her eighties, had a romantic relationship with a man who had known her—and had a crush on her—when they both were young. He lived in a nursing home in the Bronx while her apartment was in Manhattan, so they didn't get to be together often, but they spoke on the phone every day. To help me understand what this relationship meant to her, Aunt Mary told me about a conversation they'd had. She had been out one evening, attending an event on her own. Soon after she got home, her gentleman friend called. He asked how her evening had gone, and then he asked, "What did you wear?" Telling me this, Aunt Mary began to cry. "Do you know how many years it's been," she said, "since anyone asked me what I wore?"

Knowing that somewhere in the world there is someone who cares what you wore, an insignificant detail of your life that would seem unimportant to anyone else, makes you feel more connected to that person and less alone in the world. If you know you will tell someone later about something happening to you now, you begin to form the story in your mind as it is happening, hearing yourself telling it and imagining the reaction. So it's almost as if the person you'll tell it to is with you, experiencing it at the same time.

Thanks to technology, we now have an even more immediate way to bring others with us as we go about our day: snapping and sending pictures of the mundane things we are seeing. I once had occasion to witness how, and contemplate why, this could be. My husband and I had to mail a large carton, and were frustrated to discover that it was too big to fit in either the backseat or the trunk of our car. We were flummoxed, till we did something rash: we placed the large carton on the hood of our car and drove the short distance to the post office—very slowly, very carefully, and as close as possible to the sidewalk. I was not surprised to see people we passed on the street stopping to look and often to laugh. We must have made a bizarre sight, driving so slowly with a large portion of our windshield obscured by an enormous carton. But I was surprised by how many of them whipped out their phones and took pictures! Though we made an odd sight, surely it wasn't important enough to immortalize in a photo. Then I realized: having a picture to show would give more vividness when they later told someone, "I saw the funniest thing today." Or maybe they didn't wait till later but sent the photo to share the experience in real time, like poking someone standing beside them and exclaiming, "Look at that!"

Listen to Me

Knowing there is someone you can tell about your day—something that so many women treasure—is only half the story of connection. The other half is knowing that the person will listen. And listening has two parts, too. One part is seeming to be interested in what you're saying, and seeming to care about it. The other is understanding your words in the way that you meant them, and responding in the way you expect.

The act of listening itself can be precious, whether or not it comes with understanding. In this spirit, according to linguist Michal Marmorstein, it is common to hear Israeli women say about a friend, "I was her wailing wall." The metaphoric reference is to the holy wall in Jerusalem where people leave notes, which are meant to be private communications between themselves and God, by squeezing them between cracks in the stones. To be someone's wailing wall means to listen to her troubles and thoughts, secrets she would otherwise not impart to anyone. Like the sacred wall, Marmorstein explains, a listening friend is solid, strong, supportive, someone you can lean on. To be a wailing wall for a friend does not require that you necessarily understand or empathize—just that you listen.

Though simply listening can be a priceless show of caring and therefore of connection, it is even more precious to feel that you are being understood. Every time you open your mouth to speak, you are putting your personhood on the line—and entrusting it to the people you are speaking to. If they respond to what you say in the way you expect, their response reassures you that your words were reasonable and appropriate, and that you are a right sort of person. It's especially gratifying when this approval seems based on real understanding, of your words and therefore of you. It's in that spirit that a woman said of a friend, "She gets me. When I'm with her I can be myself."

A number of women commented that being close friends means that both can be themselves when they are together—as one woman put it, you can be "exactly who you are, without any façade." An Omani woman, for example, explained that true friends behave "naturally" in each other's homes. If someone persists in being formal—the Arabic word is *rasmy,* which is more or less what might be referred to in English as "standing on ceremony"—then it's "like she's not herself, I'm not myself," and "unless I am myself in front of someone, then she's not a friend, not a true friend." And being a true friend, she went on, also means you can tell each other things you might not even tell a sister, because "it's like being a friend with yourself."

A woman who said of a friend "She got me" went on to say, "She got me and all my quirks, and I got her and all her quirks and we were fine with it." There's a world of acceptance in that comment, "We were fine with it." It means you won't be rejected once a friend sees your frailties: you're accepted despite your weaknesses. Being yourself can also mean letting others see when you're unhappy. This, too, contrasts with a fear of rejection—the fear that lies behind the adage "Laugh, and the world laughs with you; cry, and you cry alone." With true friends, as with family, that should not apply. And often it doesn't. Elizabeth arrived at a friend's birthday party so upset that she had a meltdown—right in front of the party guests, who were all her friends. "I didn't feel embarrassed or ashamed," she said. The next day: "I wrote the host a funny text that said, 'Please fall apart at my birthday party. You have an open invitation to cry at my party.'" Her friend texted back, "I love you so much. You're so real. That's why we love you." Telling me about this, Elizabeth summed up, "And that to me is friendship." Her friend's response reflected the reciprocity of showing vulnerability. It is a gift not only to the one who has the meltdown but also to the ones who witness it. Friendship is the opposite of "cry, and you cry alone." Instead, "See a friend cry—or let a friend see you cry—and you both are less alone."

Honestly

A word that many women used to explain their appreciation for friends who reveal, and to whom they can reveal, vulnerability is "honest." For example, a woman, telling a friend (in an email) how much their friendship has meant to her, wrote, "These emails allow us to speak with depth and honesty, and not hide the more painful parts of our lives, and I cherish this true and honest connection we have."

Sometimes, though, "honest" meant saying negative things that a friend needs to hear, often about appearance. This, too, reminded me of family relationships, like the mother who told her daughter, before criticizing her, "I'm telling you because no one else will." One woman, for example, said that a friendship was born when she delivered bad news—

honestly. She knows this, because her friend told her: "The moment she knew that we were good friends is when she got a haircut that she thought was ugly and she asked me if it was ugly, and I said it was. That's how she knew." Another young woman, Rosalys, recalls telling a friend the truth about an even more intimate aspect of her appearance. The friend went through a phase of not wearing a bra. Rosalys recalls, "I was like, 'You need to wear a bra!' She was like, 'No, but my boobs are small.' I'm like, 'People can tell. Some girls have nice perky boobs that it doesn't show, but yours, unfortunately, are not that perky.'" Rosalys explained, "I'd rather be honest than have her looking like a hot mess." That's a true friend. And failing to tell a friend something that no one else will, but that she needs to hear, can seem like a failure of friendship.

Here is evidence of the assumption that friends will at least try to stop you from doing something that won't be good for you. Gloria Vanderbilt and her son Anderson Cooper were guests on NPR's *The Diane Rehm Show*, discussing a book they had written together. Vanderbilt was talking about a disastrous decision she'd made: at twenty-one, she married the sixty-three-year-old conductor Leopold Stokowski and, as she put it, "turned my life over to him." Her son asked, "Did any of your friends ever say, 'Wait a minute. You're twenty-one, you're beautiful, you have money on your own, and you're going to marry this sixty-three-year-old guy?' Did anybody—any friend—ever say, 'What's up with that?'" His mother replied, simply, "No." Diane Rehm then expressed her own incredulity: "Nobody did?" It is striking that Cooper didn't question his mother's judgment; he might well have asked, "Didn't you think, 'Wait a minute. I'm twenty-one, I'm beautiful, I have money on my own, and I'm going to marry this sixty-three-year-old guy?'" He seemed to accept that a twenty-one-year-old might make a foolish decision like that; what surprised him was that a friend didn't point it out. His question and Diane Rehm's repetition of it are eloquent testimony to the belief that a friend should at least caution you about, if not stop you from, doing something unwise.

There are cross-cultural differences in when and how a friend should be honest. In her book *Cultural Misunderstandings: The French-American Experience,* Raymonde Carroll notes that French and American notions of friendship result in differing habits and expectations in this regard. If an American feels that she has made a mistake or done something wrong, she might tell a friend about it, expecting the friend to say that what she did wasn't so bad, and she must have had good reasons for doing it. This will restore her self-confidence and make her feel better. In the same situation, Carroll writes, a French woman would be expected to take her friend's perspective—by agreeing that she'd made a mistake! Then she'd help her friend figure out how to repair the damage. Being told, "Yeah, what you did was pretty stupid," would, presumably, make an American feel worse, not just about her mistake but also about her friend. Why is she piling on? A friend should be supportive! According to Carroll, a French friend *is* being supportive, the French way. The one who made the mistake would leave the conversation saying, "Thank you. I feel much better. I knew it was time for me to let you set me straight." In other words, because you are my friend, I knew you'd be honest.

Please Come In

The place where people typically end the day is home, and home is where the archetypal family resides. So one way that friends can feel like family is by sharing a home, as college students do in dorms or young adults do in shared apartments. Like family, a roommate is there to return to—and report to—at the end of the day. You wouldn't call a friend to tell her you're out of sorts because the supermarket ran out of your favorite cereal, but you can tell your roommate as you're unpacking the groceries—or don't have to, because she was shopping with you. A similar feeling can come from being a frequent visitor in a friend's home, or just from how comfortable you feel when you're there. One woman put it this way:

"When other people visit, I can't bear it if they stay more than a few days. But she can stay a week. I can say, 'I need alone time now. Go away.'"

"Like family" can mean dropping in and making plans without planning. You might call up and say, "I just made lasagna. Why don't you come over for dinner?" Or you can invite yourself: "I'm feeling kind of low. Can I come to your house for dinner?" What makes it like family isn't only the spur-of-the-moment nature of the arrangements, but also the locale: the ease with which you're invited to—or are welcome in without being invited to—the most private place, another person's home. It's a physical analogue to talking about personal topics and private feelings. The notion that entering someone's home means you are family is quite literal in the kingdom of Tonga, according to an anthropologist who has worked there. Susan Philips explains that in Tonga, usually only family members are invited into people's homes. Others are greeted and entertained on the porch or close to their homes, but they generally don't cross the threshold. (Philips did notice exceptions, such as older men with no women in their household allowing younger men to come in and hang out.) This doesn't mean that women can't socialize with other women they're close to at home, because the norm in Tonga is for "friends" (Philips noted that this is not a commonly used term) to be drawn from relatives, so friends are welcome in family homes—as relatives.

In societies where friends cross the threshold, doing so can have a similar meaning. Fathiya Al Rashdi explains that close friends in Oman will be in each other's homes often, maybe daily, and will say to each other, "Feel free. This is your house." This sounds rather like the English expression "Make yourself at home," but it seems to be meant more literally, as a close friend might open the refrigerator door to take food if she's hungry; though she'll probably ask first, she knows her friend will say, "Don't ask. Just go and get it." This, too, is part of what, Al Rashdi explains, contributes to the feeling of being yourself around a friend: "You behave naturally, as if you're one of my sisters at home."

Dining In, Dining Out

Though I don't share the worry that we are losing the ability to know what a true friend is, there is a concern I do have: the increasing tendency for friends to share meals in restaurants rather than homes. I have seen this change in my own life. When I was living in New York in the 1970s, teaching remedial writing and freshman composition, I found myself in a circle of friends who were single, like me. Then I moved to Berkeley to attend graduate school and became part of another group of friends. Both of these groups rarely ate in restaurants. We gathered for dinner at our respective homes, on a rotating basis. When I think of those dinners, I remember little of the food we ate, but vividly recall the conversations we had—not the specific topics, but the tenor: the raucous laughter, the sense of delight in each other's company. We regularly multiplied food offerings and shifted locales so we could extend the conversation. Before dinner, we'd gather in living rooms, where appetizers were arrayed. We moved to a table for dinner, and after dessert, we either stayed at the table or went back to the living room. Sometimes we extended the evening beyond dessert by bringing out bottles of cheap liqueur so the tasting and commenting and talking could continue after the meal had ended. Now, when I meet friends for lunch, tea, or dinner, we meet in restaurants, where it's harder to hear and unseemly to laugh too loudly, and there is an expectation that the gathering will end soon after the meal is finished and the bill paid.

I said that I don't remember the topics my friends and I discussed at our many dinners in each other's homes, but that is not entirely accurate. I remember the topic of one conversation not only because of how much we laughed but because it entailed our making public something that is about as private as a topic can be. No, not sex, but toilets. Somehow we ended up talking about how we fold toilet paper! Some were saying they just bunched the paper up, while others tried to describe the ways they folded it. But showing is easier than telling, so our host brought out a roll of toilet paper, and each of us demonstrated how we'd handle the squares of paper if we were alone in the bathroom. I remember this evening because it was so funny—and so intimate. We were bringing into a public sphere something that we normally attended to only in private, talking openly about something that we rarely—I'd venture to say, never—talk about. The effect was a precious element of friendship: reminding each other of our shared humanity. It's impossible to imagine a conversation like that taking place in a restaurant.

Socializing in restaurants is a counterpoint to the breakdown in boundaries between inside and outside that comes with social media. Just as I worry that this breakdown means people and spirits invade our homes that would be better kept outside, I also worry that the intimacy and closeness of friends may be diminished, as socializing that used to be done in our homes is increasingly—at least for those who can afford to eat in restaurants—moving into public spaces.

The Making of Friendship

We often ask why couples break up, but we rarely ask why they got together in the first place, as if love is not only its own justification but also its own explanation. The same is true of friendship. When I interviewed women for this book, I always asked if they'd experienced cutoffs but rarely asked why a particular friend became one. Fortunately, many of those I spoke to told me anyway. I realized, on rereading the transcripts, that the creation of friendship is as interesting as why friendships end. Maybe it's more interesting, because the beginning of friendship is more mysterious and less talked about. How does an acquaintance become a friend? How does a friend become a close friend? Sometimes it's by acting like one—in word or in deed.

We speak differently to friends than to strangers, and to close friends than to casual ones. In English we have just one word, "you," to address another person, but in many languages there are two forms of "you," one formal or distant, like French *vous* and Spanish *usted*, and another for those who are more familiar (there's that word "like family"), in both French and Spanish, *tu*. If *tu* is the way you address someone you are friends with, then switching from *vous* or *usted* to *tu* can be a way to signal, and help create, the friendship. Among Korean married women, this can be done by choosing a third pronoun, according to the research of Minju Kim. Kim recorded conversations to observe how Korean women with children addressed one another in friendly conversation. In Korean culture, only family members can use first names; the traditional way for friends to address each other would be the equivalent of "Ken's mom," using the name of their oldest child. (To a more senior woman or in a more formal situation, it would be the equivalent of the more formal "Ken's mother.") Kim explains that it is becoming common for married women, when speaking with friends, to use a pronoun, *caki*, where English would use "you." And since this term is used between close friends, using it can be a way to become close friends.

These verbal means of creating closeness are built into languages that have formal and informal variants of "you." In any language, closeness can also be demonstrated, and therefore created, by the ideas conveyed. For example, a friendship can be deepened by, as one young woman put it, "breaking the barrier across friend domains," like a soccer friend with whom she no longer talks about soccer, or coworkers who talk not only about work but also about their families. And someone for whom a part of friendship is being able to complain might move an acquaintance in that direction by complaining to her. Another way might be by offering a tidbit of personal information. It might be something trivial, like "I can't believe how much chocolate I ate today!" A response like "I know! Once I get started eating chocolate, I can't stop" brings you a step closer. The rejoinder "I know, I'm the same way" implies "I like you, I approve of you, you are not alone in your experience of the world." But if a friend says something like "Why did you?" or "How could you?" or "You'd better be careful or you won't be able to fit into your clothes!" it might have the opposite effect. The implication instead is "There is something wrong with you." A response like that makes you take a step back.

How Can You Say That?

If talking can create a path to friendship, it can also place a barrier in that path. Patty and Eva were having a filling-in-our-lives conversation that could lead to a growing friendship. At one point, Patty said that after college she'd joined a challenging Outward Bound program because her college boyfriend was doing it. "You do things for the strangest reasons," Eva said. Patty felt slapped down. She hadn't expected any response to that detail at all; she'd assumed that her motive for joining the group was typical of girls that age. Hearing this response, with its implication that there was something wrong with her, Patty made a mental note that she might not want to get closer to Eva after all.

This exchange, though it was fleeting and relatively insignificant, is a window into ways that conversation can reinforce or undermine your sense that all's right with the world and with your place in it. The sociologist C. Wright Mills coined the term "vocabulary of motives" to describe the way people in a given culture agree on what it makes sense to say. For example, in a society where marriages are arranged, a woman might say that her parents chose her husband because he came from a good family, and others would nod, accepting this as a reasonable motive. If a woman in the United States today said the same thing, most Americans would react with puzzlement if not downright incredulity. They'd probably think she was joking. The reverse would be true if someone gave falling in love as a reason: unquestioning acceptance by most in the United States, incredulity—or perhaps either disapproval or congratulations—in a society where arranged marriages are the norm. While this is an extreme example, just about everything we say in everyday conversation is either accepted as reasonable or questioned as odd, providing a continual feedback loop that either reinforces or calls into question our sense of ourselves as fitting in the world we inhabit. We may relish responses which indicate that what we said was unexpected, but that's generally because we intended to provoke such a response. It's when we're sure we're saying something unexceptional that it's unnerving to see a listener recoil.

Both the potential gain and the risk are greater when the tidbit of information offered is not something trivial, like eating chocolate or taking part in a summer program, but something deeply personal. One woman hit upon a way to find out how a friend would respond to her painful family history—and therefore how close a friend she'd likely become—through joking. She could pinpoint the evening when a close friendship began:

> It came out one night that we had both had challenging or hard aspects of our childhoods, but it came out by joking about it. Here was someone who shared the experience and could joke about it in the same dark way. Those little jokes led us to more serious conversations, opening up to each other. Neither had opened up to many others before. It was like, If I can talk to you about this, I can talk to you about anything.

The decision to reveal something that makes you vulnerable is a tricky one. You have much to gain if your listener is understanding and even more to gain if she has experienced something similar, but you have much to lose if what you reveal is potentially compromising. For example, dealing with a challenge like depression is not only painful but isolating if you think you're the only one in the world who has it. Suzanna had found great solace when she spoke to a friend about her depression and learned that the friend experienced it, too. Had she not broached the subject, she never would have known that. But taking the risk of mentioning it could have had a very different effect, as it did with another friend, Meredith.

Suzanna was having a conversation with Meredith that began much like many similar conversations she had taken part in before: antidepressants are being overprescribed; it's crazy that almost everyone is taking them, and they're even being given to children. Suzanna agreed with these observations, but she also knew that antidepressants could be invaluable, because they had been to her. Though she rarely mentioned her depression to anyone other than her immediate family and closest friends, she decided to take a risk, because she liked Meredith and thought they might become even better friends. "I agree in general," Suzanna said, "but they do have a place. They can really help people who suffer from depression. I know that because I take them myself. I've struggled with depression my whole life, and they have made a huge difference for me." Meredith responded, "What? You take them too? But you were just saying they're overprescribed!" Suzanna immediately regretted having talked about herself. Her attempt to get closer to Meredith had convinced her instead that they'd never be close friends. She resolved to be more careful about letting anyone outside her family know about her history of depression.

How to Become a Friend

A close friendship can also be created when acquaintances begin doing things that close friends do. A woman recalls that when her mother became seriously ill, several women with whom she was friendly stepped up to help care for her mother. After her mother died, she realized that her relationships with these women had progressed from friendly to friends.

When I first moved to Washington, I met someone who became a close friend. We spoke to each other every day, reporting on what we'd done and what we were thinking. Any evening that we both had no other plans, we had dinner together at her home or mine. How did we go from a chance meeting when we were both looking at the same apartment for rent to being pretty much inseparable? I recall a turning point. She had gone on a trip, and told me when she was returning. I said I'd try to meet her at the airport, and I did. I could tell by the look on her face when she emerged from the terminal and saw me standing by my car, waving, that she was really pleased I had come—and surprised. Taking the time to drive to the airport to meet someone is something only close friends do; by doing it, I was showing that I felt our friendship was that close—and making it so.

Claudia was with her friend Linda, who was also a neighbor. She was lying on Linda's bed as Linda was going through her closet, trying things on, deciding what to include in her fall wardrobe and what to give away. When Claudia realized she was hungry, she asked if there was anything to eat, then went and got it. Claudia described this scene to me, to illustrate how precious this friendship was, because she felt that, before Linda, she didn't know how to be a friend. Both her mother and her husband had discouraged her from having friends, and girls she had befriended in elementary and high school had turned on her suddenly, so she had taken to hanging out with boys instead: they were easier, and she didn't have to worry that they'd betray her. She said, of Linda, "She taught me how to be a friend." When I asked how she did that, Claudia said, "By being one to me."

It began one night when Claudia had a particularly nasty argument with her husband, who drove away from the house in anger, leaving her alone. Suddenly she heard a knock on the door. It was her neighbor, asking, "Are you okay? I just want to check on you." Though it was a long time before their friendship developed, Claudia sees that knock on her door as the first step, even though she didn't open it that night. Linda's knock gave her the idea that if someone is in distress, it's okay to reach out and ask, "Are you all right?"—if not by knocking on the door, then with a phone call or a text. Until then, Claudia had assumed that no one wants to be intruded upon. By not reaching out, she thought she was giving people their space. Thanks to Linda, she began to see that there is something that can be more precious than space: connection.

Over time, Claudia opened the door to Linda—both literally and figuratively. Linda would come over and ask for an egg or a cup of milk that she needed for a recipe. Claudia realized she was happy to give her one, and happy to know that she, too, could intrude to ask for something she needed. Then Linda began asking if Claudia wanted to go to a movie. Claudia's first response was automatic; she said no. But Linda kept asking until Claudia tried saying yes—and found she enjoyed it. She and Linda started taking walks together, and going to lunch. One day it dawned on Claudia that she had a friend. A close friend. And she was being a friend: one who could lie on Linda's bed while she was trying on clothes from her closet, as they talked about the clothes and their body shapes. I love what Claudia said about that day: "I felt like 95 percent myself." Maybe it's impossible to be 100 percent yourself with another person; there's always that little part that you keep private. But 95 percent gets you pretty close to feeling you're with a true friend.

For Claudia, learning to be friends with Linda meant unlearning what her mother had taught her: not to trust outsiders, not to open the door. Sometimes a friend can be like family in a way that the family you grew up with wasn't able to be.

Instant Friends, Instant Family: A Senior Residence

A context in which friends become like family without longevity is the rarefied world of a senior residence. The forms these friendships can take highlight ways that friends can be like family—and ways that they can't. I talked to nearly a dozen women, ranging in age from late seventies to late nineties, who live in such residences. There was something I heard from almost all of them: they are genuinely fond of the friends they have made among fellow residents, but a new friendship cannot replicate the depth and comfort of friends who knew you before you retired, knew your children when they were small, saw you through both joyful and painful life passages, and know your past without your having to fill them in or explain. Yet in many ways, new friends could and did take the place of family.

Eleanor Maccoby, a retired psychology professor, described how women at the retirement community where she lives—and most residents are women—often become best friends who function for each other much like married couples or relatives:

> If you were trying to decide whether to sign up for the coming season of a theater, you would call your friend and find out if she's interested in subscribing together. If you're both taking the bus to some excursion, the one who gets on the bus first saves the seat next to her, and others who know you would honor that and walk past that empty seat. Your friend is the person who will drive you to the emergency room if you need to go there, and if you find yourself in the hospital or the care center, she'll visit you there and ask if there is anything she can bring over: Do you want your special pillow? Do you need extra underwear? The same sort of thing that a sister or a daughter would do if she lived nearby. Each knows what the other likes to eat for dinner. If your friend didn't notice something on the menu you know she would like, you point it out. Or the opposite: "No, you won't want that because it has a spicy sauce." And you can talk about what to wear for this or that occasion, where to shop for this or that, and where you might order something by mail.

"What a funny catalog it is," she mused, "when you think about what constitutes intimacy among friends."

Finding friends who can, at least partly, take the place of family is easier for seniors who live in a senior residence than it is for seniors who move to a new city but still live on their own, as many do, either to be nearer to children and grandchildren or to enjoy a better climate. As one woman who did that explained to me, one of the hardest things about such a move is the challenge of leaving old friends and making new ones:

"You tire more easily, so it's hard to invest a lot of energy in making new friends. Plus, people you meet already have friends—and busy lives. They're not looking for new ones. Even if you do make friends, they know so little about who you are. You can't exactly catch them up on your whole life." She also mentioned ageism: young people don't want to be friends with old people—especially old women. And old friends get sick, stop driving, and, worst of all, pass away.

There's Nothing to Say at a Time Like This

A life passage when friends, like family, are essential is the death of a loved one—and those times are challenging for friends, too. Just figuring out what to say can be daunting, since it seems so important to say the right thing but so hard to know what the right thing is. I spoke to people who had lost family members—a sibling, life partner, child, spouse, or parent—and asked how friends had been helpful or less so, especially in words. One reason it's so difficult to decide what to say became immediately clear: comments and questions that some appreciated were not appreciated by others. Among the most frequent was the question "How are you doing?" One woman said she valued that question as an invitation to talk about her husband and thereby, in a nebulous but precious way, bring him back. But others said that the question was impossible to answer, since how they were doing changed from day to day—or moment to moment. Better, they said, to ask, "How are you doing today?" or even "How are you doing right now?"

Everyone agreed that "Let me know if there is anything I can do," while appreciated as an expression of concern, is not as helpful as suggesting something specific, like "Can I bring dinner over on Thursday?"—or, even better, just do it: show up with dinner. Among the questions most often asked of those who have lost a spouse—and among the most resented—was "Will you sell the house?" It reinforces the awful feeling that your life, as you know it, is over. Words clearly intended to comfort can fail at that task. Feelings of guilt seem to be universal: I should have done more, done something different, done something! And it's common for friends to reassure: "You did all you could." "How do they know?" someone who lost a brother objected. Worst of all, he said, it shuts down the conversation by implying, You mustn't think about what you could have done differently. But thinking—and talking—about what he could have done differently was exactly what he needed to do.

I myself benefited from this young man's insights when I received a text from a friend telling me that her life partner had died. It was not a surprise; I had visited him in hospice, with her, not long before. I immediately texted back—but then paced the house with phone in hand wondering if I should also call. Since we weren't best friends, would a call be intrusive? I had pretty much decided to give her more time, maybe call later or the next day, when I heard in my head the voice of the man who had lost his brother: "Why are people so afraid of intruding?" and his advice: "It's always better to reach out." So I called. My bereaved friend got off the phone quickly but then immediately called back and said, "You called at the perfect time." Together with two of her partner's close friends, she was in the process of composing a notice she needed to put out, and she patched me into their conference call. Together we all worked out the wording, and when they typed it up, I caught a couple of typos (my forte). I was so very glad that there was something concrete I could do, and that I had called.

Another of this young man's observations has stuck with me, too. Why, he asked, will people spend money and time to attend weddings, bachelor parties, and showers, but not funerals? Just showing up for the funeral is something concrete they can do. And why, he went on, did friends start acting like nothing had changed only six months—or three months or one!—after a death, going back to business as usual and expecting the bereaved to do the same? Many religions and cultures have agreed-upon boundaries to measure time: a week of deep mourning; a month or forty days of slightly less intense mourning; a year of formal observance like wearing black or saying daily prayers. In the absence of such customs, it's too easy for friends to move on—and thereby move away—too soon.

Considering how many of the things people say turn out to be wrong, it's not surprising that many friends choose to say nothing, yet that may be the worst choice of all. A common impulse is to avoid mentioning the person who died, out of fear that raising the subject would open a wound. But the cumulative effect is that everyone is acting as if the person who died never lived, so it can feel like the loved one is being wiped out all over again. The conversations I had with those who had recently suffered terrible losses convinced me that friends could make a huge difference just by showing up: reach out, say something, listen, send texts or emails even if they're not always answered—and don't always expect an answer. Just don't disappear. It may be enough just to be there, like family.

Like Family—For Better, for Worse

A woman observed that when her husband died, "the friends who came through in a big way are the ones who have sisters. Other close friends just didn't know how. They don't have sisters." By watching out for her the way sisters watch out for each other, she felt, the friends who "came through in a big way" were treating her like family.

There is another way that friendships can be like family, and particularly like sisters, the family relationship that most closely resembles women friends. If a friend reminds you of a sister, it can shape the way you react to that friend, for better or worse. Say you are an older sister who always felt protective of your younger sister; you might get along especially well with a friend who had a protective older sister: you automatically watch out for her, and if she enjoyed the protection of her sister, it will feel right to her, too. But if she chafed in response to her sister's protectiveness—experienced it as condescending or overbearing—then your similar gestures toward her might get her back up. And if you saw your younger sister as spoiled and annoying, then it's your back that might be up. Your place in the family, and the way it meshes or clashes with a friend's, can be a hidden but powerful force shaping, or even de-railing, the friendship. That happened with my friend Wendy and me—and our conversation about it afterward taught me a great deal about how family patterns and styles can affect friendships, and about how discussing it can be enlightening and even healing.

I don't like it when guests in my home try to help without asking. I don't mind if they offer to help, though I almost always decline their of-fers. But when they just get up and do things, especially in the kitchen, I feel my ire rising. I know that many people appreciate such generous pitching in, but it makes me feel as if my role as host is being usurped. It makes me feel incompetent—the way I felt growing up with two more competent older sisters.

My husband and I were hosting an out-of-town guest, Victor, who of-fered to repay our hospitality by preparing dinner one night. Since we rarely cook, we gladly accepted his offer and invited our friend Wendy to share in the feast, because we had been dinner guests in her home many times and saw this as a chance to reciprocate. But when the evening got underway, I found myself in a series of awkward exchanges with Wendy. And the troubles seemed to reflect my and Wendy's places in our families—though, when we discussed it later, Wendy pointed out that the communication styles of the families we grew up in played a role as well.

While Victor was preparing dinner, Wendy, my husband, and I were seated at a table within view of the kitchen, enjoying wine, cheese, and conversation. Shortly after the evening began, Wendy called out to Vic-tor, asking if he wanted cheese on a cracker, and he said he did. I was chagrined. Wendy's offer made me realize that I had been remiss as a host: I should have offered Victor an appetizer while he cooked. My dis-comfort increased as I saw Wendy cutting cheese to place on a cracker for Victor. I felt that it was my house, my guest, and my cheese, so I should do it. I leapt up and brought Victor a cracker with cheese, though when he said thank you, I said, "You should thank Wendy. She's the one who thought of it."

I felt relieved that I'd managed to maintain my role of host, yet had acknowledged Wendy's superior thoughtfulness. But my discomfort wasn't over; it had barely begun. There followed a subtle power struggle— or, you might say, a connection struggle—as Wendy continued to offer, and sometimes deliver, cheese and crackers to Victor, and I tried, with mixed success, to stay one step ahead of her. At one point I could see that Wendy was overdoing it, and I asked Victor if he wanted more. When he said, "No, I've had enough," I felt a sense of relief that my struggle with Wendy had ended, and even inwardly gloated (I hoped it remained in- ward) to have put a stop to her incursions and demonstrated that at least in the matter of discerning my guest's desires, I had shown myself to be the better rather than the inadequate host.

Unfortunately—frustratingly—similar struggles ensued as the evening progressed. Wendy tried to help in various ways—clear the table, retrieve items from the kitchen that someone wanted—all efforts that I knew were well intended and would no doubt have been appreciated by a dif- ferent host, but which I experienced as intrusive. Each time, I told her to please sit down, that I didn't want her to help, but then she'd be up again. At one point, when she rose from the table and made it into the kitchen, I actually grabbed her arm and pulled her back to the table. It was all done good-naturedly, with humor, but I was genuinely rattled. To account for my reaction, I explained that I always felt incompetent around my older sisters, especially in the kitchen. And I added that when I visit others' homes, I stay out of the kitchen because I don't want to risk making my hosts feel the way I feel when guests do too much to help— uncomfortable, even angry.

I stopped short of saying, "You're making me angry." So I was taken aback when Wendy said, "You remind me of my sister. She'll just sit there and do nothing, too." This comment made me realize that Wendy—and other friends, perhaps especially those who are older sisters—might not appreciate my respectful hands-off approach when I am a guest in their homes, but might think I'm being lazy and self-indulgent, just sitting there doing nothing.

Because I am very fond of Wendy—and because I was writing this book—I decided to ask her about her view of that evening. Our conversation was a revelation to both of us. Like me, Wendy was surprised and troubled to realize that what she intended to be helpful could be off-putting. She agreed that it partly reflected her sense of responsibility as the oldest (she has a younger brother as well as a younger sister), but also, perhaps even more, she traced it to her parents' style. Just the other day, Wendy said, she had been a dinner guest at her parents' home. When the dinner ended, she got up and cleared the table, though her mother told her not to. She washed the dishes, as her mother chastened, "Stop it!" Then she cleaned the kitchen, to the tune of her mother's admonitions that she shouldn't. And when she was done, her mother said, "Thank you." Wendy explained how her place in the sibling constellation worked together with her family's style: "I'm the oldest and feel responsible and in my family 'no' doesn't mean 'no,' and 'Don't do the dishes' doesn't mean that. It means, 'You really don't have to do them and I don't want to ask you to do them and you shouldn't do them because you are the guest but thank you for doing them anyway!'"

As Wendy and I discussed our contrasting views of that evening in the context of our family's styles (my mother tended to be direct in saying what she meant, so I had learned to take her and others at their word), we both felt as if a light had been turned on in a dark room. I had been baffled by Wendy's continuing to help when I kept saying I didn't want her to. It had never occurred to me that she might think I didn't really mean it. And it had never occurred to her that I did. Our different assumptions about how people mean (or don't mean) what they say, which we'd learned in our families, together with our experiences as youngest and oldest sisters, had laid a trap that we'd stepped into together. We both modified our habits as a result: Wendy tells me that now when she is a guest and the host rejects her offers to help, she backs off after one or two tries—and is greatly relieved that she does not always have to do the work. She has even stopped doing all the work at her parents' home. For my part, I now make a second or even a third offer. And we both learned another lesson, too: that talking about a troubling interaction can shed light on what caused it—and strengthen a friendship.

Like Family: What It Means to Be Close

A friend can be as close as (or closer than) family. I came across evidence of this in a personal account that provides a rare window onto ways that close friends are like family, and what it means to be close. John Elder Robison, who has written memoirs about living with autism, experienced an astonishing transformation. Because of his autism, he had been unable to perceive others' emotions. At the age of fifty, he underwent an experimental procedure by which magnetic pulses applied to his brain awakened in him this ability. But the effects of this awakening did not, as Robison had expected, bring him closer to everyone in his life. In an essay based on his book *Switched On,* he recounts his dismay at discovering that others' emotions, once he perceived them, could take hold in him, too. Especially revealing was how his newfound awareness affected his casual as compared to his close relationships: "My ability to engage casual friends and strangers was enhanced," he writes. "But with family and close friends, the results were more mixed. I found myself unsettled by absorbing the emotions of people I was close to."

Robison's experience sheds light on the double-edged sword of closeness—the implications of literally "sharing" emotions: on one hand, his relationships deepened with those he was close to, as he became more keenly aware of their feelings and also "showed feelings I had never expressed." His autism had denied Robison the satisfaction of that kind of connection, but it had also insulated him from its risks: the pain of feeling others' negative emotions and of becoming more aware of his own by articulating them. That this effect was the same for family and close friends, but not for casual friends and strangers, underscores how friends can be like family—for better and also for worse.

To tell me how far back a friendship goes, or how deep it is, women often said, "She was at my wedding"—or, even more significant, "She was *in* my wedding": like a family member, taking part in the ceremony. You may have become friends because of geography or chance, and your lives may have subsequently taken different directions, but at some point, you stop asking whether you have much—or anything—in common because you've known each other so long, so consistently, that each of you is just there, like family. And, as with family, there is enormous power in just being there.

A woman who ran a women's theater group told me how the group healed the young daughter of one of their members—just by letting her be there. The girl was in the grip of anorexia, and her mother didn't want to leave her home alone while she and the other members of the group developed a theater piece about mothers and daughters. She asked if she could bring her daughter, and promised the girl wouldn't be any trouble. The group's leader said "Of course," though she feared that having an onlooker would make the other members self-conscious. Her fear turned out to be unfounded: the emaciated girl sat quietly, wrapped in a shawl, in a large overstuffed chair that happened to be in the rehearsal space. She seemed to disappear in the chair and the shawl, and the members of the group forgot she was there. As they worked together to develop the play, the women gradually built trust as women in all-women groups can do: they opened their hearts and their lives to each other as they turned the painful and precious relationships with their own mothers into riveting theater. And as she watched, the silent teenager gradually improved. She began eating, and putting on weight, and when the play opened, she baked a cake for the group—and ate it with them. Just being there, as the women became like a family by developing the play, made her part of their family, too—a family that helped her find health in a way that her own family, at that time in their lives, weren't able to do.

Sometimes we come to see friends as family because they fill roles that the family we were born into can't fill, because of what they themselves are going through, or because they live far away or feel too different or are too difficult to deal with. Holes left by rejecting (or rejected) relatives—or left by relatives lost to distance, death, or circumstance—can be filled by friends who are like family. But family-like friends don't have to be filling holes at all. I feel very lucky to have two sisters I adore and am very close to, and also a friend who is like a brother. And I know, from the many women I was privileged to interview for this book, that my experience is not unusual. Though friends, like family, can sometimes cause grief, they can also, like family, provide comfort and solace in troubled times, and, for all times, a precious sense that we are not alone in the world.

Epilogue

My husband and I were having dinner with another couple when my cell phone buzzed in my pocket. I was not going to answer it, but when I took the phone out to shut it off, I glanced at the screen, and a feeling of dread came over me. The number belonged to my longtime friend Richard and his husband, Paul. Richard had been in the hospital, and his discharge had been delayed. If Paul was calling, it wasn't good. Still, I put off listening to the message until our dinner was over. Then I discovered that my sense of foreboding had been justified. Richard had died, suddenly and unexpectedly, one day after leaving the hospital. His heart had given out. When I spoke at his funeral, I said that Richard's passing left a hole in my life that could never be filled. That feeling, too, turned out to be right. And it made me think of the many people who told me that a longtime friend who died could never be replaced. I've been pondering why that is so.

In the early years of our friendship, Richard and I were both living alone, so we spent many hours together, just the two of us. We talked about our partners when we had them, and about finding a partner when we didn't. We confided in each other when we met or dated men we thought might lead to promising relationships, and comforted each other when our hopes were dashed. The intimacy that grows of ongoing conversations like those can only be created in that way. For one thing, it's the topics and how deeply you feel about them. Politics, plays, travel, restaurants, movies, or sports, no matter how strongly you feel about them, don't have the same deep implications for your life as the everyday triumphs, hurts, connections, confusions, comforts, and misunderstandings that make up human relationships.

Even more, when you're single, the friend you are talking to has a primacy that, when you are part of a couple, is usually reserved for your partner. If revealing secrets is a bedrock of close relationships, the right to reveal your secrets is no longer yours alone when your first fealty is to a partner who might not want the secrets of your relationship revealed. You yourself may not want to give friends a negative impression of your partner, because you're all going to spend time together, and you don't want friends to harbor—or, even worse, express—resentment, or even let it slip that they know something unflattering about your partner. That's why conversation among couples is generally about impersonal topics. When you talk to a friend as a single person, you can be present in a naked-soul way that is impossible when there is a person to whom you owe greater loyalty, whether or not that person is in the room.

For the last two decades of our friendship, Richard and I no longer met one on one; we got together with our husbands. But the intimacy of our first decade of friendship had laid down roots that supported the conversations we had as couples, no matter the topic. Just seeing each other happily married gave us joy, because we knew and remembered the disappointments, heart pain, and yearnings that had led us there. I thought of the many women I had spoken to who told me, about longtime friends, "I saw her through her divorce, her cancer, her remarriage." I could imagine the conversations that must have accompanied those life passages. The depth of such friendships can come only with time. And with time can come their loss.

When a close friendship ends, it can feel like a death: you lose forever the experiences, the jokes, the references that you shared. Even worse is the actual death of a dear friend. A woman in her seventies who was mourning her lifelong best friend said that her mind simply could not grasp the loss: "I think, She's dead. Then I get a sense, She can't be dead.

She's dead. She can't be dead." The worst part was not being able to call up her friend and tell her how terrible she felt about her dying: "I can't accept that she's gone and that she left me to deal with my life without her on my own."

When friends die, a part of you dies with them. If the friend was someone who knew you when you were young, is that a part of you that dies? Your younger self? Your real self? As I've gotten older, I've become convinced that the people we were when we were young are who we still are—who we *really* are. The trappings of age—the graying or thinning hair, the lines and sags in our faces—are like masks laid over our true selves. I believe that one reason romances often blossom between people who reconnect after decades through social media, or at high school or college reunions, is that they see beneath those masks—see each other as they were when they were young, as they still feel themselves to be. In a similar way, friends who knew you when you were young help keep alive your own true self. And friends at any age and any stage who truly see you, truly hear you, are also helping you see and know your own true self.

Acknowledgments

Though they appear at the end of the book, these acknowledgments are anything but an afterthought. Throughout the long process that has led to this book's publication, I have been keenly aware and deeply appreciative of the many people who contributed in so many ways. I am grateful for this chance to thank them.

The book would not—could not—exist without the recollections and insights of those who gave me permission to incorporate their experiences and to quote their words. I therefore begin by thanking the more than eighty who took time for extended conversations, and also the many others with whom I spoke casually on the topic during the time I was researching and writing: Carolyn Adger, Fathiya Al Rashdi, Ruth Ames, Linda Lehr Anning, Caren Anton, Maureen Arrigo, Ashley Behnke, Melissa Bell, Mitch Boucher, Tovah Boucher, Joslyn Burchett, Tavia Burchett, Jo Ann Hoeppner Cruz, Anne Dauer, Sonali Deraniyagala, Holly DiClemente, Vasiliki Dimopoulos, Caitlin Elizondo, Anne-Marie Finnell, Ellie Flavell, Maria Friedrich, Neha Ghanshamdas, Serena Gleklen, Karl Goldstein, Enrique Granados, Harriet Grant, Rose Hayden, Kleio Helidonis, Adrienne Isaac, Leslie Jacobson, Rachel Jacobson, Caleen Sinnette Jennings, Jessica Jennings, Vicki Judson, Betty Kaplan, Kitty Kelley, Joann Kobin, Aisulu Kulbayeva, Whitaker Lader, Maria Leon, Betsy Lerner, Marion Lewenstein, Ricki Libby, Jennifer Litchman, Kate Lucey, Maria Lyon, Eleanor Maccoby, Alison Mackey, Addie Macovski, Devra Marcus, Ruth

Marcus, Michal Marmorstein, Beth Marx, Nancy Marx, Lucy McBride, Jill Barrett Melnicki, Sheila Meyer, Noelle Miesfeld, Kyoko Mori, Judy Mueller, Jennifer Nycz, Karen O'Hara, Daniel Ornstein, Kaley Palanjian, Catherine Payling, Elba Peralta, Micah Perks, Rebekah Perks, Robin L. Perry, Joy Peyton, Livia Polanyi, Mackenzie Price, Dimitra K. Rallis, Vivian Ramos, Phyllis Richman, Yerlyn Rojas, Ronda Rolfes, Barbara Rosenfeld, Barbara Ross, Amalia Rubin, Gabriela Rubin, Elisabeth Ness Schneider, Riley Shay, Nancy Sherman, Natalie Singal, Sheila Slaughter, Peter Malamud Smith, Sarah Emily Smith, Nancy Stanwood, Katarina Starcevic, Elaine Tanay, Mimi Tannen, Naomi Tannen, Julia Thompson, Catherine Tinsley, Allison Treanor, Jeanine Turner, Patty Wallens, Michelle C. Wang, Martha Weiss, Mona Wexler, Elisabeth Wichmann-Emory, Stephanie Wolfram, Haru Yamada, Inbal Yassur, and Mika Yassur.

I am grateful as well to Addie Macovski, Kate Murray, Joy Peyton, and Susan Philips for connecting me with others who could provide unique perspectives. In addition, Joslyn Burchett, Caitlin Elizondo, and Katarina Starcevic, students who joined me in a small working group during the spring term 2015, interviewed their own friends or relatives, and Aisulu Kulbayeva interviewed women in a small village in Kazakhstan. To them, and to those they interviewed, I extend thanks.

It was my friend Elizabeth Drew who first suggested that my next book should be about women friends—and kept reminding me until I had committed to writing it. I am grateful for her suggestion, her insistence, her thoughts on the topic, and the term for a concept I knew from the start I wanted to include but did not have a word for: poaching.

In writing this, as with my previous books, I drew on the training I received from my professors at the University of California, Berkeley: Wallace Chafe, the late John Gumperz, and Robin Lakoff. I was inordinately fortunate to attend Berkeley at a magical time, when the field of linguistics was turning attention to the language of everyday conversation. All three of these giants were leaders in this turn. Robin Lakoff was pioneering the field of gender and language and devising a theory of communicative style; indeed, her course at a Linguistic Institute at the

University of Michigan in 1973 played a major role in inspiring me to seek a doctorate in linguistics, and I decided to pursue it at Berkeley because she was there. John Gumperz was founding the field that came to be known as interactional sociolinguistics. The term that he hired me full-time to help him write up his research gave me a deep understanding of the theories and methods he was developing. Wally Chafe, for his part, was expanding the field of semantics to explore language and cognition. By including me in the "story group"—professors and graduate students at Berkeley and Stanford who brought the perspectives of a range of disciplines to the study of narrative—and in a research project devoted to analyzing how people tell about personal experience, Chafe provided yet a third pillar on which my approach to analyzing language in interaction has stood. As if the privilege of working with these three mentors were not bounty enough, it was also my exceptional good fortune that my time at Berkeley coincided with the visiting professorship of the late University of Michigan anthropological linguist A. L. Becker. Pete Becker's Introduction to Linguistics course at the 1973 Linguistic Institute had also played a major role in convincing me that linguistics holds a key to understanding how people use language in their lives. His deeply humanistic view of language—or, rather, of "languaging," the word he suggests more accurately reflects the way people shape and are shaped by the words we speak—has informed and inspired all my work.

I also cannot imagine having done the research and writing I've been able to accomplish had it not been for the support and intellectual community provided by Georgetown University, from my immediate colleagues in the Sociolinguistics Program and the Linguistics Department to the deans, provosts, and presidents from whose leadership and generosity I have personally benefited. For their support while I was working on this book, I am grateful to Dean Chester Gillis, Provost Robert Groves, and President John DeGioia. An aspect of the university's generosity has been the assistants provided since my appointment to a university professorship. As I was researching and writing this book, my assistant Kate Murray has been helpful in innumerable ways. For the many tasks she performed, and the generous spirit in which she performed them, I offer heartfelt thanks.

Perhaps the most bountiful gift that Georgetown has given me is the heart and soul of the university, its students. Over the nearly four decades I have taught here, students in my classes have enlightened me with their insights, their enthusiasm, and a treasure trove of examples from their own lives that they described in class discussion or analyzed in written assignments. Those whose specific examples I've included in this book—with their permission—are either named in connection with their examples or included in the list of names that appears above. But I want to thank all the students in all the classes I've taught over these many years. In particular, for insight into how they use social media, I am indebted to the students who took part in classes I've taught on that specific subject.

I also want to thank those who read and commented on drafts: Cynthia Gordon for the chapter on conversational style, and Harriet Grant, Kate Murray, and Naomi Tannen for the entire manuscript. My sister Naomi has been an uber-reader for all my books, commenting on every level, from finding typos to pointing out aspects I overlooked to contributing her own related examples. (The title of my book *You Just Don't Understand* was her suggestion.) For comments on an early draft but also for advocacy and wise counsel at every stage, I have relied on Suzanne Gluck, my agent extraordinaire. How fortunate I am to have had such a gifted and dedicated guide by my side for three decades. I am also grateful to my wonderful editor, Marnie Cochran. This is a better book thanks to her careful and perceptive reading of drafts. I came to rely on her judgment—and also her responsiveness. Knowing how email can fracture attention and shatter concentration, I have been filled with appreciation, even awe, at the swiftness with which she always responds to my queries.

Above all—the foundation on which all else rests—is my family. My sisters Mimi Tannen and Naomi Tannen, who are also my closest friends, talked to me about their own friendships; put me in touch with their friends; were graciously understanding when I had to cancel plans to work on the book; and helped me think through ideas as well as titles. My in-laws, Addie and Al Macovski, have been unflagging sources of love and support from the moment my husband brought me into their lives. Before she died, my mother said that it eased her mind to know that after she and my father were gone, I'd still have Addie and Al. She was right. Finally, I call on words to thank the person for whom words always seem inadequate to express the full measure of my gratitude to and for him—my partner in life and in love for over thirty years—my husband, Michael Macovski.

Notes

Introduction

xiv **Jeanne Safer, a psychoanalyst:** Jeanne Safer, *The Golden Condom and Other Essays on Love Lost and Found* (New York: Picador, 2016). The quotes are from pp. 8, 10.

xv **UCLA psychologist Shelley Taylor:** Taylor's now classic book is *The Tending Instinct: How Nurturing Is Essential for Who We Are and How We Live* (New York: Henry Holt, 2002). She has written many subsequent articles, expanding on her ideas and reporting experimental research supporting them, such as "Tend and Befriend: Biobehavioral Bases of Affiliation Under Stress," *Current Directions in Psychological Science* 15(2006): 6.273–77. Her model has also been supported by the research of others, such as Jennifer Byrd-Craven, Brandon J. Auer, and Shelia M. Kennison, "Sex Differences in Salivary Cortisol Responses to Sex-Linked Stressors: A Test of the Tend-and-Befriend Model," *Adaptive Human Behavior and Physiology* 1(2015): 4.408–20.

xv **Rodlescia Sneed and Sheldon Cohen:** Carnegie Mellon University press release, "Negative Social Interactions Increase Hypertension Risk in Older Adults," May 28, 2014. The subjects of the study were all aged fifty-one or older. Among women, negative encounters with extended family members also were associated with hypertension, but negative encounters with partners and children were not. It's an interesting suggestion that troubles with friends, as with extended family members, can be more upsetting than those with immediate family.

1. Women Friends Talking

4 **changed the life of . . . Maya:** The segment of *This American Life* originally aired on May 9, 2014.

9   "I've been playing poker": Jeffrey Zaslow, *The Girls from Ames: A Story of Women and a Forty-Year Friendship* (New York: Penguin, 2009). The quote is from p. xii.

14   "Miss Tempy's Watchers": Sarah Orne Jewett, "Missy Tempy's Watchers," *Atlantic Monthly*, March 1888, pp. 289–95. The quote is from p. 289.

15   In *The Social Sex*: Marilyn Yalom with Theresa Donovan Brown, *The Social Sex: A History of Female Friendship* (New York: Harper Perennial, 2015). The quote is from p. 110.

18   A new kind of taxi service: *New York Times*, November 12, 2014, p. A20.

22   novel aptly titled *Friendship*: Emily Gould, *Friendship* (New York: Picador, 2014). The quotes are from pp. 253–55.

29   Fiction writer Cynthia Ozick: Cynthia Ozick, "The Novel's Evil Tongue," *New York Times Book Review*, December 16, 2015.

37   Myrna Goldenberg observed: Myrna Goldenberg, "Lessons Learned from Gentle Heroism: Women's Holocaust Narratives," in "The Holocaust: Remembering for the Future," special issue, *Annals of the American Academy of Political and Social Science* 548(November 1996): 78–93.

37   Joan Ringelheim . . . quotes: "Women and the Holocaust: A Reconsideration of Research," in Carol Rittner and John K. Roth, eds., *Different Voices: Women and the Holocaust* (St. Paul: Paragon House, 1993), pp. 374–405. The quote is from p. 381.

37   Isabella Leitner said: Isabel Leitner, *Fragments of Isabella: A Memoir of Auschwitz* (New York: Open Road Media, 1978).

38   Jenna Wortham feels: Jenna Wortham, "B.F.F. Tattoos," *New York Times Magazine*, May 29, 2016, pp. 20–21.

2. That's Not What I Meant!

44   while men tend to interrupt: Deborah James and Sandra Clarke, "Women, Men, and Interruptions: A Critical Review," in *Gender and Conversational Interaction*, ed. Deborah Tannen (New York and Oxford: Oxford University Press, 1993), pp. 231–80.

44   A linguist, Alice Greenwood: Alice Greenwood, "Discourse Variation and Social Comfort: A Study of Topic Initiation and Interruption Patterns in the Dinner Conversation of Pre-adolescent Children" (PhD dissertation, City University of New York, 1989).

45   High-Involvement and High-Considerateness Styles: I developed this framework in my dissertation, which became my book *Conversational Style: Analyzing Talk Among Friends* (New York and Oxford: Oxford University Press, [1986] 2005). It was based on analysis of a Thanksgiving

dinner conversation among six friends, three of whom had been raised in New York City, two in Southern California, and one London, England. In the study, I contrasted the conversational styles of the three New Yorkers (I was one), which I characterized as high-involvement, with those of the two Californians and the British speaker, which I characterized as high-considerateness.

47   **Robin Lakoff, on what she called communicative style:** Lakoff explains this system in the book that launched the field of women and language: *Language and Woman's Place* (New York: Harper and Row, 1975).

59   **according to linguist Haru Yamada:** Yamada describes *haragei*, "belly talk," in *Different Games, Different Rules: Why Americans and Japanese Misunderstand Each Other* (New York and Oxford: Oxford University Press, 1997), p. 17.

60   **French and American expectations of friendship:** Raymonde Carroll, *Cultural Misunderstandings: The French-American Experience,* trans. Carol Volk (Chicago and London: University of Chicago Press, 1988). The quotes are from pp. 75, 77.

61   **Bharati Mukherjee:** Bharati Mukherjee, "Romance and Ritual," in Elizabeth Benedict, ed., *Me, My Hair, and I: Twenty-Seven Women Untangle an Obsession* (Chapel Hill: Algonquin Books of Chapel Hill, 2015), pp. 75–84. The quote is from p. 83.

62   *See What I Mean: Differences Between Deaf and Hearing Cultures:* Thomas K. Holcomb and Anna Mindess, Treehouse Video, 2001.

68   **Complementary Schismogenesis:** Gregory Bateson introduced this term and concept in an essay, "A Theory of Play and Fantasy," which is reprinted in his collection *Steps to an Ecology of Mind* (New York: Ballantine, 1972), pp. 177–93.

76   **researchers took a number of parrots:** Natalie Angier, "Pretty (Smart) Bird," *New York Times,* March 22, 2016, pp. D1, D5. Timothy Wright's quote, "a little immigrant enclave," is from p. D5. Angier's article is based on the book *Parrots of the Wild: A Natural History of the World's Most Captivating Birds* by Catherine A. Toft and Timothy F. Wright (Oakland: University of California Press, 2015).

3. "We're a Lot Alike," "We're Very Different"

78   **like introverts and extraverts, or like someone shy and someone outgoing:** I initially thought of these two polarities as synonymous. Helen Fisher pointed out to me that they are distinct; an introvert can be outgoing, and an extravert can be reserved. One polarity is about

sociability; the other is about whether one gets or loses energy in social situations.

79 **from a workplace training video that I made:** The clips of children playing were recorded for and are included in a training video, *Talking 9 to 5: Women and Men in the Workplace,* which is based on my book *Talking from 9 to 5: Women and Men at Work* (New York: HarperCollins, 1994). The video was made by and is distributed by ChartHouse International. It is available at http://www.fishphilosophy.com/product/talking9to5/.

93 **Joyce gave her a two-hundred-page manuscript:** Joyce Carol Oates, *The Lost Landscape: A Writer's Coming of Age* (New York: HarperCollins, 2015). The quotes are from pp. 160–61.

94 **Laura Bush and Michelle Obama:** Mark Landler, "Bush-Obama Rapport Recalls a Lost Virtue: Political Civility," *New York Times,* September 26, 2016, p. A17.

94 **Grete Stern and Hella Fixel:** Angelika Brechelmacher, "Contemporary Witnesses—the Memories of Hella Fixel and Grete Stern," in Angelika Brechelmacher, Bertrand Perz, and Regina Wonisch, eds. *Post41: Reports from Litzmannstadt Ghetto* (Vienna: Mandelbaum Verlag, n.d.), pp. 285–96.

98 **The Cline of Person:** A. L. Becker with I Gusti Ngurah Oka, "Person in Kawi: Exploration of an Elementary Semantic Dimension," in A. L. Becker, *Beyond Translation: Essays Toward a Modern Philology* (Ann Arbor: University of Michigan Press, 1995), pp. 109–36.

4. The Same—or Better?

105 **Rosie Schaap recalls:** Rosie Schaap, "Kozmic Hippie Hair Breakdown Blues," in Elizabeth Benedict, ed., *Me, My Hair, and I: Twenty-Seven Women Untangle an Obsession* (Chapel Hill: Algonquin Books of Chapel Hill, 2015), pp. 67–74. The quotes are from p. 72.

106 *The Lost Landscape*: Joyce Carol Oates, *The Lost Landscape: A Writer's Coming of Age* (New York: HarperCollins, 2015). The quotes are from pp. 123, 124.

110 **two German marathon runners:** Christopher Clarey, "Hand in Hand: Did Their Finish Cross a Line?" *New York Times,* August 17, 2016, p. B10.

114 **Hanwool Choe studied messages:** Hanwool Choe, "Type Your Listenership: An Exploration of Listenership in Instant Messages" (master's thesis, Georgetown University, 2015).

119 *You Are One of Them*: Elliott Holt, *You Are One of Them* (New York: Penguin, 2013). The Hide-and-Seek episode is from pp. 57–59, the Marco Polo dream from pp. 125–26.

5. FOBLO, FOGKO, and the Safe Embrace of Women in Groups

124 **Jeffrey Zaslow gives an example:** Jeffrey Zaslow, *The Girls from Ames: A Story of Women and a Forty-Year Friendship* (New York: Penguin, 2009). The account is from p. 179.

125 **the United States's "Women's Eight":** *New York Times*, August 14, 2016, pp. SP1, 13. The quotes are from those two pages, respectively.

130 **Linguist Amy Sheldon observed:** Amy Sheldon, " 'You Can Be the Baby Brother, but You Aren't Born Yet': Preschool Girls' Negotiation for Power and Access in Pretend Play," *Research on Language and Social Interaction* 29(1996): 1.57–80.

131 **Saint Augustine . . . cautioned nuns:** Marilyn Yalom with Theresa Donovan Brown, *The Social Sex: A History of Female Friendship* (New York: Harper Perennial, 2015). The quote is from p. 50.

137 **Sociologist Donna Eder observed:** Donna Eder, "Serious and Playful Disputes: Variation in Conflict Talk Among Female Adolescents," in Allen Grimshaw, ed., *Conflict Talk* (Cambridge: Cambridge University Press, 1990), pp. 67–84.

139 *Ephesian Matron* **by Walter Charleton:** Evelyn Fox Keller, *Reflections on Gender and Science* (New Haven: Yale University Press, 1985), p. 60. Keller cites this passage in the context of arguing that, historically, science was framed as "rational" in specific contrast to witchcraft, which was associated with female sexuality.

146 **Minnesota Senator Amy Klobuchar said:** Laura Bassett, "Men Got Us Into the Shutdown, Women Got Us Out," *Huffington Post*, October 16, 2013, 04:24 P.M. ET, updated October 20, 2013.

6. Too Close for Comfort

147 **In *The Prophet*, Kahlil Gibran wrote:** The poem is "On Love." *The Prophet* (New York: Alfred A. Knopf, 1923).

147 **Hildegard of Bingen:** Marilyn Yalom with Theresa Donovan Brown, *The Social Sex: A History of Female Friendship* (New York: Harper Perennial, 2015). The quote is from p. 57.

148 **Speaking . . . on NPR's *The Diane Rehm Show*:** The book, by Elena Dunkle and Clare B. Dunkle, is *Elena Vanishing: A Memoir* (San Francisco: Chronicle Books, 2015). The authors appeared on *The Diane Rehm Show* on May 20, 2015.

152   **A cartoon on BuzzFeed:** "Friendship Realities" by Rubyetc is number 10 of "Ten Comics About Friendship That Are Way Too Real." It can be retrieved at https://www.buzzfeed.com/maritsapatrinos/comics-about -friendship?utm_term=.lo0n0ERa0#.pqvKYX2NY. I am grateful to Kaley Palanjian for bringing this cartoon to my attention.

159   **In *The Bridge Ladies,* Betsy Lerner quotes:** Betsy Lerner, *The Bridge Ladies: A Memoir* (New York: HarperCollins, 2016). The anecdote appears on pp. 60–61.

166   **Joy Williams's short story "Train":** Joy Williams, *The Visiting Privilege: New and Collected Stories* (New York: Alfred A. Knopf, 2015), pp. 63–77. The quotes are from pp. 63, 65, 70, 75.

168   **"They Were All to Be Pitied":** I translated this story by Elli Alexiou from the Greek and published it with an essay about Alexiou in *The Charioteer,* nos. 22–23 (1980–81): 147–51.

172   **"After such knowledge, what forgiveness?"** The line is from T. S. Eliot's poem "Gerontion," first published in 1920 and available in numerous collections and anthologies.

174   **"I was angry with my friend":** William Blake, "A Poison Tree," in *Songs of Experience,* first published in 1794.

178   **Robert Worth describes:** Robert Worth, *A Rage for Order: The Middle East in Turmoil, from Tahrir Square to ISIS* (New York: Farrar, Straus and Giroux, 2016). The quotation is from p. 94.

7. "Like" It or Not

205   **Girls and women tend to text:** A few of these studies are Deborah Kirby Forgays, Ira Hyman, and Jessie Schreiber, "Texting Everywhere for Everything: Gender and Age Differences in Cell Phone Etiquette and Use," *Computers in Human Behavior* 31(2014): 314–21; A. Goumi, O. Volckaert-Legrier, A. Bert-Erboul, and J. Bernicot, "SMS Length and Function: A Comparative Study of 13- to 18-Year-Old Girls and Boys," *European Review of Applied Psychology* 61(2011): 4.175–84; Amanda M. Kimbrough, Rosanna E. Guadagno, Nicole L. Muscanell, and Janeann Dill, "Gender Differences in Mediated Communication: Women Connect More Than Do Men," *Computers in Human Behavior* 29(2013): 3.896–900; Amanda Lenhart, Rich Ling, Scott Campbell, and Kristen Purcell, "Teens and Mobile Phones," *Pew Research Center,* April 20, 2010, http://pewinternet.org /Reports/2010/Teens-and-Mobile-Phones.aspx; Rich Ling, Troels Fibæk Bertel, and Pål Roe Sundsøy, "The Socio-demographics of Texting: An Analysis of Traffic Data," *New Media & Society* 14(2011): 2.281–98. My own article on this topic is "The Medium Is the Metamessage: Conversa-

tional Style in New Media Interaction," in Deborah Tannen and Anna Marie Trester, eds., *Discourse 2.0: Language and New Media* (Washington, D.C.: Georgetown University Press, 2013), pp. 99–117.

206   **Fathiya Al Rashdi compared messages:** Fathiya Al Rashdi, "Forms and Functions of Emojis in WhatsApp Interaction Among Omanis" (PhD dissertation, Georgetown University, 2015).

209   **pictures of themselves on . . . Instagram:** That women are more active users of Instagram than men is reported and discussed by Hannah Seligson in "Why Are More Women Than Men on Instagram?" *Atlantic,* June 7, 2016. See also "Men Catch Up with Women on Overall Social Media Use," Pew Research Center website posted August 28, 2015, http://www.pewresearch.org/fact-tank/2015/08/28/men-catch-up-with-women-on-overall-social-media-use/, where Monica Anderson writes, "Pinterest, Facebook and Instagram have a larger female user base, while online discussion forums like Reddit, Digg or Slashdot attract a greater share of male users."

210   **Reading a *New York Times* article:** Valeriya Safronova, "The Finstagram Rebellion," *New York Times,* November 19, 2015, pp. D2, D12.

8. My Friend, My Sister, My Self

226   **Gloria Vanderbilt and her son Anderson Cooper:** Vanderbilt and Cooper discussed their book, *The Rainbow Comes and Goes,* on *The Diane Rehm Show,* March 31, 2016.

227   **In her book *Cultural Misunderstandings*:** Raymonde Carroll, *Cultural Misunderstandings: The French-American Experience,* trans. Carol Volk (Chicago and London: University of Chicago Press, 1988). The quote is from p. 79.

231   **the research of Minju Kim:** Minju Kim, "Women's Talk, Mother's Work: Korean Mothers' Address Terms, Solidarity, and Power," *Discourse Studies* 17(2015): 5.551–82. The quotes are from p. 555.

232   **"vocabulary of motives":** C. Wright Mills, "Situated Action and Vocabularies of Motives," in *Symbolic Interaction,* ed. Jerome G. Manis and Bernard N. Meltzer (Boston: Allyn and Bacon, 1967), pp. 355–66.

244   **John Elder Robison:** John Elder Robison, "Life in a Harsh New Light," *New York Times,* March 22, 2016, p. D6.

Index

About the Author

DEBORAH TANNEN is University Professor and Professor of Linguistics at Georgetown University. Among her many books, *You Just Don't Understand: Women and Men in Conversation* was on the *New York Times* bestseller list for nearly four years, including eight months as #1, and has been translated into thirty-one languages. Her books *You're Wearing THAT?: Understanding Mothers and Daughters in Conversation* and *You Were Always Mom's Favorite!: Sisters in Conversation Throughout Their Lives* were also *New York Times* bestsellers. Her book *Talking from 9 to 5: Women and Men at Work* was a *New York Times* business bestseller; *The Argument Culture: Stopping America's War of Words* won the Common Ground book award; and *I Only Say This Because I Love You: Talking to Your Parents, Partner, Sibs, and Kids When You're All Adults* won a Books for a Better Life award, as did *You Were Always Mom's Favorite!* She has written for and been featured in most major magazines and newspapers, including *The New York Times, The Washington Post, USA Today, Time, Newsweek,* and the *Harvard Business Review*. She is a frequent guest on television and radio news and information shows, including *The Colbert Report, 20/20, Today, Good Morning America, The Oprah Winfrey Show, Charlie Rose,* and NPR's *Morning Edition, All Things Considered,* and *Fresh Air*. She has been McGraw Distinguished Lecturer at Princeton University; has twice been a fellow at the Center for Advanced Study in the Behavioral Sciences at Stanford; and spent a term in residence at the Institute for Advanced Study in Princeton, New Jersey.

In addition to her books and articles about language in personal and public life, she has published poems, short stories, and essays. Her play *An Act of Devotion* is included in *The Best American Short Plays: 1993–1994*. It was produced together with her play *Sisters* by Horizons Theatre in Arlington, Virginia.

deborahtannen.com

Deborah Tannen on Video and Audio

Training Video

Talking 9 to 5: Women and Men in the Workplace
ChartHouse International Learning Corporation
www.fishphilosophy.com/product/talking9to5/ 800-328-3789

Educational Lectures on Video

He Said, She Said: Gender, Language, and Communication

Deborah Tannen: In Depth companion video

That's Not What I Meant!: Language, Culture, and Meaning

Deborah Tannen: 1 on 1 companion video

Into the Classroom Media
www.classroommedia.com
800-732-7946

Educational Lectures on Audio

Communication Matters I: He Said/She Said: Women, Men and Language

Communication Matters II: That's Not What I Meant! The Sociolinguistics of Everyday Conversation

Each is a series of fourteen lectures and accompanying study guide

Recorded Books
Modern Scholar Series
www.recordedbooks.com 877-732-2898

About the Type

This book was set in Legacy, a typeface family designed by Ronald Arnholm (b. 1939) and issued in digital form by ITC in 1992. Both its serifed and unserifed versions are based on an original type created by the French punchcutter Nicholas Jenson in the late fifteenth century. While Legacy tends to differ from Jenson's original in its proportions, it maintains much of the latter's characteristic modulations in stroke.